Mark Twain at the Gallows

Mark Twain at the Gallows

Crime and Justice in His Western Writing, 1861–1873

JARROD D. ROARK

McFarland & Company, Inc., Publishers
Jefferson, North Carolina

LIBRARY OF CONGRESS CATALOGUING-IN-PUBLICATION DATA

Names: Roark, Jarrod D., 1974– author.
Title: Mark Twain at the gallows : crime and justice in his Western writing, 1861–1873 / Jarrod D. Roark.
Description: Jefferson, North Carolina : McFarland & Company, Inc., Publishers, 2019 | Includes bibliographical references and index.
Identifiers: LCCN 2019033829 | ISBN 9781476679730 (paperback : acid free paper) | ISBN 9781476638058 (ebook)
Subjects: LCSH: Twain, Mark, 1835–1910—Criticism and interpretation. | West (U.S.)—In literature. | Crime in literature. | West (U.S.)—Intellectual life—19th century.
Classification: LCC PS1342.W48 R58 2019 | DDC 818/.409—dc23
LC record available at https://lccn.loc.gov/2019033829

BRITISH LIBRARY CATALOGUING DATA ARE AVAILABLE

ISBN (print) 978-1-4766-7973-0
ISBN (ebook) 978-1-4766-3805-8

© 2019 Jarrod D. Roark. All rights reserved

No part of this book may be reproduced or transmitted in any form or by any means, electronic or mechanical, including photocopying or recording, or by any information storage and retrieval system, without permission in writing from the publisher.

Front cover image: Mark Twain circa 1864 and background images © 2019 Everett Historical/Shutterstock

Printed in the United States of America

McFarland & Company, Inc., Publishers
  Box 611, Jefferson, North Carolina 28640
    www.mcfarlandpub.com

For my wife, my sons, my daughter,
my students, my teachers

Table of Contents

Acknowledgments	ix
Abbreviations Used	xiii
Introduction: Mark Twain's Periodical Murders	1
1. "We Pine for Murder": Mark Twain's Sensational Journalism and "Philosophic Observation," 1862–1866	13
2. The Space Betwixt the Garden and the Devil: Mark Twain's "Personal" and "Public" Reports on Stages and Coaches, 1862–1864	51
3. Exposing Hackmen and Demoralizers: Mark Twain's Punishment of Metropolitan Beasts, 1864	80
4. Between Law and Outlaw: Mark Twain's Anti-Gallows Sentiment, 1861–1872	109
5. Laura: Mark Twain's Conflation of Gender Performance and Judgment, 1863–1873	146
Afterword: Mark Twain's Contradictory "Messiness": Murderer, Judge and Hangman	180
Chapter Notes	189
Bibliography	205
Index	213

Acknowledgments

Al Swearengen in *Deadwood* once advised Merrick the journalist that the "world ends when you're dead. Until then, you got more punishment in store." Seems like an apt description for writing a book, especially because we welcome the punishment as pleasure. These years researching and writing have certainly offered me both. But I'm grateful for those years researching violence, crime, punishment, and justice in mining camps in the West. Swearengen would be proud.

Many of the ideas in this book I developed while working on my dissertation, which means this book could not exist without five fine folks on my advisory committee who guided me beyond intention to completion. Many thanks to John Cyril Barton, Jennifer Phegley, John Herron, Anthony Sze-Fai Shiu, and Diane Mutti Burke. I would also like to thank Miriam Forman-Brunell and Stephen Dilks, who helped shape this project by reading essays that became chapters.

I thank my current students and colleagues at St. Teresa's Academy, especially my English Department colleagues, Kelly Fast, Barb McCormick, Liz Baker, and Nan Bone, for support, freedom, and friendship. I would also like to thank Mark Luce, Shane Foster, Liz Bartow, members of the Gates Committee, and the family members who bestow the Betsy Brooks Crumm Award for supporting my research with questions, fellowships, and grants during my time teaching at The Barstow School.

In the past few years, I have met several kind and generous Twain scholars at conferences, especially at the American Literature Association conferences, at the Mark Twain Conference in Hannibal, Missouri, and at the International Conference on the State of Mark Twain Studies in

Elmira. Some of these scholars have listened to me read papers and offered suggestions, or read drafts of essays that grew into chapters in this study. I thank particularly scholars in The Mark Twain Circle of America: John Bird, Ann M. Ryan, Lawrence Howe, Chad Rohman, Kerry Driscoll, James Caron, Joe Csicsila, Hal Bush, Susan K. Harris, Jim Leonard, Linda A. Morris, Henry Sweets, Cindy Lovell, Bruce Michelson, Tom Quirk, James Leonard, Gary Scharnhorst, and Lawrence Berkove, who gave me my first advice for writing about Twain, and who passed away in 2018.

This project has also benefited from the generous financial support of various institutions and programs. I would like to thank the University of Missouri–Kansas City and the College of Arts and Sciences for a Chancellor's Doctoral Fellowship and the School of Graduate Studies for travel funds, including the Interdisciplinary Doctoral Travel Grant. The Women's and Gender Studies Program also financed my research with a grant, and I would like to thank especially Dr. Virginia Blanton, Dr. Linda Mitchell, and Dr. Brenda Bethman for their support. Thanks also to the PCA/ACA for awarding me a Michael Schoeneke Travel Grant. Additional thanks go to the English and History departments at UMKC for travel support. I am also indebted to Sherry Neuerburg in the UMKC English Department, Amy K. Brost in the History Department, and Connie Mahone, Nancy Hoover, and Quincy Bennett in the School of Graduate Studies. Each of these women has answered my questions and helped alleviate my stress.

Many archivists and librarians have helped me find sources and discover new ones. Among these researchers I thank especially Chris Driggs at the Nevada State Library and Archives and Neda Salem and Robert Hirst at the Mark Twain Papers housed in the Bancroft Library at Berkeley. Several folks also helped me find images for this project, and I'm grateful for their time: Melissa Martin at the Mark Twain Papers, Eve Brant at *Harper's*, Karalea Clough at the Nevada Historical Society, Jennifer Griffiths at the Fenimore Art Museum, and the staff at the Bancroft Library.

I must also thank the *Mark Twain Annual* and Wiley-Blackwell for allowing me to employ for this book parts of an essay, "Mark Twain's 'Laura': A Conflation of Western Gender Performance and Justice, 1863–1873." © 2011 Jarrod Roark, in the fifth chapter. The method for this book contained within the introduction also benefits from an additional essay published in the *Mark Twain Annual*, "Beneath Mark Twain: Detecting Sensational Residues in Twain's Early Writing." © 2014 Penn State Press. This article is used by permission of The Pennsylvania State University

Press. And thanks to McFarland and David Alff for bringing this manuscript into print.

Finally, I thank my children, Jacob, Brogan, Sloan, and Quaid, for teaching me about fatherhood—a pursuit much more arduous and joyful than writing a book. To my friends Jeremy and Amber, Bil and Val, I offer thanks for living life with me, for music, for birthdays. To my wife, Jessica, you are a loving poem.

Abbreviations Used

MTP   Mark Twain Papers, Bancroft Library at the University of California, Berkeley
SLC   Samuel Langhorne Clemens
RI   *Roughing It*

Introduction: Mark Twain's Periodical Murders

> "Nothing in the world affords a newspaper reporter so much satisfaction as gathering up the details of a bloody and mysterious murder, and writing them up with aggravated circumstantiality. He takes a living delight in this labor of love."—Mark Twain, from "The Killing of Julius Caesar 'Localized'" (1865)

Murder made Mark Twain. Desperados, lynch mobs, failed and drunk husbands, prostitutes and johns, judges, and even the gallows provided Twain the "bloody and mysterious" murders he transformed into literary accounts that sold newspapers in the West. When Samuel Clemens left Missouri by overland stagecoach with his older brother Orion on July 26, 1861, Sam could not have known that the page of his western notoriety would be written in the blood of criminals and their victims. The color of hard silver had originally appealed to Clemens more than viscous red. Though Clemens did not find fortunes in the silver mines of Nevada Territory as he had hoped, he did find fame, but not until after February 1863, and as a journalist for Virginia City, Nevada's *Territorial Enterprise*, where he first signed his pseudonym "Mark Twain."[1] In the West, he continually reported with both judgment and humor on violence in newspapers and letters, and eventually, after he left the West, in books. Even if Clemens, like other western emigrants, did not welcome the presence of actual violence in his daily life, he certainly enjoyed reading about murder and entertaining his readers with inventive ways to describe bloodshed. He once wrote humorously to his mother that he had greedily saved a letter from her to read at the end of the day, for it contained details of a murder in his home state. His paragraph ends with a simple statement about his own tastes in reading that he must have known was true for most readers of periodicals and sensational journalism and fiction in the 1860s: "I like murders—especially when I can read them in bed & smoke."²

"Beneath" Mark Twain: A Framework of Interrogation

This purpose of this book is not to write a history of the American West, nor to write a biography of Mark Twain, though elements of both exist. Rather, it describes Mark Twain's journalism, letters to friends and family, and fiction that responded to cultural anxieties about crime, punishment, and gender in the West between 1862 and 1873. Though James E. Caron analyzes roughly the same period in his excellent *Mark Twain: Unsanctified Newspaper Reporter* (Columbia: University of Missouri Press, 2008), Caron expresses the "unsanctified" qualities of Clemens's humor that helped create "Mark Twain," the "vehicle by which Sam Clemens expressed his comic genius."³ Instead of viewing the comedic vehicle, I analyze the violent conduit present in Twain's western writing and connect it with cultural events in the West. His writing from this period reflects a style, ethic, and publishing practice that began in the sensational periodical marketplace of antebellum America and England and continued to be popular throughout the mid–nineteenth century. Sensational literature depended

"Sam Clemens," 1863, age 27, Carson City, Nevada (courtesy Mark Twain Papers, Bancroft Library).

on violence and sexuality. Twain tended to avoid overt sexuality in his western writing, however, he often celebrated and exposed the gore spilled by criminals. Twain's graphic discourse of violence, in addition to his application of humor, gained him recognition, and revulsion, from editors, readers, and eventually fame. Ultimately, a verdict emerges: Twain's early western writing and the writing he produced about the West in the early 1870s should be understood as a reflection of his personal and developing anxieties about justice and femininity and masculinity; as hopes or criticisms written in letters, journalism, and fiction; as literary productions meant to sell papers or books and ultimately "Mark Twain"; and as literature written within a lineage of sensational literature that thrived in antebellum America and continued to flourish in the periodical marketplace of the 1860s.[4]

In recent years, scholars have complicated Mark Twain's neat and secure placement with William Dean Howells and Henry James in the genre of literary Realism, a movement that rejected Romance.[5] "Beneath" Mark Twain invokes the title of David S. Reynolds's study of sensational literature, *Beneath the American Renaissance: The Subversive Imagination in the Age of Emerson and Melville* (1988). His book argues that popular literature by writers such as George Lippard, George Thompson, and others existed "beneath" the works of Emerson, Thoreau, Whitman, Hawthorne, and Melville. F.O. Matthiessen called the publication of works by these authors during the five years between 1850 and 1855 the "American Renaissance." His analysis of this period, *American Renaissance: Art and Expression in the Age of Emerson and Whitman* (1941), inspired Reynolds's response that invokes Matthiessen's. Reynolds burrows beneath these works to analyze "the process by which hitherto neglected popular modes and stereotypes were imported into literary texts" and to unearth "forgotten writings" that are "worthy of study on their own."[6] Though Mark Twain's more popular and famous writing includes fictional characters named Huck Finn, Tom Sawyer, Hank Morgan, or even memorable depictions of the Mississippi River, this inquiry delves "beneath" such book-length narratives to evaluate Clemens's violent, often didactic, journalism, personal and published letters, and two books, *Roughing It* (1872) and *The Gilded Age* (1873), that developed from his experiences in the West. In these violent and sensational works composed by a young Mark Twain, we see a Trinitarian literary persona emerge: Twain the Murderer, Twain the Judge, and Twain the Hangman. The three work in concert to offer extra-legal, indeed, extra-literary responses to crime and punishment meant to be received by an audience: his family, his friends, his newspaper readership, and ultimately a Trans-Atlantic marketplace.

But Samuel Clemens's beginnings are simple, for they are violent. What he saw in Nevada Territory and California in the 1860s may have shocked him: "ugly" bullet wounds that welcomed a lead ball but did not release it; spines severed and organs punctured; a hanged man whose limp hands streaked with purple; another man's silenced scream and bitter tears on the gallows; a bitten, bleeding, raped woman; pornographic French playing cards peddled in shops; "unbonnetted" girls forced into prostitution by a cowardly monster who marked himself a man in the catalogue but sold for much less in court. These were the real stories, starring real people. What Clemens imagined, newspaper editors thought worse: an insane man who rides a horse into town with a nearly severed head hanging from atop a thing once known as a husband and father, who recently bludgeoned his wife to death and slayed most of his children. But Clemens did not consider his fictitious violence worse than the realities of the West or in any way shocking. Like the actual violence on which he reported, his invented violence within a sensational periodical marketplace was normal, regular, expected. Literary violence reflected a literal image of the West: men were often "beasts" or "demoralizers," and women were sometimes victims and other times sexualized or subversive. Writing about violence, rather than crafting humor, allowed Clemens to show his readers these realities and provided one effective method for Clemens to create a man who sold himself as a writer, whose inkwell brimmed with blood.

The Periodical Marketplace

By the time Clemens began writing journalism and crafting what he called the "sensation hoax" for Virginia City's *Territorial Enterprise* in 1862, Americans had been devouring sensational novels, stories, and journalism for two decades by such American writers as George Lippard, George Thompson, Edward Zane Carroll Judson, Sr., better known as "Ned Buntline," Emerson Bennett, and John Rollin Ridge, who sometimes wrote as "Yellow Bird," his translated Cherokee name. These writers, though only a few among many linked to the nineteenth-century Transatlantic genre of sensational fiction, were concerned with social reform in antebellum America, but they gained readership by writing tales about murderers, rapists, legal and extra-legal executions. Lippard's famous novel *The Quaker City; or, The Monks of Monk Hall: A Romance of Philadelphia Life, Mystery, and Crime* (1845), Thompson's *City Crimes; or Life in New York and Boston. A Volume for Everybody: Being a Mirror of Fashion, a Picture of Poverty, and a Startling Revelation of the Secret Crimes of Great Cities* (1849) and *The House Breaker* (1848), Buntline's *The Mysteries and Miseries of New York* (1848), Bennett's *Mike Fink: A Legend of the Ohio* (1853), and Ridge's *The Life and Adventures of Joaquin Murieta, the Celebrated California Bandit* (1854) include murderers, romantic criminals, abused characters, and heroes striving to right these intimate wrongs, which symbolize larger social ills such as inequality between the sexes and violence in the domestic space.[7]

Like Twain, antebellum writers of sensational fiction often began careers in newspaper writing or editing, and continued to be involved in periodical publishing even after publishing novels. In 1841, George Lippard began writing "city sketches and courtroom accounts" for a daily paper, the *Spirit of the Times*. Two years later, the *Citizen Soldier: A Weekly Newspaper Devoted to the Interests of the Volunteers and Militias of the United States* hired him as editor for what would become a "family story paper."[8] Similarly, in the mid–1850s, George Thompson sometimes edited *The Broadway Belle, and Mirror of the Times*, a weekly periodical published in New York and devoted to humor writing.[9] He published at least twelve books between 1855 and 1858. His final books, The Jack Harold series, were published in the last three years of his life until the series, and his life, ended in 1873.[10] Ned Buntline also worked in periodicals and in the second half of the 1840s began his own story paper, *Ned Buntline's Own*.[11] He first published the paper in the South and then moved it to New York. Emerson Bennett's writing was published in *The Saturday Evening Post*, the *National Weekly Story Paper*, and the *New York Ledger*—all weekly papers—and he edited his own *Emerson Bennett's Weekly* in 1879 and 1880.[12] When Clemens moved West and began writing for Nevada and California newspapers such as Virginia City's *Territorial Enterprise* or San Francisco's *Daily Morning Call*, among others, Bennett was still writing sensational novels, often set in the West. *Wild Scenes on the Frontiers; or, Heroes of the West* (1859) and *The League of Miami* (1860) were in print at the same time Clemens traveled West. Bennett went on to publish more than fifty novels. Buntline published numerous books before the Civil War and continued to publish and gain popularity with his *Buffalo Bill, the King of the Border Men*, serially published beginning in 1869. Clemens had certainly read Bennett's fiction. Twain's narrator in *Roughing*

It (1872) mocks "the scholarly savages in the *Last of the Mohicans*," who speak with grammatical accuracy "like a hunter or a mountaineer as a Broadway clerk might make after eating an edition of Emerson Bennett's works."[13] In 1853, Bennett published an appropriate example of this kind of book, *Mike Fink: A Legend of the Ohio*.[14] The title character is a less noble Davy Crockett adventurer in the West and boatman of the Ohio and Mississippi Rivers, just as Samuel Clemens became in the late 1850s. Also worthy of note is the manner in which the publishers of these books advertised other works the publishers thought readers might also purchase. For example, the following year, Bennett published another of his popular, sensational frontier tales, *The Bride of the Wilderness* (1854). After the end of the novel, a series of advertisements appear for transatlantic sensation books by this publisher, T.B. Peterson. The ad's copy informs the reader, "In this catalogue will be found the latest publications by the most popular & celebrated writers in the world." Listed authors include Alexandre Dumas, W. Harrison Ainsworth, Thackeray, Eugene Sue, and—printed one name after the other—Emerson Bennett and George Lippard. Finally, also in the 1850s, John Rollin Ridge served as editor for western newspapers, including the Sacramento *Bee*, and published in California periodicals, such as the daily *Alta California* and the literary weekly *Golden Era*.[15] Ridge died in 1867 after writing no other sensational hits. His *Poems* was published posthumously in 1868. In the 1860s, Twain published in both San Francisco periodicals, the *Golden Era* and *Alta California*, just as Ridge had a decade earlier.

The periodical marketplace of the 1860s, and even of antebellum America, depended on the cheap printing of factual reporting, humor writing, sensational fiction, and sentimental narratives. During this period, Clemens wrote for a variety of periodicals, some of which were daily newspapers and others weekly literary magazines. Between September of 1862 and June 1864, he reported full-time for the *Enterprise*, which was published daily, except Monday, and for a proportionately high male readership. Clemens's published work garnered the attention of local editors, and in July 1863, when he still lived in Virginia City, Clemens began contributing pieces to San Francisco's *Daily Morning Call*. Within a couple of months, in the spring of 1864, Clemens moved to San Francisco, where he became a full-time reporter for the *Daily Morning Call* from June to October 1864.

Between 1864 and 1867, Clemens contributed to a number of literary periodicals, published weekly, and other papers with varying degrees of literary merit. Clemens hoped to publish in the better variety, but sometimes wrote for the more sensational, as well.[16] During this period, Clemens continued his contributions to the established sensational *Enterprise* and became the San Francisco correspondent for the new sensational *Dramatic Chronicle*. He also began submitting correspondences for the *Californian*, the new weekly literary journal that Charles Henry Webb founded and Clemens's friend Bret Harte edited.[17] Webb began the weekly literary magazine to compete with the weekly literary journal the *Golden Era*, founded the previous decade by Rollin Daggett and J. Macdonough Foard.

Twain's western journalism, and his writing just after he left the West, participated in a marketplace with publications that had developed from periodicals such as the Boston weekly *Flag of Our Union*, the New York weekly *Frank Leslie's Illustrated Newspaper*, the *National Police Gazette*, which in 1850 serialized Thompson's *City Crimes*,[18] and the California *Police Gazette*, which in 1859 serialized a pirated version of Ridge's *Joaquin Murieta*,[19] the *New-York Tribune*, and the sensational *New York Herald*. James Gordon Bennett began publishing the daily *Herald* in New York in 1835. On November 20, 1867, the *Herald* published Twain's letter about the *Quaker City* excursion, of which a modified version later appeared in *The Innocents Abroad*.[20] Two months later, on January 24, 1868, Twain wrote to his mother and sister explaining his interaction with the *Herald*:

> This is a good week for me. I stopped in the *Herald* office as I came through New York, to see the boys on the staff, & young James Gordon Bennett asked me to write impersonally twice a week for the *Herald*, & said if I would, I might have full swing, & abuse anybody & everybody I wanted to. I said I must have the very fullest possible swing, & he said, All right. I said "It's a contract"—& that settled *that* matter. I'll make it a point to write *one* letter a week, anyhow.[21]

For Twain, having "full swing" to "abuse anybody & everybody" meant that he had the freedom to write with humor but also with sensation. In fact, Bennett and the editors on staff expected such literary techniques to appear on the pages of the sensationally driven *Herald*. Though *Innocents Abroad*, nor the travel letter published in the *Herald*, was a highly sensational text, Twain's writing benefited from the techniques pioneered by journalists and fiction writers published in papers such as the *Herald*, and these periodicals sold issues because of the violence and sensation their pages contained.

Isaac Clarke Pray, who wrote Bennett's memoirs, noted that Bennett's "means to attract the public to the *Herald*" included publishing mockeries of politicians and people in power and humorous and violent pieces that might "convulse the people with laughter" and "startle the gaping opposition editors, at breakfast."²² Such language is reminiscent of Twain's when he wrote in 1868 a letter to the *Territorial Enterprise* commenting on the "slaughter" and "mutilation" in those early newspaper pieces, years after writing some of his most sensational hoaxes, "Petrified Man," "A Bloody Massacre Near Carson," and "Horrible Affair."²³ According to Twain:

> To find a petrified man, or break a stranger's leg, or cave an imaginary mine, or discover some dead Indians in a Gold Hill tunnel, or massacre a family at Dutch Nick's, were feats and calamities that we never hesitated about devising when the public needed matters of thrilling interest for breakfast. The seemingly tranquil ENTERPRISE office was a ghastly factory of slaughter, mutilation and general destruction in those days.²⁴

Twain's western journalism, like Bennett's *Herald* in the East, responded formally to social issues such as crime and politics. Furthermore, Twain's journalism—like that of Spear, James Gordon Bennett, Emerson Bennett, George Thompson, Ned Buntline, John Rollin Ridge, and George Lippard—gained popularity because it critiqued violence while it instructed and entertained.

Certainly, Twain recognized the usefulness of sensation in attracting readers. He tried to change the hearts and minds of his readers and those with whom his readers conversed by entertaining and instructing. Sometimes, as a journalist, he entertained and shocked more than he instructed. Sometimes, when he wrote hoaxes, his readers were confused. Though Twain wrote these hoaxes with enough facts to convince readers to pay attention to various social concerns, such as the corruption of a water company, the murder of innocent men, or the cowardly acts of a lynch mob, he also invented scenes, details, and extreme violence "when the public needed matters of thrilling interest for breakfast." As a reporter in the West, he needed to thrill so that he could criticize western culture, even if his writing conflated fact and fiction.

Twain, of course, was not writing these sensational or regionally inspired pieces in isolation. Charles Farrar Browne, born in 1834 one year before Clemens, was better known by his *nom de plume,* Artemus Ward. He performed in Virginia City, Nevada, which Twain attended, and after the two became friends, Ward recommended Twain's "Jumping Frog" story for publication in the November 1865 issue of Henry Clapp, Jr.'s *New York Saturday Press.* Bret Harte, born in New York in 1836, first published in *The Californian*, edited by Charles Henry Webb. Harte became the editor there and hired Twain to submit regular correspondences. In 1868, Harte accepted a position as editor for the California literary magazine *The Overland Monthly*. He became famous for publishing a short story, "The Luck of Roaring Camp" (1868).

Clemens, Ward, and Harte were born within two years of each other and shared similar career paths. Like Clemens's western writing that frequently gauged gender norms or criticized legal and sometimes extralegal justice, Harte's writing "challenged social norms and conventional values."[26] These men influenced each other, as did the journalists and editors who worked at the *Territorial Enterprise*, where Joe Goodman gave Clemens his first job in journalism. He owned and edited the paper with his business partner. One year before he hired Clemens, Goodman hired William Wright, better known as "Dan De Quille," who mentored Clemens at the paper. De Quille influenced Clemens's writing style that combined fact with fiction, also known as the hoax. De Quille remained on staff long after Twain had left and never gained the fame or notoriety of his protégé, but he did publish a classic, *The Big Bonanza* (1876). Sam P. Davis, Fred Hart, Thomas Fitch, Rollin Dagget, C.C. Goodwin, Alf Doten, Arthur McEwen, just to name a few western writers, also contributed to the growth and style of journalism, hoaxes, fiction, poetry, and memoirs in the American West. Principal among these writers, Twain used the "ghastly factory of slaughter, mutilation and general destruction" of newspaper writing in Nevada and then in California as a machine to affect the thinking of his readers, especially concerning violence and justice in the West. Perhaps the mere presence of crime, murder, vigilance committee hangings, and capital punishment indicates that society, even an embryonic western society, is an absurd concept. And, an absurd concept, as violent and sensational as the concept called society, is worth judging.

Overview of Chapters

The first chapter, "'We Pine for Murder': Mark Twain's Sensational Journalism and 'Philosophic Observation,' 1862–1866," analyzes the violent crime on which Twain reported, often from his position as a "philosophic observer." As a journalist, he became the "voice of the people," which he displayed not only in how he wrote about crime but also in how he viewed his role as a writer. As his "voice" developed, so did his signature. With the creation of his *nom de plume*, "Mark Twain," Clemens participated in a style of journalism that reflected his goals to offer philosophical judgments for the people and to entertain the people. "Mark Twain" allowed him to "lie," to play, to offer his readers philosophies in addition to facts. Such writing illustrates how his use of violence, rather than humor, reflected his philosophies and gained him national attention.

The second chapter, "The Space Betwixt the Garden and the Devil: Mark Twain's 'Personal' and 'Public' Reports on Stages and Coaches, 1862–1864," begins in 1862, like the previous chapter, but rather than discuss the voice and philosophy of Twain's early journalism, this chapter illustrates how Twain's "personal" and "public" sentiments about California and Nevada Territory and their spaces—cities and countryside—demonstrate Twain's political views of the West and his anxieties about the women in his family traveling West. The violence on the road in both regions reflected his views, and the views of the newspapers for which he wrote, of the regional and national politics that influenced this violence. Between 1862 and 1864, Nevada was Twain's "hell," but he "liked" it and his time there (mostly). California was supposed to be the "Garden of Eden reproduced," and yet the political violence, and the "drudgery" of his newspaper job, created for Twain a paradise lost (frequently). Furthermore, Twain's letters often reflect personal anxieties about financial successes and failures, safety, and gender roles, which complement his "public" judgments that appeared in journalism.

The third chapter, "Exposing Hackmen and Demoralizers: Mark Twain's Punishment of Metropolitan Beasts, 1864," is a companion of the previous chapter, for it too views violence of the same period and region and includes examples of attacks on transportation, this time within hacks (taxis). These legal cases, at their most sensational level, involve men seducing and raping women. Like the sensational periodical publishing of writers such as George Lippard, Twain's journalistic accounts of sexualized violence warn female newspaper readers to beware of the male beasts lurking in the city and within hacks. But the violence and abuse did not end within the hacks. Twain also reported on the "epidemic" of "obscenity" and "demoralization" that infested the city. Once again, men abused women and lured women and girls into a troubling existence that finally marked California as a kind of fallen Eden. But some women Twain judged as imposters, as women willing to appear chaste in court after they had participated in the immoral or illegal behaviors for which Twain had eviscerated men. He describes these hackmen and subversive men as "beasts" and agents of "villainy" who torment women in a space not quite domestic, not completely public, but enclosed and transitional. In treatments of hacks occupied by women, Twain complicates the construction of the West through his reports of violent crimes performed by men against women. The abuse of women's bodies, then, becomes a symbol for the destruction of Twain's "Garden of Eden reproduced" and a narrative for his readers to assign meaning to such violence as a "guide to living."

The fourth chapter, "Between Law and Outlaw: Mark Twain's Anti-Gallows Sentiment, 1861–1872," builds on the discussion of crime and punishment, introduces Twain's views on legal and extra-legal justice, and positions Twain as a conflicted anti-gallows proponent. This chapter uses legal and extra-legal punishment as evidence for his view that "valuable" murderers do not deserve to be hanged. Twain offered complex views of hanging between 1861, during the events of *Roughing It* when Twain sided with outlaws and desperadoes such as J.A. Slade rather than with vigilance committees, judges, and juries, and 1871, when Twain was revising *Roughing It* in Elmira, New York, during a famous death penalty case before the New York Supreme Court. This chapter examines depictions of three men's stories—Edward Howard Rulloff, and Joseph A. Slade and Captain Ned Blakely from *Roughing It*, two heroic criminals who have entered into Twain's mythic storytelling—that illustrate the tension between Twain's distrust of governments that execute criminals and his admiration of strong, yet flawed "badmen," These case studies also illustrate Twain's rhetorical strategies that relied on the "feeling" of his readers. He wanted for these criminals, these "badmen," redemption, not retribution. In these reflections, he hoped to entertain but also to inspire people to question the law and representations of legal and extra-legal violence.

The fifth chapter, "Laura: Mark Twain's Conflation of Gender Performance and Judgment, 1863–1873," also witnesses the development of Twain's view of punishment, but largely concerning female victims and subversive women. According to Twain, men who abused and murdered women, even prostitutes, deserved death. To complicate this view, however, I include the legal case that influenced Twain's literary depiction of a legal decision that ultimately saw a female murderer go free, even though she was guilty of murder. Twain's western journalism and letters (when he lived in Nevada and California in his mid-twenties to early thirties) and *The Gilded Age* position Twain's literary view of women in more complicated, sometimes conflicting, ways than scholars have previously noted—as subversive women who performed both masculine and feminine roles, which finally conflated into one multi-vocal female character, Laura Hawkins. Or, to represent this lineage in reverse, Twain had been thinking and writing about subversive women for ten years prior to creating Laura Hawkins. His inspection, judgment, and inscription of these western women are evident in his 1873 female creation. Twain used these women's performances, and the performances of the men (including Twain) who judged these women, to complicate his ideas about femininity and justice and to build toward a culminating literary judgment of women in *The Gilded Age*.

The afterword shows a final view of Mark Twain, the petitioner for human rights who also performed as a literary Murderer, Judge, and Hangman. We see such contradictions in news items in 1862, and we see their development in *The Gilded Age* (1873), *The Adventures of Huckleberry Finn* (1884), *A Connecticut Yankee in King Arthur's Court* (1889), and *Pudd'nhead Wilson* (1894). Twain, like other sensational writers and journalists within this book, asked his readers to look at "Look at what a sight!" (to quote Hank Morgan); he then advanced a pathos so that readers could consider the horror of the violence, understand its cause, and seek justice, even if mobs and courts did not. Finally, then, this book does not avoid these contradictions or seek "a verdict that resolves all conflict." Rather, it exploits these conflicts by viewing Twain's western writing within a context that relied on contradiction: sensational literary responses to violent crime and punishment, whether journalistic or fictional, always involve the use and celebration of violence. Because of sensational literature's relationship to violence, Mark Twain's sensational western writing relied on, and became popular because of, Twain's criticisms of regional violence and his exposure of the men, actual or fictional, who abused and raped women or planted lead balls that bloomed with blood and gore in the bodies of men.

1

"We Pine for Murder": Mark Twain's Sensational Journalism and "Philosophic Observation," 1862–1866

The muzzle of the pistol might have felt cool against his flesh, but Samuel Clemens was not thinking about the pistol's steel or the circular character it printed on the page of his head. He was pondering his failure. Samuel Clemens sat alone, in the darkness of his rented crib in San Francisco, and later thought, "I wasn't man enough to pull the trigger."[1] Though he had recently read the editor of the New York *Round Table*'s praise for the "foremost among the merry gentlemen of the California press," who "signs himself 'Mark Twain,'" published on September 9, 1865, and reprinted on October 18 in the San Francisco *Dramatic Chronicle*, the twenty-nine-year-old journalist was in debt. Clemens was overworked and underpaid, depressed, and wanted earthly rewards. The New York editor seemed to offer Clemens a prediction and a warning: "if he will husband his recourses and not kill with overwork the mental goose that has given us these golden eggs, he may one day take rank among the brightest of our wits."[2]

Clemens both feared being overworked and dreamed of being famous. In an October 1865 letter to his brother and sister-in-law, Clemens admitted that he had been "sighing after vain possibilities" and striving "for a fame," though he had not succeeded. Now, he even questioned his faith. He wrote that he had "a religion—but you will call it blasphemy. It is that there is a God for the rich man but none for the poor."[3] He closed this letter with the thought that led him to push the pistol to his head: "If I do not get out of debt in 3 months,—pistols or poison for one—exit *me*. {There's a text for a sermon on Self-Murder—Proceed.}"[4]

In November, his first story, "Jim Smiley and his Jumping Frog," was published in *The New-York Saturday Press*, a weekly literary newspaper. The paper had become well known for publishing work by established and newer American and British writers such as Walt Whitman, Ralph Waldo Emerson, Horatio Alger, Jr., James Russell Lowell, Wilkie Collins, Charles Dickens, and William Dean Howells. A few months later, in March 1866, Clemens sailed to the Sandwich Islands for a five-month excursion as the correspondent for the Virginia City *Union*. These reports and letters gave him more opportunities for fame. On June 2, 1866, the *Saturday Press* published "A Strange Dream," a sketch, set near the Kilauea crater in Hawaii, about a fictional quest for "the corpse of the warrior King."[5] This success, and others that year, allowed Mark Twain to leave the West and seek national fame, rather than the regional kind, in New York. This transition permitted the "gentlemen of the California press," born Samuel Clemens and reinvented as "Mark Twain," to publish his sensational writing that reflected his criticisms of crime, criminals, and violence for a broader audience.[6] The success that Twain had enjoyed in Nevada, California, and the entire West, however, was vast, important, and based on his use of humor, but also on his reports on crime with a discourse of violence.

Between September 1862 and May 1864 he published over one hundred reports and news items in the Nevada's *Territorial Enterprise*. Nearly half of those contain reports on crime and violence. Similarly, of the approximately 470 local items Clemens wrote for San Francisco's *Call*, identified by Edgar Branch, approximately half contain reports on crime or violence. When Clemens dented his head with a pistol near the end of 1865, he had failed in the mines, but he had already gained much popularity for crafting combinations of sensational, violent, satirical, and humorous journalism, while simultaneously reflecting his anxieties about power, crime, and especially his masculine identity. After all, he admitted that he was not "man enough to pull the trigger" and cause "Self-Murder." Though this admission to his family in a letter is the only evidence to support Clemens's claim that he contemplated suicide, the claim, not the event, bears the greater significance. For even if the event never occurred, Clemens still thought that reporting with sensational language to his family the disaster of his external set of circumstances, coupled with an emotional response to them, would appeal to his readers, even if they numbered only two.

This chapter traces the gruesome historical and literary timeline in Clemens's life beginning in 1862 and ending in 1867. The climax of this timeline—the moment when he considered adding his own skull to that list of gore—as related in the letter to his brother and sister-in-law in October 1865—offers a view of Clemens on a precipice. At that moment, he did not know if he would fail or succeed as a writer. By beginning here, at the climax of this timeline, and then returning to the beginning, three years of Clemens's literary ambitions and experiments building toward this moment solidify like blood spilled in the saloons of the West. Though Clemens feared these ambitions would not come, he experienced their fruition after 1865. During this period, Samuel Clemens's responses to violence, and later Mark Twain's, display his "indifference to 'news'"[7] that instead operated as a "philosophic observation."[8] The entertaining, yet critical voice allowed him to perform as his readers' *vox populi*, a collective "voice of the people," meant to entertain, to deliver morals and ethics to the region, or to reflect the morals and ethics of a region to its readers. His refusal to report simply the facts, and his readership's desire for sensation, allowed Twain to develop a fictional and sensational style that satirized social relations in the West. Such stylistic development, first news items and then with hoaxes, instructed readers. These readers, then, became Twain's deposit for assigning meaning to violence, and "Mark Twain," his performative penname, allowed him to "lie," to play, to offer competing discourses.

Personas and Pronouns

If "Mark Twain" created for himself a persona as a kind of "badman," an agent of immorality, as a "violent outlaw whose weapon of choice was a pen,"[9] as Joseph Coulombe has argued, perhaps Twain also advanced with his outlaw ethic a morality. To create this persona, a desperado with a pen, Twain wrote about murders, executions, and violent criminals in his journalism and in his hoaxes. But Clemens also functioned as a kind of preacher, writing about criminals (sinners), crimes (sins and vices), what to avoid, and how to avoid such dangers in what was supposed to be a western utopia and escape from the East. Though Clemens had always wanted to deliver meaning to people, he had not always wanted to be a writer. He initially had "two powerful ambitions"—to become a riverboat pilot, which he did become in 1859, and a preacher, which he did not become. He explains in the same letter he wrote to Orion and Mollie that rather than having a "call" to preach the gospel, he has one to write: "I *have* had a 'call' to [literature], of a low order," which he hopes will "excite the laughter of God's creatures."[10] This view of a writer, then, is similar to the role of a preacher. Both deliver meaning to people and capture their attentions. Though delivering God's "message" might have been a more "powerful ambition," delivering a moral philosophy—indeed judgments, about violent men and their crimes—also satisfied a high ambition. His contemporaries noticed this trait. It was likely Charles Henry Webb who called Twain the "Moralist of the Main."[11]

Even before becoming "Twain," Clemens had learned early on as a journalist in Nevada Territory (and then in California) that murder attracted readers. Sensation sold. Clemens's initial fascination with masculine violence in a new region led to his writing about violence for his newspaper readership that he was assigned to satisfy. Many of the hoaxes, sensational news items, and his reviews of theatrical performances first printed in the *Enterprise* were reprinted elsewhere, for example in the *Stockton Daily Independent* and the *Unionville Humboldt Register*. *The Californian*, edited by Charles Henry Webb who noticed Twain's literary style, and the California literary magazine *The Overland Monthly*, edited by Twain's friend Bret Harte, were popular in the West. Harte, like Twain, became a famous writer because of his newspaper and story publishing in the West. In "Free Fight," a story printed in Virginia City's *Territorial Enterprise* and dated January 6, 1863, Clemens describes a disappointing brawl in Virginia City:

> A beautiful and ably conducted free fight came off in C street yesterday afternoon, but as nobody was killed or mortally wounded in a manner sufficiently fatal to cause death, no particular interest attaches to the matter, and we shall not publish the details. We pine for murder—these fist fights are of no consequence to anybody.[12]

Here, Clemens's ironic voice slithers among the prose, biting, hissing at the harmlessness of a fist fight when compared with a murder, and yet he releases enough venom to deliver his social critique—within the masculine mining town, a fist fight has lost its sensational appeal. Now, readers "pine for murder." Because Clemens was in the process of crafting for himself a persona of literary desperado, his language delivers both sensation and social satire. In fact, his persona was not only a literary desperado, but also his name, Mark Twain, became famous for its relationship to badmen, crime, violence, and the regional reception of infamous men.

But Clemens also considered himself to be the witness for and the voice of the people. An article such as "Free Fight" offers the first evidence for this growing persona. Branch and Hirst call this newspaper clipping "less an item of news than a philosophic observation."[13] The comment and the clipping both support my claim that Clemens understood his role as reporter and his ambition to preach an ideology, or against one—that his audience does not view simple "fist fights" as sensational or even frightening. Facts mattered, but his readers wanted to "eat a man for breakfast." Clemens used this phrase in his journalism, and in *Roughing It*, a book constructed from his newspaper articles and clippings, to describe the desires of the people in the West. Of course, he was a participant in this culture and most especially an observer of it. By commenting on the audience's dissatisfaction with a brawl, and then building a narrative technique that supplies readers with the violence he thinks they want, he then has constructed a literary form that contains competing discourses. In this way, his technique defies the logic of a sermon, for a sermon should deliver monologic discourse like a lecture. Clemens, however, did not position himself in the role of a lecturer only, for he included himself within the position of the audience by using the pronoun "we." He, like his audience, feared not a fight and in fact was bored by it. Such facts no longer astonished.

A news item, such as "Free Fight," offers facts but also an accumulation of deposited voices in the collective "we" within a constructed narrative. Contained by this framework, then, such a voice is not unlike Clemens's view of a sermon's voice. While this idea might seem contradictory, the competing discourses can be separated. On the one hand, neither Samuel Clemens nor Mark Twain is a preacher (I) instructing readers or listeners (they) to do one thing or another. He comments on the crime and the state of the boredom with or expectation of crime. On the other hand, any delivered message with a narrative is a production. For example, in his letter that lists his failed ambition to be a preacher, he encourages his brother to become one instead and calls his brother's good and truthful sermon a "literary production." Clemens continues to write to Orion, "I will read your sermons with sincere pleasure, but only as literary gems."[14] If a sermon is a production that delivers truth through literature or a narrative, certainly a news item is also a production that delivers a fact through storytelling. Yet unlike a sermon that offers concerned instruction for the righteous and judgment for sinners, Clemens's narrative suppresses concern for an injured person. Instead, the journalist delivers a masculine realization that a fight does not satisfy an appetite for murder and by doing so judges his audience. But whose voice delivers these claims, Samuel Clemens the journalist, the resident, or the collective "we"? The journalist is the preacher, and "we" represents an audience in the West of which all are a part. Because "Twain" assumed the role of a "violent outlaw whose weapon of choice was a pen," the act of writing, unlike the act of preaching, is not necessarily positive, pious, or truthful. Such a dialogic form provides complication in the reception of meaning but also a method of analysis. As an example of Clemens's competing discourses, "Free Fight," then, supplies an early example to use as a model for Clemens's layered journalism, just before he began signing his articles "Mark Twain"[15] and willingly performed as a named preacher or a judge.

In July 1863, Clemens, now usually writing as Mark Twain, still lived in Virginia City and published articles in its premier newspaper, the *Territorial Enterprise*, yet he also contributed pieces to San Francisco's *Daily Morning Call*. I have selected a few articles that offer Twain's views of saloon shootings, of which some were accidental, that do not deliver a clichéd view of a showdown. These acts of violence in and around saloons display the kinds of quarrels in which men engaged and how these arguments were settled, often with a pistol. A letter offering Twain's "philosophic observation" on this topic appeared under the section, "'Mark Twain' Letter. [From Our Regular Correspondent.]."[16] This "local item," titled "Man Shot," delivers violence with sarcasm and humor and offers the young journalist's attempt to report some facts and his failure to report all:

> The good order and freedom from disturbance which prevailed yesterday, were the subject of general remark. I hardly think old citizens were fooled by it though. If they did not speak of it openly, many of them must have been speculating inwardly as to what man we were likely to have for breakfast. The fearful question was solved—or almost solved—just before midnight. Two Irishmen got to fighting in the San Francisco Saloon, and the proprietor of the establishment, Mike Millenovich, attempted to separate them. Two policemen—McGee and Scott—came in, attracted by the noise, and a general row ensued, in the course of which nine pistol shots were fired, one of which broke Millenovich's arm, and another entered his side, inflicting an ugly and probably fatal wound. I get this meagre and unsatisfactory statement from an eye-witness, who says "they made it so warm for him in there that he don't rightly know much about it." I entertain a similar opinion myself. Another witness tells me several outsiders were wounded by chance shots, but I have been unable to stumble upon any such.[17]

Buried in the middle of this piece lies the body of Mike Millenovich, the saloon owner, which will likely become a corpse. Twain notes that of the nine fired pistol rounds, two struck Millenovich's body. The first broke his arm, and the second produced in his side "an ugly and probably fatal wound." We are left to imagine exactly what "ugly" signifies, but it must indicate an open wound, from close range with a large, lead ball, perhaps from a .36 caliber Colt 1851 Navy Revolver (like the one Clemens supposedly brought with him to Nevada Territory), or from a larger .44 caliber Colt Walker or Dragoon, or the more recent Colt Model 1860. The blood and gore produced by any of these pistols certainly would have dressed the wound in ugly color. And yet the murder of a saloon proprietor draws no surprise or pity from the writer. In fact, the shootout does not constitute a murder but rather a disturbance.

Twain begins by describing the "disturbance," on a day, like any other, when citizens awoke and wondered when the violence for the day would commence. The phrase "speculating inwardly as to what man we were likely to have for breakfast" positions violence as both expected and awaited, as regular and satisfying as a breakfast meal. It also connects newspaper reading with the act of eating in the morning. Though Twain's tone about having a man "for breakfast" is humorous, every issue of the *Call* did include reports on and lists of crimes committed that day. Most of these local items and short columns appeared on pages two, three, and four of the paper with larger stories filling the first page. In the four months he reported full-time for the paper, between June and October 1864, Twain published hundreds of short news items that contained rapes, assaults, robberies, and murders. It is no exaggeration to say that five to ten such items appeared each morning in the paper. Even though this shooting in "Man Shot" occurred in San Francisco, such violence was common in many nineteenth-century mining towns in Nevada and California. Perhaps the regularity of violence could reduce the sensational nature of such stories, but according to Ronald M. James, "the constant threat of violence" could also create readiness in western inhabitants and prevent violence.[18] People carried guns, and used them, as a way to prevent being the victim of stories like the man in "Man Shot." Of course, the "Two Irishmen" in this story carried guns, which did not prevent the act of violence. Citizens expected to read about murder in the "daily morning" papers as they ate breakfast. Twain made certain he gave it to them.

"Them" is an important pronoun to use here, for in "Man Shot," unlike in "Free Fight," Twain's pronoun use divides himself (I) from the people (them). For example, in the statement, "I hardly think old citizens were fooled by it though. If they did not speak of it openly, many of them must have been speculating inwardly as to what man we were likely to have for breakfast," Twain uses "I" to insert his commentary about the shooting that "they," the spectators, witnessed. And yet he does use "we," as he did in "Free Fight," to include himself in his audience, his readers. "They" refers to the people at the scene of the crime, whereas "we" refers to the external state of being of readers digesting the news of the crime the morning after it occurred. As a person in the crowd at the crime scene, Twain was an "I" gathering facts in opposition to the witnesses: "Another witness tells me several outsiders were wounded by chance shots, but I have been unable to stumble upon any such." Not until he relates these facts and discoveries for his audience does he become a participant in the act of consuming that which the "I" reporter has discovered. Because of these competing roles, the reporter at the scene is not the philosopher. The writer is the philosopher, for he is constructing an "observation" and a judgment about the general state of crimes that occur each day in the region. The observation, then, is the "literary production."

Twain reproduced his "literary production" of the regularity of violence like breakfast when describing a similar culture in California's Sacramento Valley once he left Nevada Territory for a vacation in San Francisco in spring of 1863. This time allowed him to make professional acquaintances that led to gaining his job as a Nevada correspondent for the *Daily Morning Call*, beginning in July. Years later, in *Roughing It*, Twain's narrator recalls this time in California. He describes the mining culture as having crowded streets, "labor, laughter, music, dancing, swearing, fighting, shooting, stabbing—a bloody inquest and a man for breakfast every morning—*everything* that delights and adorns existence."[19] The literary violence in the mining community was fun, for Twain, but also perhaps for the readers of the newspaper articles that described the music and dancing, and also the shooting and stabbing. In this culture, like in Nevada Territory, citizens expected to eat a man for breakfast. Again, because of the expectation of violence, inhabitants carried guns as prevention for crime. And yet, by the early 1860s, the "sheriff, police, and courts were usually able to hold crime in check." Twain had plenty of crime to report. Furthermore, the presence of a sheriff or marshal did not guarantee the eradication of crime. In *Roughing It*, for example, Twain notes a robbery whose "perpetrator" was in fact the marshal.[20] The shooter, of course, is a man, and so too is the owner of the saloon, who tries to break up the fight. For his heroic efforts, the saloon owner is shot twice, which inflicted "an ugly and probably fatal wound." The eyewitness, from whom Twain learns little, escaped the saloon in fear. Another witness suggested that many innocent "outsiders" were also wounded, but Twain the observer, perhaps in this case more than a reporter, could not or would not find anyone who was wounded to corroborate the account. Such refusal to investigate the potential victims and instead focus on the violence and masculine acts of men suggests that Twain or his readers were interested in the facts of the potential wounded. Twain and his audience, the "we," wanted murder on the pages as much as the inhabitants, "they," did not want murder in reality.

Certainly, Twain's audience included women as well as men, but Twain did not mention any women in "Man Shot." Everyone in the story is a man, including the eyewitness who offered the "unsatisfactory statement." Twain used the male pronoun "him" to describe this witness, but the second witness receives no gender identification. Perhaps this unreliable witness was a woman, or perhaps such details were unimportant. Though we know that men outnumbered women in the West, especially in mining communities in the 1860s, women did live in the West. For example, in 1860 3,016 people lived in Storey County, Nevada, of which Virginia City is the county seat. Ninety-five percent, or 2,857, of these were men, and 5 percent, or 159, were women. In 1862, Twain's first year writing for Virginia City's *Territorial Enterprise*, the population had grown to 4,498. Fifteen percent, or 655, of these inhabitants were women. By 1870, 31 percent of the 11,319 inhabitants were women.[21] Still, at this point in Twain's writing career, he diminished the significance of women's numbers in the region. In *Roughing It*, his narrator notes that Sacramento Valley has "an assemblage of two hundred thousand *young* men—not simpering, dainty, kid-gloved weaklings, but stalwart, muscular, dauntless young braves, brimful of push and energy, and royally endowed with every attribute that goes to make up a peerless and magnificent manhood.... No women, no children."[22] This description of the West and its men anticipates Frederick Jackson Turner's frontier thesis (1893) or Theodore Roosevelt's four volumes of *Winning of the West* (1889–1896). Frederick Jackson Turner, in particular, credited the growth of the frontier to the conquering force of strong men like the ones Twain describes. These men possess a "coarseness and strength combined with acuteness and inquisitiveness; that practical, inventive turn of mind, quick to find expedients; that masterful grasp of material things, lacking in the artistic but powerful to effect great ends; that restless, nervous energy."[23]

Twain, like Frederick Jackson Turner three decades later, celebrates this romanticized aspect of the culture inhabited by hearty men. But, according to his reports on violence, these strong men—though capable miners, pioneers, and businessmen—are also capable murderers. Twain, in fact, rejoices, and uses multiple exclamation points to emphasize this point, at the "wild, free, disorderly" culture. It was a "grotesque society! *Men*—only swarming hosts of stalwart *men*—nothing juvenile, nothing feminine, visible anywhere!"[24] In this masculine society, men talked of violence, even when there existed none to witness. Twain wrote of this lust for violence in "Man Shot," but he also wrote an item about this kind of cultural discussion on the same day he published "Man Shot." In "False Report," the journalist reports that a rumor has been spreading that a local businessman "had been shot and very effectually killed." No one would have been surprised to hear this news, in this "wild, free, disorderly" culture—no one except the businessman. Twain reports that he saw the rumored victim and "asked him about it at church this morning. He said there was no truth in the rumor."[25] Twain had learned, and was continuing to develop, a dialogic style that relied on the telling of fact blended with humor. He also had learned by 1863, when he was writing for papers in Nevada and California, that violence in reality was a gift for his journalism. In *Roughing It*, Twain's narrator remembers discovering this truth and "wrote up the murder with a hungry attention to details."[26] Joseph Goodman, his boss at the *Enterprise*, encouraged such a practice, which gave Twain great pride. He congratulated and challenged himself, noting, "I felt that I could take my pen and murder all the immigrants on the plains if need be and the interests of the paper demanded it."[27] As bad as murders were for the community and the growth of a region, they were good for paper sales. Murders supplied Twain with his subject. From the topic he developed his journalistic and literary voices. The performative voice of Twain allowed the journalist the freedom to resort to violence if "the interests of the paper demanded it." Indeed, he celebrated the murders his pen wrote onto the pages of the papers. Twain needed to "murder" for the benefit of the paper that reflected and guided the interests of its readership.

Performing the "Voice of the People": The Journalist Who "Came and Saw"

In 1862, Samuel Clemens had not yet settled on the *nom de plume* "Mark Twain." This public creation of the new persona did not occur until

February 1863. Even in these early days, he saw his job as a journalist as a reporter of facts, but, more importantly, as a reflector of people's concerns. His journalistic voice represented the citizens' interests, and not only the interests of men. In order to do be the *vox populi*, "voice of the people," he needed to give the people what they wanted. Clemens's readers wanted violence, at least in the papers.

Twain did not prescribe, nor did he function as the literal voice of the people. In an 1886 speech to the members of the Typothetae, an American association of master printers, Twain remembered his early newspaper and printer days in the 1850s. During his address, he chastised a columnist of the paper (a glorified subscriber who contributed articles) for often writing a "long primer" and then signed them "'Junius,' or 'Veritas,' or 'Vox Populi,' or some other high-sounding rot."[28] Twain rejected such prescriptions. Rather, the evidence supports the idea that Twain wanted to be the people's voice and considered this ambition a goal of journalism. Such an analysis renders a view of Twain's thinking at the time. To gain access to this thinking, we must analyze the articles that include all or some of the following methods: journalism that appropriated first-person collective pronouns, stories that produced meanings for Twain's readership that included the "I" voice, humorous judgments, criticisms, and mockeries of criminals or law enforcement, and pseudonyms that reflect his desire to go and witness events for the people. And yet he avoided the "high-sounding rot" of a self-righteous editor or preacher who believed a truth and delivered it to the people so that they should all believe it, too.[29] Twain's reluctance to report "truth" and instead blend facts with sensation allowed him to administer a journalistic, common and popular voice, rather than a voice of prescription.

A journalist first must witness by going and seeing. He then must report and instruct readers about what he has learned. In this way, Twain connected his work to the people reading his articles and living in the region about which he wrote. In these reports, he also seems to know and to judge his cultural consumers, his readership. By examining these factual murder cases and popular journalism that responded to violence, we see that Twain's discourse, ending with a signature that unifies his voice with the people's, offers a performative voice where a formalized audience, a readership, existed. According to Judith Butler, performativity is a "repetition and a ritual" that allows, perhaps even commands, inhabitants within a singular culture to share an understanding of what is being performed.[30] Butler has even more explicitly discussed how speech "acts" or "performs" certain authorities. While she has analyzed political discourse, particularly hate speech, I apply her view that "speech is finally constrained neither by its specific speaker nor its originating context" to Twain's performative voice in his early journalism and hoaxes.[31] Twain wanted be the people's voice, and he adopted a satirical yet judgmental style to offer his "philosophic observations." Whereas a judge "pronounces" a sentence that reflects his legal legitimacy and authority, Twain pronounces judgments that do not illustrate his "uncontested power,"[32] but instead show *how* he contests power. Twain performs, or reclaims, power in his factual reporting that contains facts but, more importantly, facts told in exaggerated ways that depend on graphically described murders. Though his audience was not a congregation, as it might have been had he become a preacher, his readers did receive his teachings each day. These local and regional readers migrated to the West, worked in mining towns, and participated in the growth of new culture, which Twain judged. These westerners also lived within a violent culture. In a representative month, June 1863, 167 crimes appeared in Virginia City, Nevada, where Twain lived and wrote. While sixty-six of these were "drunk and disorderly" charges, only about twenty did not involve violence.[33] Crimes appeared each day in the papers, but because Twain *wanted* be the people's voice, that is, a voice of instruction that excited "God's creatures," he adopted a style of enjoyment and judgment to offer his "philosophic observations," not his moralistic prescriptions.

Clemens published numerous stories about these displays of masculinity that intensified under the conditions and pressures within mining towns, but also under the influence of alcohol. Two such stories appeared in "Brutal Affrays in Washoe," April 19, 1864, *Territorial Enterprise*. I have selected one line from each story and placed emphasis on the phrases concerning alcohol: "The parties have always heretofore been good friends, but both at the time of the affray were somewhat under the *influence of liquor*." In the second item, Twain notes that by viewing "the evidence before the Justice, it appears that the attack was entirely unprovoked, and *whisky is the only cause that can be assigned for the assault*."[34] While many murders did occur because of lost tempers, sometimes the death was accidental. But an earlier case, in 1862 about the accidental murder of an emigrant from Baltimore, became the subject of one of Clemens's first articles about a saloon shooting. The event began when two men started to share a drink at the bar, but when one man, Peyton, insulted the other, Wooley, he retorted and then found Peyton drawing a pistol. Wooley caught Peyton's arm, but the pistol fired. An innocent man, the Baltimore emigrant, was accidently shot during the scuffle. While this article is not especially sensational, it does report the facts that would cause a reader to understand the dangers that might occur within a western saloon. The tone also laments the loss of an easterner who loved his mother, whose friends spoke "in the highest terms of him," whose death is tragic because he happened to be reading a newspaper inside of a saloon. Like "Man Shot," "Another Innocent Man Killed" contains judgment toward subjects involved in a saloon shootout:

> A man named Samuel L. Franklin was shot by another named Peyton, between the hours of nine and ten o'clock on Sunday evening last. Peyton drew his pistol to shoot a man named Wooley, but Wooley caught his arm, and in the scuffle that ensued the pistol was discharged, almost instantly killing Franklin who was seated in a chair reading a newspaper. The ball struck the unfortunate man near the navel, passed through his body and lodged under the skin to the left of the spine, causing death in about ten minutes. Mr. Franklin was a native of Baltimore, Md., and had been in the Territory about four months. He bad been in Humboldt part of this time and had reached this place but about four weeks before the accident resulting in his death. He was a man of remarkably fine personal appearance and but about 27 years of age. On his person was found letters from his mother begging of him to return to her at his home in the States, and mourning over the "long absence" of her "dear boy." The following evidence was giving before the Coroner's jury: JAMES H. WOOLEY. Being duly sworn said the affair occurred on C street at Mr. McCoy's saloon, somewhere near 9 o'clock; between the hours of nine and ten o'clock. I had met Peyton at Mac's saloon, the first thing that occurred between him and me was when Mr. Williams came into the house and wanted me to take a drink with him, I did and this man Peyton was sitting in a chair on standing up—, he said to me when I was about to sit down "you are such a good-natured cuss I want you to take a drink with me"; "Well," said I, "Yes, I will take a drink with you"; he then commenced talking with me in a slanging manner, and I took it for a long time in good sport-, he called me an "ill bred, low-bred pup"; I then turned around and said to him, "I am as well bred a gentleman as you are, sir"; he then stood at the corner of the counter; he jumped back, put his hand in his side pocket and drew his pistol; I then started for him and caught his pistol hand by the wrist—, I struck his hand down towards the floor to prevent his hitting me or anybody else, I held his hand between my legs when the pistol went off while between my legs, shooting a person immediately behind me the person was Mr. Franklin. Mr. W. STAFFORD, being sworn, said: He was in the saloon at the time of the shooting occurred; they (Peyton and Wooley) came up to the bar and took a drink together and stood joking together; I saw Peyton step back toward the back end of the saloon; I saw him draw his pistol; he drew it from his side pocket, cooked it and presented it at Wooley, Wooley jumped and seized his arm, when a scuffle ensued; Mr. Williams ran up to them, and at this moment the pistol was discharged the man Franklin was sitting in a chair. A number of other witnesses were examined, the tenor of whose evidence was the same as

that given above. A verdict was given and in accordance with the facts as above shown, Peyton was committed by a Coroner's warrant to the custody of the Sheriff to await the action of the Grand Jury which will be in session on Monday next, and is now lodged in the county jail. Persons who were acquainted with the deceased, speak in the highest terms of him. He was no drinker or frequenter of saloons, and merely went into the one in which he met his death on account of the chilliness of the night, while awaiting the return of a friend with whom he had been talking some time in the street, and who recollected some business it was necessary for him to attend to on B street. Deceased was well known and had many friends in San Francisco. His funeral took place yesterday afternoon at 4 o'clock. The expenses of the funeral were paid by a subscription raised among our citizens.[35]

Clemens begins the article by presenting the facts of the case, who is involved, and the outcome of the victim, Samuel L. Franklin. The murder is simple, accidental, and tragic. Two men quarrel, a pistol is drawn, neither man is wounded, and an innocent man is shot and then dies ten minutes later. There is, however, a brief discussion of violence that once again allows the reader to imagine the progress of a bullet through the body of Franklin. The ball enters through his naval, which is likely Twain's euphemistic way to describe a gut shot, a painful and gory wound. The ball, again probably a .44 caliber round from one of various Colt pistols, "passed" through the body of the victim and "lodged" near his spine. Such a wound undoubtedly produced a great deal of agony in Franklin—intestinal bleeding, destruction of soft tissue and organs, and a buried lead ball near the spine, close but not likely close enough to paralyze the victim. Franklin bled and writhed in pain for ten minutes before he died. And then, as if more interested in the outcome than the murder, Clemens abandons the violence and performs a legal role. For the rest of the article, Clemens relates the story as he heard it in court, as a court reporter, listening to the testimonies of two men—James H. Wooley, the intended victim, and Mr. W. Stafford, a witness, both sworn before the Coroner's jury. Clemens used this method to gain "evidence" for his journalism in both Nevada Territory and in California. By using these legal testimonies, Clemens was able to reconstruct a scene about which readers wanted to learn.

Also significant is the journalist's tone. Unlike so many of his articles about murder, here, Clemens offers no humor. Though some scholars have noted that Mark Twain's early writing was crude or lacked variation, Clemens is clearly withholding the kinds of judgments he railed against other murderers and victims of murder. The reason seems to be simply that Franklin was innocent, in addition to being an emigrant from the East. He is a victim but not because he has committed a crime or entertained unethical behaviors. Instead, he has placed himself in harm's way. In fact, Franklin "was no drinker or frequenter of saloons, and merely went into the one in which he met his death on account of the chilliness of night." He was only waiting for his friend in the saloon to escape the cold. Apparently, the readers of the paper shared Clemens's sorrow for the victim, for the citizens who read the paper paid for Franklin's funeral. This shared sorrow, as indicated by the closing phrase "our citizens," contains once again a collective pronoun that aligns Clemens's voice with his readers.' None found humor in the abuse of the innocent that day, and Clemens used no humor to deliver that reverence.[36]

Though it is not clear if Clemens attended Franklin's funeral, we do know that he and other reporters frequently attended funerals to glean additional details for their writing. In *Roughing It*, for example, Twain's narrator explains, "that in order to know a community, one must observe the style of its funerals and know what manner of men they bury with most ceremony. I cannot say which class we buried with most eclat [*sic*] in our 'flush times,' the distinguished public benefactor or the distinguished rough."[37] Twain's idea that the community regarded desperados with as much or more éclat at a funeral than a citizen of note might also be complicated by suggesting that Twain could mean that citizens in the West, in rough mining towns, pined for murder and for sensation. The funeral of an infamous badman, or even of a common murderer, might draw as much public attention as the ceremony for a respected man.[38] Funerals of murderers, then, allowed Twain the journalist an additional opportunity to glean facts, grab headlines, and gain readers interested in eating a man for breakfast and then burying a man after dinner. As we might now expect, Twain did not always deliver the details of such a funeral with reverent diction. Twain did report the facts, what he saw and heard, but he also inserted a certain amount of humor and irony by choosing the exact details on which to focus.

As one who came, saw, reported, and reflected the voice of the people, Clemens the journalist, and sometimes the letter writer, delivered the facts and advice in this story, not only as a method for citizens to understand the town's cultural violence, but also as a way to entertain readers through violence. Though Clemens and his readers pined for such details, no one wanted to experience the violence first hand. In this way, stories about shootings and "affrays," allowed Clemens and his readers to participate safely in the mockery of cowards or greedy men.[39] The story of Franklin, in "Another Innocent Man Killed," and others in this section, supports the view that Clemens the journalist reflected his readership's concerns and interests and also influenced those readers. These articles, though not always humorous, display his ambition to "excite" the people by becoming part of the people. He gained that right as a journalist because he was a part of the culture, an observer and a witness. Though Clemens's *vox populi* delivered violence, it also transmitted his "philosophic observation."

Some criminal men were judged in court and sentenced to time in jail or prison. Others found extra-legal retribution and death rather than legal correction and life. According to Mark Twain in the next article, "Offices," murder occurred frequently in Virginia City, "four murders in the first degree a month," and yet the murderer might go unpunished. In a cynical tone, the reporter laments, "we never convict anybody." Again, Twain appropriates the collective first-person as a method to include himself in the community suffering from the crimes and not as the reporter delivering facts. Indeed, attempted murder garners a criminal a reprimand and a request to the leave the region. Though he "feels badly," the criminal rejects this "punishment" and remains in the area—just another criminal to perform future crimes. In the following article, the journalist delivers his disdain for such legal inaction, relying on a discourse of judgment and feeling:

> We average about four murders in the first degree a month, in Virginia, but we never convict anybody. The murder of Abel, by his brother Cain, would rank as an eminently justifiable homicide up there in Storey county. When a man merely attempts to kill another, there, and fails in his object, our Police-Judge handles him with pitiless severity. He has him instantly arrested, gives him some good advice, and requests him to leave the country. This has been found to have a very salutary effect. The criminal goes home and thinks the matter over profoundly, and concludes to stay with us. But he feels badly—he feels very badly, for days and days together.[40]

The short article contains not only Twain's signature irony and humor, but also his darker sentiment—his lamentation for crime and how legal justice seems ineffective. The people need for criminals to be punished. When a judge exiles a criminal to another county, the badman "feels badly," but he does not stop being a badman. Twain closes this article with sarcasm, yet he has finished writing about this topic with criticism. Though Twain has included himself in the audience's perspective of suffering criminals, he also acts as a replacement for legal punishment. Throughout the article, Twain's satirical tone withholds judgment, but the message is clear: criminals should be punished. In this particular article, however, Twain's role is not to offer judgment but instead to suggest the absurdity of a situation no one wants to experience. Men like Twain's unnamed criminal exist in reality. The police and judge must handle him. Twain cannot punish. He can only mock, deride, chastise, and "excite" readers to feel. Feeling, after all, is threaded throughout the article. The criminal may feel "badly" in place of feeling punishment. But the readers also feel something when reading Twain's words. Readers can either share Twain's outrage or reject it. Yet the "facts," according to the journalist, suggest that "we" should all feel something and should "convict anybody."

Lawrence I. Berkove has argued that such shootings were common in western mining towns, for the brutal or the disorderly imposed an extralegal order. Journalists then used such violence to support codes of masculinity and "heroic values."[41] But Twain also configured such a story to show how manliness failed to protect the innocent or to enact justice. Vengeance succeeded in that such violence discouraged a man from drawing a pistol when he should not. According to Wells Drury, newspaper editor for the *Virginia Evening Bulletin*, "When every man is the judge of his own conduct and is swiftly resentful of even the slightest insult, the standard of behavior is necessarily marked by a high degree of punctilious courtesy."[42] Still, some men, especially under the influence of alcohol, were dangerous and needed judgment, even if that judgment were journalistic rather than legal.

One month later, Twain wrote another short article about a murder and robbery in which the police were slow to act: "A teamster was murdered and robbed on the public highway, between Carson and Virginia, to-day. Our sprightly and efficient officers are on the alert. They calculate to inquire into this thing next week. They are tired of these daily outrages in sight of town, you know."[43] Twain's criticism of the inefficient legal justice system becomes obvious, here, through his use of irony. The officers, in fact, are not "sprightly" or "efficient," for they will not "inquire into this thing" until the following week. This kind of legal tolerance of crime causes Twain to note that officers are "tired of these daily outrages," not because Twain believes this to be true of the police. This statement is true for him, and for the citizens of the town. Here, his mockery of the police overshadows his reverence for the victim. The victim bears no name, and Twain seems more interested in addressing the problem in the police force than the problem of crime. Furthermore, his direct address in the second person, "you know," allows the reader to receive the light reporting as if it were an anecdote that reflects a truth or a circumstance, perhaps even "high-sounding rot," rather than a news item reporting facts. Such discourse is not a judgment. It is an urging for the police to act, signed by a collective voice or audience that is irritated with the police force's ineffective presence. Rather than the police "factually" being "tired of these daily outrages," Twain and his audience are "actually" tired of such crime.

Performing "Mark Twain": A Name and a Voice

Throughout 1863 and 1864, Samuel Clemens the journalist, now signing "Mark Twain" at the end of his work since February 1863, published articles that complicated his use of names. Twain valued his constructed penname and the way he signed an article as a way to reflect his role as a reporter. But he also paid special attention to the names of criminals and "badmen" as a way to "preach" about the dangers of such men or to assign some form of heroic respect to villains. Such factual or "official" reports fall into two broad categories: First, Twain's journalistic views on violence that seem to lack enough sensation to sell papers, in which he inserts sarcasm meant to instruct the people about codes of justice or masculinity. These cases often include saloons as settings, and Twain seems to play with the convention of the shootout within or outside of the saloon. Second, his reports portray men seeking vengeance against men who have wronged them, which again reflects the potential concerns of the people. Naming a thing gives it power, perhaps, but a name also denotes meaning within Twain's discourse of instruction that relies on violence. These "observations" also develop to include a signature "Mark Twain" style and salutation that allowed the writer to offer "unofficial" discourse that combined fact and fiction. Such articles offered two options for reducing violence. The first solution was a legal one—to hire a police force equal to the task of capturing or killing criminals. The captured needed to appear in court and receive appropriate and harsh punishment. The dead would receive a well-attended funeral. The second solution involved extra-legal justice. Both outcomes seemed satisfactory to Twain. Reports on the legal solution provide an example of this aspect of the culture and Twain's interaction with it. A simple, yet effective, example of this kind of reporting appears in the following article: "We had fifty extra policemen on duty all day. They were kept busy."[44] Though these two sentences offer no details about the types of crime or their frequency, the implicit message is that disorder existed that day.

A longer article with details about a murder, and yet inside another

1. "We Pine for Murder" 31

saloon, appeared four months later, in July 1864. According to Twain, "a volunteer soldier named John Barrett shot and killed an ex cab driver named John McGowan, in a cellar saloon." Twain then shifts to "official" report, as discovered through legal testimony:

> Capt. Douglas testified that he found one bullet hole in the floor of the saloon, one through the bar, and one through the partition, which passed through and struck the Clay street wall; (the fourth killed McGowan); and the weapon the prisoner held in his hand when he gave himself up, was a new patent Colt's six-shooter, with two chambers still loaded. Witness went after Dr. Boyce and another physician, and the former arrived a few minutes before McGowan died. Witness also sent for the Coroner, and remained until the body was removed.
>
> Coroner Sheldon said he visited the prisoner, who confessed that he shot deceased, and explained the circumstances of the case. He held a post-mortem examination of McGowan's body, and found that the ball had entered just at the edge of the hair, about the centre of the forehead, and lodged at the base and in the substance of the brain, behind the right ear. He exhibited the ball, which was much flattened, and also the pistol, which bore Barrett's name on the sheath. The case was submitted to the jury without waiting for the witness Hunter, who could not be found. The verdict returned was that deceased, a native of New York City, aged about thirty years, and named James McGowan, came to his death by a pistol shot fired by John Barrett, on the morning of the 6th of July.[45]

Though the police did not arrive in time to save the victim from the murderer's gunshot, they did arrest the murderer, John Barrett, and removed him from the streets to prevent more violence. And the violence here is like what we have previously seen—a large caliber round, in this case a .44 caliber round from a "new patent Colt's six-shooter," certainly the Colt Army Model 1860, that has traveled throughout the body of the victim. The "ball entered" the skull at the forehead near the hairline, which must have created an enormous hole and subsequent parting of the hair like a cranium's red sea. The ball then "lodged at the base" of the brain "behind the right ear," a specific, darkly humorous image that reflects an unheeded warning of violence. With all of this forensic evidence, police seem capable of detecting evidence to make a case against Barrett, for Twain does not criticize the officers' methods or chastise their inefficient action even while he describes the progress of the pistol's ball. Twain did not withhold such criticisms at any point during his career as a journalist. When the police did not act with skill and precision, as did this article's "Capt. Douglas," Twain introduced a second option for criminals being brought to justice.

If the police force or courts were inefficient or ineffective, the citizens might raise a vigilance committee to administer justice extra-legally. This outcome, too, agreed with Twain. The following two articles illustrate Twain's disdain for the legal justice system when a notable desperado or repeat offender haunted the town. In other words, everyone knew the man, and the name, Jack McNabb, for he was a "notorious desperado." If he was a known criminal, for his crimes appeared in the papers on numerous occasions, then shouldn't the justice system be able to contain him? Apparently not. Such criminals did, however, offer Twain additional opportunities to write articles that people wanted to read, not just because they contained violence, but also because they contained Twain's signature judgment and the names of victims and criminals.[46] Two such articles about the same desperado, Jack McNabb, appeared just six months apart. In the first, we see that the citizens desired to hang McNabb, before and after the criminal was arrested, because of the "infestation" of criminals:

> This afternoon, Jack McNabb, a notorious desperado, shot at a negro. He was not arrested. Afterwards, he created a disturbance, and Officers Watson and Birdsall tried to arrest him, when he shot Birdsall in the breast, and a special officer, named Burns, in the arm. Birdsall is not expected to live till morning. The people wanted to hang McNabb, but were prevented by the officers. Gen. Van Bokkelen, Territorial Provost-Marshal, asserted his authority, guarded the jail, and closed the saloons and stores. The city is infested with thieves, assassins and incendiaries. There is some little talk of a Vigilance Committee.[47]

The citizens wanted to raise a vigilance committee, for McNabb had shot an innocent man and then continued to act violently toward the arresting officers. McNabb shot one officer, who later died from the wound. The officer, Birdsall, is shot in the "breast," the kind of wound a bird might experience from a hunter's shotgun blast. We see pellets spreading across the breast of this bird, exploding feathers and meat, rupturing organs, and causing an agonizing wound that will end in death the next morning.

Six months later, McNabb appeared once again in Twain's writing. This time, McNabb turned himself in after the shooting, but not because officers pursued him or arrested him. Instead, a brave (or reckless) stranger settled with pistols what the police had failed to do in September of 1863:

> A shooting scrape occurred at the Clipper Saloon, B street, on Sunday night, between Jack McNabb and a stranger whose name we could not learn. According to the story of an eye-witness, the stranger was abusing a harmless individual known as "Drunken Jimmy," when McNabb came up and remonstrated against such treatment of an inoffensive man.... The stranger drew a revolver, fired two shots, received one in return, and then cleared out. One of the stranger's shots damaged McNabb's vest to some extent, and passed through a couple of letters in his pocket, but did no injury to his person, while the ball from the latter's pistol peeled a strip from the stranger's forehead which a small

amount of doctoring will restore. After the occurrences McNabb gave himself up to Marshal Perry.[48]

In this scene, McNabb has engaged in a shootout, and he eventually turns himself in to the police, but McNabb actually appears to be the more noble of the aggressive men. McNabb has "remonstrated" against the stranger for abusing "Drunken Jimmy," a harmless and helpless patron of the saloon whose souvenir from the fray includes a "peeled" strip of forehead flesh from the pistol's ball. Twain's journalism, even the pieces assembled to create *Roughing It*, often display both criticism of and support for the desperado if these men represent courage, masculinity, and what Twain called "usefulness." The badman, in Twain's writing, might act nobly in one scene and vilely in another. But their acts had gained them a name, a reputation—something that Twain desired. The letter to his brother about "Self-Murder" includes Clemens's ambition to become a great writer, known in the East. But because he and his brother were both badly in debt, Clemens also joked that Orion "had better shove this [letter] in the stove—for if we strike a bargain I don't want any absurd 'literary remains' & 'unpublished letters of Mark Twain' published after I am planted." Such a letter that relates the ambitions of a young writer embarrassed Clemens. Better to burn the letters than sell these writings for money.[49] But these men Twain named and discussed, and gave them a reputation, as a mix of local irritants, social dangers, and as romantic heroes when they enacted justice that officers could not. Still, Twain noted that McNabb deserved to be punished. And Twain gave him a *name*—Jack McNabb, "a notorious desperado."

In a letter to his sister dated March 18, 1864, Twain discusses his opinion of the role of names in journalism:

> Pamela, you wouldn't do for a local reporter—because you don't appreciate the interest that attaches to *names*. An item is of no use unless it speaks of some *person*, & not then, unless that person's *name* is distinctly mentioned. The most interesting letter one can write, to an absent friend, is one that treats of *persons* he has been acquainted with, rather than the public events of the day.[50]

For Twain, a story without a name was useless, in that the interesting part of the story is what happens to the people. A person who does something important enough to be named, even committing a crime, was probably a gift for a journalist, especially for Twain. After all, his ambition beyond being a reporter was to write literature. Initially, he became a reporter for two reasons: as a means to make an income, which he expressed in a letter to his brother: "I'll write as many letters a week as they want, for $10 a week—my board must be paid."⁵¹ Twain also wanted to gain notoriety. In a letter to his mother and sister, Clemens notes his ambition to gain notoriety as a writer and become known beyond Virginia City:

> Ma, you have given my vanity a deadly thrust. Behold, I am prone to boast of having the widest reputation as a local editor, of any man on the Pacific coast, & you gravely come forward & tell me "if I work hard & attend closely to my business, I may *aspire* to a place on a big San Francisco daily, some day." There's a comment on human vanity for you! Why, blast it, I was under the impression that I could get such a situation as that any time I asked for it.⁵²

According to Clemens, he can "boast of having the widest reputation as a local editor," but he wants more. He wants not fame in San Francisco, for that seems too easy. Instead, he wants something beyond the Pacific Coast—fame in the East and nationally, which, to use the religious discourse of a preacher, produces "a comment on human vanity." And yet, in order for Twain to achieve this attention, he knew that his name mattered, and that the names of the agents in his stories mattered.

Though Twain often mentioned the names of notable desperados, he did not always give names to those who were arrested or extra-legally hanged after their first offense. In other words, these criminals had no reputation and did not warrant Twain's literary treatment. They were unknown people, and therefore "the person's *name*" was not "distinctly mentioned." This kind of literary treatment can be seen in two vignettes in the same article as the one starring McNabb:

> A man was arrested on Sunday, on B street, who was crazy drunk, and rushing about the streets with a big knife, offering to attack everybody who came in his way. He was placed in the lock-up after some difficulty, though he was so wild it took the Sheriff and some three or four men to get him to the station-house.

> Gurtey, the man who was shot a few nights ago ... is not in a fair way of recovery, and his physician expressed the belief that he will not die, at least not for the present; not withstanding that he has been reported dead several times, and his slayer reported hanged by the Vigilance Committee.⁵³

Though the acts of violence were important enough to print, the names of the criminals seemed not to be. The nameless murderers, dangerous as they might have been, did not warrant a name, for they were not infamous, attractors of readership. Certainly, omission of names in a news report could have been a product of space saving. Editorial economy achieved by omitting names meant that the name was not important to take extra space on a line. Furthermore, naming a person anchored a news item with details but also with people. After all, according to Twain, an "item is of no use unless it speaks of some *person*, & not then, unless that person's *name* is distinctly mentioned." Because a name on the page was familiar, even popular, Twain's readers continued to experience in print the bold and illegal deeds of a named badman, such as McNabb, and signed by a man, Mark Twain, whose *name* now appeared at the end of news items.

In another series of writings, Twain depicted the crimes and punishment of "Deputy Marshall" Jack Williams, who "had the common reputation of being a burglar, a highwayman and a desperado."[54] In *Roughing It*, "Chapter XLIX," Twain's narrator begins the chapter with an introduction and then a selection of such stories, all which involve Jack Williams. The narrator introduces these stories with one sentence explaining their sources and reason for including them in the book: "An extract or two from the newspapers of the day will furnish a photograph that can need no embellishment." In "Fatal Shooting Affray" and "Robbery and Desperate Affray," Williams shoots, kills, and bludgeons men, but in "More Cutting and Shooting," Williams has been assassinated. The journalist begins this article, reprinted in *Roughing It*, by explaining, "The devil seems to have again broken loose in our town. Pistols and guns explode and knives gleam in our streets as in early days." The narrator ends this chapter with a lament for the legal justice system: "as far as I can learn, only two persons have suffered the death penalty there. However, four or five who had no money and no political influence have been punished by imprisonment."[55] In this case, the death penalty might satisfy the various personas involved in this competing discourse. Three personas exist in the telling of this story: Samuel Clemens, the man; Mark Twain, the literary invention; and Twain's narrator in *Roughing It*, a version of Twain. Each persona plays with a social application of justice and violence. Years before, as a journalist, Twain often lamented a series of injustices. The younger Twain and the older one writing a book, certainly applied to his work the personal voice delivered by "Mark Twain," the voice of the people, and received by the people who comprised the formal audience known as his readers.

Twain's narrator in *Roughing It* engages in a similar critique that his journalistic persona advanced in 1863 and 1864. On the one hand, Jack Williams was "an efficient city officer," precisely because he was ruthless and "a highwayman and desperado." He was an effective enforcer of the law, however, because he was willing to break the law in order to bring criminals like himself to justice. On the other hand, Williams was also a murderer and a part of the criminal element in the West when Twain wrote for the newspapers. Twain's narrator notes several instances of lawmen engaging in crimes, including a case in which the deputy marshal committed robbery.[56] Even when lawmen did not cross the boundary into lawlessness, citizens sometimes took matters into their own hands. One such case in 1863 occurred after a quarrel over a prizefight. Six people were seriously wounded or killed in a shootout among civilians.[57] This group of citizens, however, had no leader, no man of note. Jack Williams, though, was notorious, feared, respected, and everyone knew his name.

By this time in Twain's writing career, readers and citizens of the West were also beginning to know the name Mark Twain. The performative act of self-naming granted Mark Twain authority to speak "officially" and "unofficially" and to create a persona that extended beyond the physical region. He began signing this *nom de plume* in February of 1863, just after Jack Williams had made a name for himself. If ever Twain believed a name mattered, as he did in 1864 when writing to his sister, he must have believed this truth in 1863 when he settled on a name that sounded like a man. Though *mark twain* was a nautical term for "two marks," or twelve feet, and identified the safe depth for riverboat on the river, the term also reflects Twain's playfulness with names, especially as a marker for duality.[58] "Mark Twain" became Samuel Clemens's "other," the persona that performed as witness to crimes and judge of criminals.

Later that year, a "special policeman" named Joe McGee, who was also a desperado like Williams, presumably assassinated Jack Williams. Little difference separated such a "special policeman" from a desperado, further solidifying a view now, and a realization then, that legal and extralegal justice often operated within a conflated space. According to Twain's narrator, "Williams was assassinated while sitting at a card table one night; a gun was thrust through the crack of the door and Williams dropped from his chair riddled with balls."[59] Though we are uncertain how many pistol rounds invaded Williams's body, we are certain that he gained weight from the lead and lost volume from the leaking blood—and act of open boldness by McGee. But because these men were desperadoes and law enforcers, and because they were infamous in the region, they could not hide from retribution any easier than Williams could hide from the shower of raining lead balls. Ironically, Joe McGee was killed in the same manner he had assassinated Williams, in December of 1863, while sitting inside a saloon.[60]

Twain's "narrator" reports these facts in *Roughing It*, but Twain as "journalist" also published a similar article San Francisco's *Daily Morning Call* when he worked as a correspondent from Nevada. In this short item,

Twain names the assassin of Williams as "Joe Magee," uncorrected spelling for McGee: "CARSON, December 10.—Joe Magee was assassinated in the St. Nicholas Saloon, at four o'clock this morning. The gun was fired through the window, from the street. The murderer is not known. It is thought Magee assassinated Jack Williams in Virginia last Winter. MARK TWAIN."[61] Clemens, through the use of the sobriquet "MARK TWAIN," gives authority to the suspicion that Magee is a killer. The importance of using the language "Mark Twain," like the importance of naming Magee or Williams (or even McNabb), offers a concrete meaning within a particular set of circumstances.[62] In Twain's case, the "particular" is the sensational style he developed to discuss people and events in a way that would be read. He knew that writing about infamous men attracted readers. In this way, the name of Mark Twain became associated with sensation, violence, and good story telling, even if the story fit into a local column. James E. Caron has compared these "stylistic flourishes" present in Twain's 1866 reporting about Hawaii to those "typical of a blood-and-thunder tale" that "had dominated American popular culture since midcentury."[63] Such "flourishes," or his sensational style, lived in print much earlier than 1866. Even in 1863, Mark Twain employed violent language that depended on his use of names. Perhaps "Mark Twain" evoked Twain's time on the Mississippi and was catchy compared with his other various pennames: the Reliable, W. Epaminondas Adrastus Perkins, Rambler, Grumbler, Peter Pencilcase's Son, John Snooks, Thomas Jefferson Snodgrass, A Dog-Be-Deviled Citizen, Sergeant Fathom, and Josh.[64] Certainly, Caron has analyzed how the penname "Mark Twain" reflected his desires or performative role as a journalist and a humorist or even as a *feuilletoniste*. But in the West, Clemens also constructed "Twain" to critique violence and justice, largely by employing vicious discourse in his "factual" reports and in his hoaxes.

Performing Truth and Lies, Fact and Fiction

In this same year, 1863, Mark Twain wrote two sensation hoaxes, the first in April and the second in October, which bulged past the boundary of fact into a fictional form. Though hoaxes are part journalism, they are part lie. Many scholars have analyzed these pieces to illustrate the beginning of Twain's humorous, violent writing, influenced by his time in Nevada, which continued to grow and mature once he left the West.[65] I include these hoaxes, however, to create some tension between Twain's journalistic and his fictional methods and to reflect his interest in attracting readership and entertaining them. And still, these responses to violence represent another form of "philosophic observation." Such a term reflects Twain's purpose to "say" something beyond a delivery of facts. In the case of hoaxes, the "observation" is multitudinous, for it does offer facts, conflated with fictions, so that Twain could chastise people and events in a forum that had a built-in audience—newspaper readers. But these hoaxes also emanate from his connection to his readers and his desire to attract attention. To put it another way, Twain wanted to be famous, at the expense of other newspapers, if necessary, and certainly at the cost of being known as a "journalist." In an 1863 letter to his mother, Twain discusses his writing and his recent notoriety: "I am prone to boast of having the widest reputation as a local editor." While he enjoyed this local fame, he also had ambitions to write "literature."[66] Journalism, after all, has rules. Facts must be delivered; truths must be told. But a hoax does not depend on truth, and yet it requires the manipulation of facts. Sensation hoaxes offer the highest levels of "unofficial" speech, for they mix enough factual, journalistic details to make believable the fictional account of horror and murder. As performative acts rather than reports of facts, hoaxes are lies, meant not to harm or to offer information about a factual set of circumstances. Rather, hoaxes intentionally subvert the "facts" and satirize their content to criticize and create warnings for readers in the West. Twain's journalism certainly refers to an actual and existing set of circumstances, but his writing, especially along a spectrum of more to less "official," brings about performative acts in the subversion of authority, gender, and style. Twain uses modes of discourse to entertain but also to observe and to philosophize, even if these observations are built on lies. Ironically, these lies tell the truth.

These traits are especially significant in his western journalism. As for the hoaxes, Twain invented the stories—horrific and believable tales that entertained with violence and humor without basking in actual death. And, because the publication of these hoaxes in multiple newspapers exists, as do a letter he wrote that mentions the source material for the first hoax and a published retraction for the second, we can see that he wrote these sensation pieces to expose criminals, either the violent kind or the corporate variety. In the first hoax, "Horrible Affair," dated April 1863, Twain wanted to make a personal statement about an actual double homicide (two of his "friends") and their murderer. The "five dead Indians" Twain fabricated.

For a day or two a rumor has been floating around, that five Indians had been smothered to death in a tunnel back of Gold Hill, but no one seemed to regard it in any other light than as a sensation hoax gotten up for the edification of strangers sojourning within our gates. However, we asked a Gold Hill man about it yesterday, and he said there was no shadow of a jest in it—that it was a dark and terrible reality. He gave us the following story as being the version generally accepted in Gold Hill:—That town was electrified on Sunday morning with the intelligence that a noted desperado had just murdered two Virginia policemen, and had fled in the general direction of Gold Hill. Shortly afterward, some one arrived with the exciting news that a man had been seen to run and hide in a tunnel a mile or a mile and a half west of Gold Hill. Of course it was Campbell—who else would do such a thing, on that particular morning, of all others? So a party of citizens repaired to this spot, but each felt a natural delicacy about approaching an armed and desperate man in the dark, and especially in such confined quarters; wherefore they stopped up the mouth of the tunnel, calculating to hold on to their prisoner until some one could be found whose duty would oblige him to undertake the disagreeable task of bringing forth the captive. The next day a strong posse went up, rolled away the stones from the mouth of the sepulchre, went in and found five dead Indians!—three men, one squaw and one child, who had gone in there to sleep, perhaps, and been smothered by the foul atmosphere after the tunnel had been closed up. We still hope the story may prove a fabrication, notwithstanding the positive assurances we have received that it is entirely true. The intention of the citizens was good, but the result was most unfortunate. To shut up a murderer in a tunnel was well enough, but to leave him there all night was calculated to impair his chances for a fair trial—the principle was good, but the application was unnecessarily "hefty." We have given the above story for truth—we shall continue to regard it as such until it is disproven.[67]

The darker truth of this tale is the murdered men were friends of Twain, two policemen named Dennis McMahon and Thomas Reed. The murderer was a badman of note, a fellow Missourian, like Clemens, named John Campbell. He shot the officers on the morning of April 12, 1863.[68] Before Twain sent the hoax, he wrote a letter to his mother and sister, the end of which delivered the information about the murder: "P. S. I have just heard five pistol shots down street—as such things are in my line, I will go and see about it."[69] Apparently, Twain left his desk and visited the crime scene, for, as he notes, as a journalist his job is to observe and to report. Some hours later, once he had discovered the details of the crime, he returned to his desk and finished the letter with a second postscript: "P. S. No 2–5 A. M.—The pistol did its work well—one man—a Jackson County Missourian, shot two of my friends, (police officers,) through the heart—both died within three minutes. Murderer's name is John Campbell."[70] Perhaps Twain was outraged at the murder of his two police officer friends. Certainly, he had their murders on his mind, for only a few days later appeared "Horrible Affair," the hoax based in part on these murders.

What, then, is the "horrible affair" to which Twain refers? Five innocent "Indians" die after citizens are too fearful to pursue Campbell into a cave. Instead, they stop up the "mouth of the tunnel" to trap him until officers can be found to arrest him. The next morning, no Campbell is found, only a dead "Indian" family. Newspaper readers in the early 1860s would have been familiar with the "Indian Wars," the common, expected, genocide of native peoples in California. Bret Harte, for example, reported on a particularly brutal killing in 1860 that ended with ten to forty times greater casualties. Though Harte claimed to have no "didactic purpose in his fiction," his fiction did offer cautionary tales, as did Twain's fiction and journalism.[71] And Harte's reporting on the killing of native peoples certainly reflected his disdain for genocide. So then would Twain's readers, largely emigrants wanting land and resources once occupied and used by native peoples, have understood that a dead Indian family was a horrible affair? Or perhaps the horrible affair is not the death of the family but rather the murder of the two police officers and the subsequent failure to capture the desperado Campbell and bring him to justice. Twain notes that sealing a man in a cave "was calculated to impair his chances for a fair trial," meaning that the citizens tried to execute extra-legal justice. Perhaps the tragedy is an act of the "citizens," which amounts to little more than a failed lynching. Each of these cowards "felt a natural delicacy about approaching an armed and desperate man in the dark," and instead waited for a braver sort of men, a posse, to arrive the next morning. The lynch mob of citizens appears to be devoid of a man brave enough to capture a criminal. This pusillanimous act led to the death of the five innocent people. And yet Twain's contempt seems to be less for the death of the "Indians" and more for the actions of the mob and for Campbell. Like the mob Sherburn backs down in *Huck Finn*, this mob lacks a man brave enough to bring a murderer to extra-legal justice. Possibly, then, Twain wrote this article because of his disdain for Campbell and as a lament for the deaths of two good men when so many cowardly men lived who would not avenge the deaths of men Twain admired. Campbell, though he initially escaped, was soon arrested.[72] Even though in the hoax Twain dispatched a lynch mob for Campbell, in reality Campbell received justice within the Virginia City court.

The second sensation hoax, known as "A Bloody Massacre Near Carson," was published on October 28, 1863, in the Virginia City *Territorial Enterprise*.[73] It opens with the following "sell":

The Latest Sensation.

A Victim to Jeremy Diddling Trustees—He Cuts his Throat from Ear to Ear, Scalps his Wife, and Dashes out the Brains of Six Helpless Children!

From Abram Curry, who arrived here yesterday afternoon from Carson, we have learned the following particulars concerning a bloody massacre which was committed in Ormsby county night before last. It seems that during the past six months a man named P. Hopkins, or Philip Hopkins, has been residing with his family in the old log house just at the edge of the great pine forest which lies between Empire City and Dutch Nick's.[74]

In order to make this hoax believable, especially to readers living outside the local Nevada region, Twain included actual place names, such as Empire City, Magnolia saloon, Virginia City, Gold Hill, and the Comstock lead. But the style of the piece, divided between "character speech" and "authorial speech," also allowed readers to accept a lie, a piece of fiction. Twain appropriates a "character," in that his story-telling technique depends on a new authority, not only as a reporter, but also as a reporter of the rhetoric of courtroom forensics:

> The family consisted of nine children—five girls and four boys—the oldest of the group, Mary, being nineteen years old, and the youngest, Tommy, about a year and a half. Twice in the past two months Mrs. Hopkins, while visiting in Carson, expressed fears concerning the sanity of her husband, remarking that of late he had been subject to fits of violence, and that during the prevalence of one of these he had threatened to take her life. It was Mrs. Hopkins' misfortune to be given to exaggeration, however, and but little attention was paid to what she said. About ten o'clock on Monday evening Hopkins dashed into Carson on horseback, with his throat cut from ear to ear, and bearing in his hand a reeking scalp from which the warm, smoking blood was still dripping, and fell in a dying condition in front of the Magnolia saloon. Hopkins expired in the course of five minutes, without speaking. The long red hair of the scalp he bore marked it as that of Mrs. Hopkins. A number of citizens, headed by Sheriff Gasherie, mounted at once and rode down to Hopkins' house, where a ghastly scene met their gaze. The scalpless corpse of Mrs. Hopkins lay across the threshold, with her head split open and her right hand almost severed from the wrist. Near her lay the ax with which the murderous deed had been committed.[75] In one of the bedrooms six of the children were found, one in bed and the others scattered about the floor. They were all dead. Their brains had evidently been dashed out with a club, and every mark about them seemed to have been made with a blunt instrument. The children must have struggled hard for their lives, as articles of clothing and broken furniture were strewn about the room in the utmost confusion. Julia and Emma, aged respectively fourteen and seventeen, were found in the kitchen, bruised and insensible, but it is thought their recovery is possible. The eldest girl, Mary, must have taken refuge, in her terror, in the garret, as her body was found there, frightfully mutilated, and the knife with which her wounds had been inflicted still sticking in her side. The two girls, Julia and Emma, who had recovered sufficiently to be able to talk yesterday morning, state that their father knocked them down with a billet of wood and stamped on

them. They think they were the first attacked. They further state that Hopkins had shown evidence of derangement all day, but had exhibited no violence. He flew into a passion and attempted to murder them because they advised him to go to bed and compose his mind.[76]

The description of the children's bodies, whose "brains had evidently been dashed out with a club, and every mark about them seemed to have been made with a blunt instrument," invokes a level of inspection and morbid description that relies on an application of "authority." Readers of the hoax, however, may not have registered the difference between "character speech" and "authorial speech," thus confusing the invented elements with the factual bits.[77] Such an outcome must have transpired with ease and shock. After all, the article is shocking in its violence long before it makes a point. Hopkins's failing sanity causes him to scalp his wife, split her head open, nearly sever her hand, bludgeon to death six of his children. He then rides into town holding his wife's red hair and scalp dripping "warm, smoking blood" while wearing a severed neck like a sadistic second smile. Twain as the author intended for readers to see a larger point, or, at least to share his point when he mentions Spring Valley Water Company, a San Francisco utility company that received Twain's disdain, along with San Francisco newspapers with which he had affiliations. Twain's authorial voice slips away from the voice of the people, for the people did not share Twain's outrage for the Spring Valley Water Company, at least not the people living in Nevada, beyond the reach of the San Francisco company. The final section of the hoax offers the criticism of the water company and the reason for Hopkins's insanity:

> Curry says Hopkins was about forty-two years of age, and a native of Western Pennsylvania; he was always affable and polite, and until very recently we had never heard of his ill treating his family. He had been a heavy owner in the best mines of Virginia and Gold Hill, but when the San Francisco papers exposed the game of cooking dividends in order to bolster up our stocks he grew afraid and sold out, and invested to an immense amount in the Spring Valley Water Company of San Francisco. He was advised to do this by a relative of his, one of the editors of the San Francisco Bulletin, who had suffered pecuniarily by the dividend-cooking system as applied to the Daney Mining Company recently. Hopkins had not long ceased to own in the various claims on the Comstock lead, however, when several dividends were cooked on his newly acquired property, their water totally dried up, and Spring Valley stock went down to nothing. It is presumed that this misfortune drove him mad and resulted in his killing himself and the greater portion of his family. The newspapers of San Francisco permitted this water company to go on borrowing money and cooking dividends, under cover of which cunning financiers crept out of the tottering concern, leaving the crash to come upon poor and unsuspecting stockholders,

without offering to expose the villainy at work. We hope the fearful massacre detailed above may prove the saddest result of their silence.[78]

Of course, by the time the reader arrived at the criticism, the details of the murders had overshadowed the social and political message. In this case, Twain's authority and crafted details had actually masked his larger intention. His experience as a journalist should have taught him to lead with the important information rather than burying it, and yet that same experience also had led him to understand that violence hooked the reader, not a simple criticism of a water company.

In a retraction printed on October 29, one day after the hoax first ran, Twain admitted that his intention in writing the hoax was to lambast in print the water company, not to fool readers into believing a horrible murder had occurred:

I TAKE IT ALL BACK.
The story published in the Enterprise reciting the slaughter of a family near Empire was all a fiction. It was understood to be such by all acquainted with the locality in which the alleged affair occurred. In the first place, Empire and Dutch Nick's are one, and in the next there is no "great pine forest" nearer than the Sierra Nevada mountains. But it was necessary to publish the story in order to get the fact into the San Francisco papers that the Spring Valley Water company was "cooking" dividends by borrowing money to declare them on for its stockholders. The only way you can get a fact into a San Francisco journal is to smuggle it in through some great tragedy.[79]

Richard G. Lillard has noted that Twain's retraction signals a miscommunication, a misread on the writer's part for his audience to understand his gag. Lillard calls Twain's misjudgment an "inartistic and unethical" act.[80] While Twain admitted in print that his hoax failed, the hoax did not necessarily create animosity between writer and reader. On the contrary, western readers in mining towns were accustomed to reading sensational, violent stories in the newspapers.[81]

Furthermore, though a difference exists between local news items that contain details about shootouts and affrays between drunks over mining disputes and a hoax that pits a "deranged" father as the killer of his family, a startling similarity is also present. The father, like the drunks disputing mining claims, feared foul play. A danger slithered beneath a ruffian's bullets or a father's axe—financial loss, the heavy kind, able to cause a man to lose his sanity. Indeed, the father in the hoax "had been a heavy owner in the best mines of Virginia and Gold Hill, but when the San Francisco papers exposed the game of cooking dividends in order to bolster up our stocks he grew afraid and sold out, and invested to an immense amount in the Spring Valley Water Company of San Francisco." The message, then, is not unlike the observations of the news items: financial dishonesty ruined men and caused them to act violently, even to kill their business partners or family members. If Twain wanted to attract attention, this hoax succeeded. If Twain wanted to prove a point that most readers and editors understood, then Twain failed. The cultural critique within the hoax did not deliver as clear of a meaning as did Twain's journalism. Nor did the point about the Hopkins character committing murder because he had invested in Spring Valley stock resonate with readers, as did the sensational acts of murder. Twain's technique, "to smuggle [fact] in through some great tragedy," was, in fact, so successful that no one noticed that facts had been smuggled into the tragedy. How could they, amid so much blood? The internal logic of the narrative delivered the tragedy of murder and overshadowed unethical business practices. Perhaps the external tragedy appeared after the failure of the hoax that caused Twain to "take it all back."

Though Clemens vacationed in San Francisco in the late spring of 1863, worked as the Nevada Territory correspondent for the San Francisco *Daily Morning Call* in the summer and fall of 1863, and finally became the local correspondent for the *Call*, spring through fall 1864, when Twain wrote "A Bloody Massacre Near Carson," in October 1863, he did not call California his home. In fact, he often despised the practices of California politicians and companies that seemed to degrade with corruption Nevada Territory. This hoax, then, was Twain's "voice," acting for the voice of the abused people of California, who were in danger. Here, the lie works as an illocutionary act. Because fires were a real threat in San Francisco, and Twain judged the Spring Valley Water Company's practice of "turning off the water overnight" as not only dangerous but also profit driven, the intended and illocutionary act reflects the concern of the people and Twain's criticism of a greedy company.[82] Twain also proposed a certain amount of humor for the outcome of refusing water to Californians: the act was uncivilized for metropolitan dwellers that wished to brew coffee for breakfast.[83] Twain knew the editors of San Francisco newspapers, and he believed it their responsibility to lampoon the water company. Since they did not, Twain did. According to Twain's friend and fellow journalist for the *Enterprise* William Wright, better known as Dan De Quille, Twain's "main object was to slap back at the San Francisco *Bulletin*, the editors of which had made attacks on cooked dividends in Washoe investments but had left unmentioned similar cooking done in California by the Spring

Valley Water Company of San Francisco."[84] As his technique Twain used what was tried and true in Nevada and on the staff of the *Enterprise*— explicit violence. In order to gain readers who might in fact develop some sense of outrage for a corrupt company's business practices, Twain wove into the story details of William Cornwell's actual murders at Reese River from the previous July.[85]

Even if Twain's readers were amused, editors of the newspapers that printed the hoax were not. Editors printed tirades attacking the integrity of the *Enterprise* and the architect of the story who had soiled the reputation of the territory. On October 28, the Virginia *Evening Bulletin* reported that the hoax "affected the character of the community.... God knows our Territory has a reputation of being the theater of scenes of blood and violence that really do occur bad enough to satisfy our bitterest enemies. There does not exist any need to paint our characters any blacker than they really are."[86] Although the region possessed a reputation for violence, much law did exist.[87] Twain wrote often about the police force in Virginia City and San Francisco, but he also wrote about active vigilance committees in the 1860s in California, Nevada, and other regions in the West. Vigilantes and vigilance committees play prominent roles in "Horrible Affair," "A Brisk Business in the Shooting and Slashing Way at Washoe," and "Dispatches by the State Line." One aim of both legal and extra-legal justice was to reduce violence and crime so that men from the East like Twain and his journalist contemporaries, laborers, businessmen, and politicians would continue to come to the West. The silver and gold, not to mention the land and other resources, were attractive for investors east of the Mississippi. Still, when Twain discusses vigilantes, it is because he has judged law enforcement to be ineffective. Phrases to describe these groups of vigilantes appear in these articles as a "party of citizens" who come after the murderer when the police fail, a murderer who is "reported hanged by a Vigilance Committee" after the police display a perceived incompetence, and a discussion among citizens who produce "some little talk of a Vigilance Committee" when the police become ineffective. Though contemporary editors claimed Twain's writing, and his hoax in particular, had stained the "reputation" of the Territory, Twain's violent hoax and satirical story had actually supported the reputation of the *Enterprise*. Its pages were often painted in blood. But, with the criticism of the sensation hoax, Twain actually gained free press, notoriety, and fame for having duped and frightened so many readers all over the West. The Gold Hill *Daily News's* editors, however, wanted their readers to know that, had they known the story was fiction, they would never have printed such a "sell":

> THAT "SELL."—The horrible story of a "murder," which we yesterday copied in good faith from the "Enterprise," turns out to be a mere "witticism" of Mark Twain. In short, A LIE—utterly, baseless, and without a shadow of foundation. The "Enterprise" is the pioneer newspaper of the Territory, is more widely known than any other, and having been ably and respectably conducted has heretofore been considered a reliable medium of information. The terrible tale related in its columns yesterday, and copied into ours, was believed here, and will be believed elsewhere—wherever the ENTERPRISE and the NEWS are read. It will be read with sickening horror, and the already bloody reputation of our Territory will receive another smear. When the readers of the soul-sickening story are informed that it was a mere bubble of "wit," they will feel relieved, although they may utterly fail to see the humor or "the point."[88]

Twain assumed his readers would see the humor and the point, even if the editors of competing newspapers did not. Twain later remembered this publication and its responses and called the hoax "the talk of the town" and "the talk of the territory." He intended to expose the water company by creating a sensational murder caused by one man's failure in relation to investments in such companies.[89] In this way, Twain's hoax also operates as a perlocutionary act, or a method to encourage a reader to act, to think—to do something, in this case, to warn his readers to share his view of a corrupt company. Editors, however, did not receive Twain's "LIE" as a warning with a valuable social message for Californians. Instead, they were abused by this lie that they claimed defied their ideals concerning journalistic integrity. In Twain's opinion, the editors of competing papers exposed Twain's "lie" to draw attention to their papers by playing on the reputation of the *Enterprise*.[90] Twain, then, was a "victim" of others' muckraking.

Twain, however, had not required such an application of "truth" in his hoax. The hoax's competing discourse ultimately failed to deliver his intended message, indicating that such competition had created too many possible ways to receive this message. Or, perhaps another way to view Twain's failure, within the context of "I TAKE IT ALL BACK" and "THAT "SELL," is to admit that the hoax's fictional elements defeated the competing journalistic elements. The horror and entertainment of the piece were received with more power and urgency than were the facts. He also preferred to tell a story rather than telling the truth.[91] The truth, he thought, should not be told at the sacrifice of the narrative. Fiction, after all, is always a lie. To a certain degree, all of Twain's writing was a lie, even his journalism. Twain was outraged, however, that the Gold Hill *Daily News*, when calling his "sell" a "LIE," used a smaller font for the all-majuscule letters in LIE. He thought this smallness of the font represented the editors' ideas about his smallness of talent or character.[92] A good idea, though, did not need to be impartial or "truth" in order to tell truths. Twain's sensation hoaxes and sensation items were biased. Perhaps all writing is biased, especially when the writer has constructed a persona to reflect a masculine and violent ethic espoused by many dwellers in the West.[93] And yet, if Twain did "shock the moral sense of the many readers of the Enterprise,"[94] perhaps his efforts to align himself as a reporter for the concerns of a people could never fully be realized. Because he never became the preacher, whose voice told truths and instructed, he instead became a reporter. Yet he never considered reporting and writing literature to be the same act. News was constructed from reality and constrained him within a framework of fact. Literature freed him from fact and allowed for the application of fiction without misjudging the readership that relied on factual reporting. Hoaxes, though, did not fail to deliver meaning through storytelling. Perhaps readers and editors did not agree with Twain about what those stories should mean, but the stories stuck with people. The stories even lasted beyond Twain. Dan De Quille told Twain that the hoax "will be remembered and talked about when all your other work is forgotten. The murder at Dutch Nick's will be quoted years from now as the big sell of our times."[95]

Mark Twain, embracing his literary liar persona, eventually became a literary voice for his country. But in the West, his writing performed two roles: it critiqued western culture, which helped create a literary persona that first made him popular in the West and then famous in the East and on a national scale. He wanted national attention.[96] Additionally, the literary, critical tone he developed as a journalist in the West grew into a style that had enough literary and cultural cache to report on, reflect, and subvert western, southern, northern, and national cultures. In 1864, Twain had begun a working relationship with Charles Henry Webb, owner and editor of the *Californian*, a weekly literary paper whose main contributor was Bret Harte, the other famous western humorist and friend of Twain. In a letter to his brother and sister-in-law on September 28, 1864, Twain explains that though writing for the *Californian* paid less than writing daily for the *Call*, the job was better and had a broader audience: "I only get $12 an article for the Californian, but you see it makes my wages up to what they were on the Call, when I worked at night, & the paper has an exalted reputation in the east, & is liberally copied from by papers like the Home Journal."⁹⁷ Three days earlier, he had sent his mother and sister the good news, which appears in the middle of the letter:

> I have engaged to write for the new literary paper—the "Californian"—same pay I used to receive on the "Golden Era"—one article a week, fifty dollars a month. I quit the "Era," long ago. It wasn't high-toned enough. I thought that whether I was a literary "jackleg" or not, I wouldn't class myself with that style of people, anyhow. The "Californian" circulates among the highest class of the community, & is the best weekly literary paper in the United States—& I suppose I ought to know.⁹⁸

Clemens brags here that he will now be writing for the "best weekly literary paper" and that because of his reputation, he should be able to judge such papers and choose among them. He is, after all, Mark Twain. Some periodicals were preferable to others, and he exploited this hierarchy by writing simultaneously for various publications. Because of his periodical publication, his fame would continue to grow, but in 1865 he had his doubts about his success. Real fame was drawing near, but Clemens failed to recognize it. In October, perhaps he placed a pistol to head and considered ending the potential to gain a national readership, though he would have certainly been remembered as the western sensational, violent writer who shot himself.⁹⁹

Two weeks later, Twain read the kind words of Charles Henry Webb, who, one year before, had given Twain the opportunity to reach with his writing beyond the West. Charles Henry Webb published several contributions from Twain, but in 1865, when Twain published his soon-to-be famous story, "Jim Smiley and his Jumping Frog" for Henry Clapp, Jr.'s *Saturday Press*, Henry Webb wrote a letter to the Sacramento *Union* extolling the talent of Twain and his reception in the east, especially within the New York literary community heavily influenced by Clapp and his publication. Webb notes that

> future Mark Twain scholars will puzzle over that gentleman's present hieroglyphics and occasionally eccentric expressions. Apropos, of Twain, who is a man of Mark, I am glad to see that his humor has met with recognition at the East, and that mention is made of him in that critical journal, the *Round Table*. They may talk of course humor, if they please, but in his case it is simply the strength of the soil—the germ is there and it sprouts good and strong. To my mind Mark Twain and Dan Setchell are the wild Humorists of the Pacific.¹⁰⁰

Charles Henry Webb might have saved Clemens's life, and probably saved the career of Twain, though neither man likely recognized this reality then. Though Twain might not have known if western violence would sell within a transcontinental context, he certainly knew by 1865 that his western humor could gain him national notoriety. In the October 1865 letter to his brother about "Self-Murder" and his ambitions to succeed as a writer, Twain wrote to Orion that only with new attention from eastern editors did he begin to believe that he might become a writer of note:

> *You* see in me a talent for humorous writing, & urge me to cultivate it. But I always regarded it as brotherly partiality, on your part, & attached no value to it. It is only now, when editors of standard literary papers in the distant east give me high praise, & who do not know me & cannot of course be blinded by the glamour of partiality, that I really begin to believe there must be something in it.[101]

Webb certainly helped push Twain's writing beyond the sagebrush and into the eastern metropolis. At the time, the West, as well as Twain, had entered the national imagination. When in September 1865 the New York *Round Table* characterized American humor, it noted the importance of the western humor in the development of the tradition: "The enterprising State of California, which follows as closely as she can upon the steps of her older Eastern sisters, has produced examples of our national humor which compare favorably with those already mentioned."[102] But Twain's time in the West had ended. Though the West remained and continued to influence his journalism and book-length works, he would never again report on a daily basis on western cultural violence for these same newspapers. He would use his literary style as a badman who advanced his "philosophic observations" about violence enacted by badmen, and his humorous "hieroglyphics and occasionally eccentric expressions," to critique culture and simultaneously attract readers. He was in the West, and he continued to be in the East, a kind of philosophical *vox populi* who came, saw, and reported.

Performing After the Muzzle

When Twain arrived in New York in January 1867, the bohemian culture of antebellum Greenwich Village had largely dissipated. Still, a postwar bohemia had re-emerged in New York. Twain became a part of this new culture that he called "we of Bohemia," a term used to mean an eclectic group of journalists.[103] This group contained a few writers from the West, including Artemus Ward, Twain's friend and fellow writer who had recommended Twain's story "Jim Smiley and his Jumping Frog" for Clapp's *Saturday Press* in 1865. In New York, Twain met and published alongside writers such as Walt Whitman, William Dean Howells, Anthony Trollope, and Wilkie Collins, who published not only nationally but also in transatlantic markets.[104] And these men shared a literary and social culture as close as the one Mark Twain had enjoyed in Virginia City, Nevada Territory, and in San Francisco with writers such as Bret Harte, Artemus Ward, Dan De Quille, Sam P. Davis, Joseph Goodman, and Adah Isaacs Menken. These writers had all published in the famous western newspapers and periodicals with Twain.

Twain's transition from western humorist, journalist, and writer of sensational news items and hoaxes to a New York bohemian marked his transition from a regional reporter to a book-length writer of national literary merit and fame. But the articles he published in Clapp's *Saturday Press* that helped garner a readership in New York and the East were not reflections of New York culture or even an image of a nation divided by war and reunited with its conclusion. Twains' first story published in New York paper was a tale of western lore set in a mining camp that used vernacular as part of its style. Twain's final story printed in this paper, "A Strange Dream," which was published in the last issue of the *Saturday Press*, and on its front page, is a kind of travel piece with an imaginary narrative about a "dead monarch" who "had been spirited away!"[105]

"A Strange Dream" is a strange and sensational story, though not sensational in the violent, forensic manner found in his early journalism. This story, like Twain's hoaxes, was a lie. In this way, Twain's story represented a regional transition but also a stylistic one. The style of his journalism and hoaxes in the West depended on the conflation of fact and fiction, the real and the fantastic, the violent and the sensational. And yet he usually inserted an opinion, a judgment, or a criticism, of the culture or of himself. His wry wit or satire marked Twain as a writer whose talents and desire to report on a larger culture erupted from his regional merit as a voice who mixed these styles and concerns. These stories in the *Saturday Press* grew out of his experiences in the West and because of the opportunities he was given after years of writing and publishing sensational, violent journalistic representations of this region's culture.

As the 1860s closed and the new decade opened, Twain found domestic comforts in New York and Connecticut. Here he transitioned to a book-length writer and never again lived in the region for which he had sometimes operated as a *vox populi*. And yet the West remained in his memories and allowed him, even as an easterner, to write about the violent men who had helped construct a violent space—a space Twain remembered as populated by devils.

2

The Space Betwixt the Garden and the Devil: Mark Twain's "Personal" and "Public" Reports on Stages and Coaches, 1862–1864

Mark Twain read and then considered the story printed on the page proof of chapter twenty hanging between his hands. He liked it. The tale contained no murders, hangings, rapes, or robberies that he had written about and published in newspapers in Nevada Territory and California between 1862 and 1864. Instead, the tale provided a whimsical, romantic view of the West, its excitement and mythos that the writer enjoyed. Furthermore, this mythos had attracted him and other emigrants to the region, even if the myth was not quite reality. Now in Hartford, Connecticut, in 1871, he reviewed the proofs for his manuscript about these early days of the 1860s in Nevada and California, published the following year under the title *Roughing It* (1872). He needed to know if a simple story transformed into legend about a famous stagecoach ride was a lie. Supposedly, on his trip out West by stage, Horace Greeley, editor of the *New-York Tribune*, had met another famous man, the driver Hank Monk.

According to Twain's narrator in *Roughing It*, he had heard many drivers and passengers tell the story of Greeley complaining to Hank Monk about being in a hurry on the leg between Carson City, Nevada, and Placerville, California. As the story went, Hank Monk responded with "Keep your seat, Horace, and I'll get you there on time" and whipped the horses to drive like poor devils on the plains of hell. Twain included that story in his book, and wanted to leave it, for the tale was a ridiculous yarn about overland travel, a strange even notorious stagecoach driver, and it included an influential newspaper editor in New York at a time when Twain's fame was beginning to flourish beyond the bounds of the West. Still, Twain doubted the tale's accuracy. On August 17 Twain wrote a letter to Horace Greeley, asking him to confirm the tale as myth before the book went to press: "I have said in the positive words that the famous Hank Monk anecdote refers to an episode *which never occurred*. I got this from a newspaper editor, who said he got it from you. I never knew of his telling a lie—but to make *sure* & will you please endorse his statement if you can—or deny it if you must?—so that I can leave my remark as it is; or change it if truth requires."[1] Though for the publication of his book Twain desired to get right the facts of this story, he had not minded perpetrating this mythic stagecoach ride on December 12, 1863, in a letter from Carson City, published in Nevada's Virginia City *Territorial Enterprise*. In this newspaper article, Twain wrote about a ceremony in honor of Hank Monk, in which wealthy donors presented him with a "superb gold watch," which was "gorgeously embellished with coaches and horses," and bore "for a motto Hank's famous remark to Horace Greeley: 'Keep your seat, Horace—I'll get you there on time!'" But eight years had passed, and Twain was fact checking for a book.[2]

Though no letter from Greeley in response to Twain's request exists, Twain included the story of Greeley's famous ride with Hank Monk in a humorous section that undercuts the validity of the story by exaggerating how many times he had heard others tell it—"four hundred and eighty-one or eighty-two times."[3] He also included a footnote based on what "a newspaper editor" had told Twain. The note states that the incident "*never occurred*." The editor's name is Joseph Goodman, owner and editor of the *Territorial Enterprise*. He told Twain that Greeley had said, "there was not a damned word of truth in the whole story!"[4]

The fictionalized tale about Horace Greeley's stagecoach travels symbolized Samuel Clemens's initial hope for rejuvenation in the West. Stages and coaches offered transitional and transient spaces, not domestic and not quite public, that allowed men to commit robberies, rapes, assaults, and murders. What began as Clemens's personal fear he wrote in letters to his female family members about traveling to Nevada Territory by coach amid a harsh climate and landscape, "Indian" attacks, and opportunistic "devils" in the guise of men developed into a different, more public anxiety published in newspapers. Because of the Civil War and his experiences writing for California papers, Twain's concerns shifted to include both gendered and political causes for peril in the West. In Twain's letters, the "devils" in Nevada that might grope a woman in a coach gave way to his published accounts of California and Nevada "Secessionists" and "organized" bands of robbers loyal to the Confederacy. In 1862, the traffic by overland stagecoach that Clemens reported on when he lived in Nevada had little to do with violence caused by the impending war, even though the war had displaced many western emigrants, including Clemens; indeed he had fled from it. By 1864, his reports on local and regional crime published in California papers often linked this violence to a national discussion. His "public" criticisms of local crime engage the discourse of the Civil War in subversive ways, so that his ironic tone and humor judged criminals as players in a larger cultural and political context. Glenn Hendler has argued that in the nineteenth century the novel delivered a "public sentiment" for readers to establish ways to "feel right" about a variety of issues. I extend Hendler's view of the novel to Twain's journalism, for it was received by readers who assigned meaning to the violence that Twain described. Conversely, Clemens's letters to his family offered them the ability to discover the West through his personal lens and receive a warning that begins with the method of travel within a region and among regions.[5]

Sympathy for the Devil

After deserting a brief military campaign as a member of volunteer militia, Samuel Clemens left Missouri by overland stagecoach with his brother Orion on July 26, 1861, just five days after the First Battle of Bull Run near Manassas, Virginia.[6] The brothers arrived on August 14, 1861, in Carson City. Far west of the Mississippi, in a region that must have initially seemed removed from the war in Virginia or even in Missouri, Clemens served as secretary to his brother, who was the newly appointed Secretary of Nevada Territory. Clemens and his brother had both headed West to find success. Orion also wanted to begin a new life with his family. The trip these brothers made symbolizes the migrations many men and families made in the mid-nineteenth century, and yet such migrations could only lead to a new life if the men, and then the women and children, could travel safely. And yet on this journey west Orion carried a "small-sized

Colt's revolver," and Sam was armed with a "pitiful little Smith and Wesson's seven-shooter which carried a ball like a homopathic pill, and it took the whole seven to make a dose for an adult." In this recollection later published in *Roughing It* (1872), Clemens added, "But I thought it was grand. It appeared to me to be a dangerous weapon. It had only one fault—you could not hit anything with it."[7] These pistols, though mostly insufficient to protect the brothers from male outlaws, offered them a notion of salvation on the perilous migration.

Though he hoped the land and the region would offer paradise, and not an eventual hell, he was skeptical of the region's men and characterized them as "devils."[8] Twain frequently employed the term "devil" or "Devil" in this personal writing. In fact, between September of 1861 and July 1864, he wrote the word twenty-two times in seventeen letters to family and friends to denigrate men. Such criticisms of "devils" and concerns for women were initially related to Clemens's concerns about the differences between the far West and Missouri. Still, for women from the Upper South, Clemens assumed that Missouri certainly offered a kind of security that the plains of the West, and mining towns in Nevada Territory, could not offer. After all, people performed gender within a social and economic context, which was always contained within a political context, in this case, the differences between the West and the Upper South and what the West symbolized to a nation. California entered the Union as a free state in 1850 within the Compromise of 1850 designed to avoid a war or secession. Nevada became a state, and a free one attached to the North, in 1864.

That same year, railroad travel was new to Nevada Territory and California. Horse-drawn carriages were the dominant form of transportation for men and women in the early 1860s. The First Transcontinental Railroad's construction began in 1863 and was completed in 1869. Not until 1872 did workers connect the Virginia line to the transcontinental line at Reno.[9] Luxurious, by comparison, railroad cars soon replaced the slower, less comfortable stagecoaches as the major form of transcontinental transportation. Though he thought that stagecoaches were uncomfortable, Clemens's fear for his female family members' safety surpassed his anxiety about their comfort.

While Clemens offered concerns for the safety of his mother and sister, Orion fretted about his wife, Mollie, and six-year-old daughter, Jennie, joining him. Five months after the brothers arrived in Nevada Territory, Orion wrote a letter to his wife warning her about traveling by stagecoach.

He claimed that coaches offered the threat of male passengers groping (or worse) female passengers in the dark of night travel. He cautioned his wife to be wary of a man's hand that might "wander" over her body, which, if he did not believe her to be "incorruptible," might cause him to doubt her purity and refuse to "sleep" with her. Orion admitted to his wife, "Traveling across the plains sometimes develops the d—l in people. But of all ways of traveling for a woman, the very last I have even tried is a stage."[10] When Orion wrote about developing the "devil" in people, he meant men. Men, according to Orion, would commonly pretend to be asleep during half "the time for the three weeks it will be so dark in the stage," and that she would be unable to see her own hand, let alone a man's wandering hand.[11] For Orion, the choice his wife might make to travel by stage was so wrong that he considered it immoral. The man, he expected, would perform as the "devil" might in the dark of the stage. The woman, however, should not choose to put herself inside the stage, which was the same as putting herself in the situation that might impugn her judgment and Orion's reputation. Orion closes the letter, not by pleading with his wife to be careful, but by accusing her of the possibility of infidelity even before she has made the trip. His insult, here, was meant to discourage her, for, after reading the letter she knew that her husband would not to sleep with her if she decided to travel "three weeks of dark nights, through a wilderness, with only a man acquaintance."[12] Orion did not fear "Indian" attack or potential politically motivated robberies, at least not in this letter. His anxieties were focused on female purity.

In February 1862, one month after Orion wrote to Mollie, Clemens wrote a letter to his mother, Jane, and sister, Pamela, that contains information about his poor luck mining for silver, about the terrain, and especially about the discomfort and dangers of the West, most notably for women traveling by stagecoach. Sam and Orion had hoped to find success before inviting other family members to join them. For Orion and Sam, the process was taking longer than they had hoped. Orion's wife and daughter joined him a year later. Their mother, Jane, moved in with Pamela and her husband, William A. Moffett. Jane had been a widow since 1847, and since Sam and Orion had left for the West, Jane relied on Pamela and her husband for care and support. The Civil War brought hard times to Pamela and William, however. They lived in St. Louis, where he was a merchant. His business suffered because of the closing of the river to civilian traffic, which is also the reason Clemens had left piloting a riverboat and headed West.

If the West presented opportunities for Sam and Orion, perhaps the region would be good for the rest of family. But safety came first. In the letter, Clemens urges his mother and sister to travel out West by steamer and avoid an overland coach. The long trip offered many sights to see, but travel was hot, dirty, uncomfortable, and dangerous. Desperados like Joseph A. Slade, who later in life found greater profits in protecting overland coaches than in robbing them, often raided coaches, especially coaches occupied with women travelers. While specific figures, rather than romanticized accounts, of stagecoach and carriage robberies are difficult to verify, Clemens's personal concerns were echoed by other westerners at the time. For example, in 1863 a "wave of stagecoach robberies" spread across parts of Nevada and Idaho Territories. One trader noted that "no safety for life or property" existed, which is why he, and other men, had to "protect his own." On his stagecoach journey West, Clemens had heard tales of robberies, even J. A. Slade's robberies. Clemens met Slade and feared that the desperado might murder him. Ironically, Margaret Gilbert, wife of J. A. Slade's partner, Henry Gilbert, commented that no man was safe "if it was thought he had money."[13] Of course, Clemens survived the journey West, as did many men and women. The women who lived in the region who worked as lodging-house keepers, seamstresses, and servants survived and thrived where Clemens now feared his mother and sister could not even safely visit.[14] A year prior, in 1861, in a letter to his mother just two months after arriving in Nevada Territory, Clemens answered a list of questions his mother had posed in a previous letter. Jane's third question and Clemens's response: "Third—'Are there many ladies in Carson?' Multitudes—probably the handsomest in the world."[15]

Both of these letters describe parts of Nevada to his mother and sister, but by February 1862, five months after he wrote the first letter, Nevada Territory has become a hell, and California "the Garden of Eden reproduced." At this point, his optimism about becoming wealthy in the mines began to diminish. His desires, as well as his fears, existed within a culture of westward expansion, where hope was replaced with reality. In this case, the fears associated with violence against women are related to a fear that the West might not satisfy the hopes and dreams of success. In part of the letter addressed to Pamela, Twain admits that his view of Nevada has changed, largely based on his financial failings: "Don't you know that I have expended money in this country but have made none myself? Don't you know that I have never held in my hands a gold or silver bar that belonged to me? Don't you know that its [sic] all talk and no cider so far?"[16]

2. The Space Betwixt the Garden and the Devil   57

The repetitious structure evokes a sense of desperation and loss, one that eventually drained his "organ of Hope" for Nevada mining and replaced it with a drive to become a writer instead. In the absence of wealth mined from the earth, Nevada Territory became for Clemens a hellish landscape that also allowed him to develop a sharp pitchfork for a pen.

Indeed, Nevada Territory became a lode from which Mark Twain could mine and develop his "public" writing style, begin a famous career in the West as a journalist and performer. Here he created a persona that combined the charm of life on the Mississippi with the wildness of the West, and later with the sophistication of the East. But in 1862, Clemens's Nevada was no place for a female family member or a family friend, Margaret Sexton, whom he loved. Certainly, the landscape was harsh. Nevada's famous Gold Hill mining town sat just beyond a place named "Devil's Gate." This gate symbolized the entrance to hell, a place on earth that neither Pamela, Margaret Sexton, "nor the devil either" could like, but that Clemens emphasized: "but *I* like it." He often used devil in a metaphorical sense to suggest that Nevada, or parts of Nevada such as Lake Bigler, were so lovely as to "make the Devil's mouth water if he ever visits the earth,"[17] and yet most of Nevada below the mountains was so hot, dry, and miserable that the devil would not "like the country." Clemens continues to describe the harshness of the landscape, but his dripping pen interrupts his thought. The paragraph ends abruptly after his pen's ink damages the letter:

> When it rains here, it never lets up till it has done all the raining it has got to do—and after that, there's a dry spell, you bet. Why, I have had my whiskers and moustaches so full of alkali dust that you'd have thought I worked in a starch factory and boarded in a flour barrel. And it is very healthy here. The funeral bell, with its sad accompaniments of tearful eyes, and drooping heads, and [*ink blot*] (*blast* such a pen, anyhow—I *do* think they get up pens in this country that would make the oldest man in the world cuss—if he hadn't, like me, promised that he wouldn't). But its healthy here, you know, if you wear a heavy beard. That is what I was trying to come at.[18]

Like the blemished page, the landscape was displeasing and disappointing. In fact, if the devil were to visit Nevada, he would grow "homesick and go back to hell again."[19] But Clemens was not homesick. He took advantage of the freedom found in the West. He caroused, gambled, drank and had promiscuous sex with menial and servant women. In a January 1862 letter to "Mollie," his sister-in-law, Clemens brags that he has been sleeping with various women servants in Nevada: "I don't mind sleeping with female servants as long as I am a bachelor—by *no* means—but *after*

I marry, that sort of thing will be 'played out,' you know."[20] He also wrote for a paper that compensated him well for his reports, which included public versions of his personal fears. For Clemens, and even for Orion, the real devil, at least initially, before the war had dragged for three years, was the man willing to abuse an innocent person, especially a woman, in Nevada or in California.

This same letter from February, which is less accusatory than his brother's letter sent one month earlier to his wife concerning her safety in a stagecoach and her sexual purity, offers a point similar to Orion's—the terrain is rough, the journey is long, and the men of the road are dangerous. The masculine landscape, and its inhabitants, is more perilous than the feminine sea. So much of Clemens's boyhood experience and young career was influenced by his leisure, travel, and vocation on the Mississippi River, so he thought taking a steamer to San Francisco or Sacramento, rather than a stagecoach to Carson City, was more comfortable, safer, and seemed a more appropriate form of travel for a woman.

Clemens begins his warning by drawing a distinction between California and Nevada. On the one hand, California has already become a kind of utopia in the popular imagination, especially San Francisco. Gold had attracted emigrants for thirteen years by the time Twain wrote the later, and San Francisco had already become a cosmopolitan metropolis. Nevada Territory, on the other hand, was a new mining territory, and was also a kind of hell that would make even the devil homesick. Clemens informs his mother and sister, "Any of you, or all of you, may live in California, for that is the Garden of Eden reproduced—but you shall never live in Nevada."[21] For Clemens, San Francisco's intimate location near the water enabled this Garden of Eden to offer an opportunity that a woman could never enjoy in Nevada—a safe arrival at a port city where desperadoes do not arrive from the sea. In addition, little entertainment or leisure existed in a stagecoach on the plains. A coach was small, hot, and dirty, whereas a ship offered space and comfort for women. Men, however, could actually enjoy the journey West by coach, according to Clemens. He certainly did.

Clemens then continues to contrast a man's experience traveling by coach against a woman's. He warns the women to avoid the coach but that his brother-in-law, "Mr. Moffett," would find pleasure in the journey, which becomes his second point:

> Secondly, none of you, save Mr. Moffett, shall ever cross the Plains. If you were only going to Pike's Peak, a little matter of 700 miles from St. Joe, you might

take the coach, and I wouldn't say a word. But I consider it over 2,000 miles from St. Joe to Carson, and the first 6 or 800 miles is mere Fourth of July, compared to the balance of the route. But Lord bless you, a *man* enjoys every foot of it. If you ever come here or to California, it must be by sea, you know. Mr. Moffett must come by overland *coach*, though, by all means. He would consider it the jolliest little trip he ever took in his life.[22]

For a man to have a jolly trip, however, he would have to cross the plains, alone, without women or children. The overland coach, compared with a wagon train, was fast though less hospitable for a family. However, a coach was also supposed to be less prone to attack by "Indians," such as the Snake Indian attack on a large wagon train between Pike's Peak and Nevada. Clemens reported anonymously on this attack for the *Enterprise* on October 1, 1862, which offered details about the murdered men and women.[23] Even in February, when he urged his family to avoid the overland coach, he also offered a final warning about wagon trains: "Don't you say a word to me about 'trains' across the plains. Because I am down on that arrangement. That sort of thing is 'played out,' you know. The Overland Coach or the Mail Steamer is the thing."[24] Wagon trains were slow and vulnerable to "Indian" attacks, though overland coaches were private and offered more intimate dangers from men against women. Here again Clemens emphasizes the differences between female and male perceptions of the landscape and traveling long distances to cross it. Danger and discomfort offered men a certain kind of fun in a region, perhaps, unlike the one they had left behind. For women, the possibility of having "the jolliest little trip" of their lives seemed unlikely to Clemens.

As evidence for his claims, Clemens follows this warning to his mother and sister by referring to J. Ross Browne's three-part series, "A Peep at Washoe," which appeared in *Harper's New Monthly Magazine* from December 1860 to February 1861. Even before heading west, Clemens had started to develop his "personal" perception of the region. The foundation of these beliefs came from growing up in a conservative Missouri home led by his mother, and older siblings after his father died in 1847. But as a young man, he had also read about the West. He was especially interested in the travel writing that appeared *Harper's*. Like many readers of the magazine learning about the West, he had read articles written by J. Ross Browne. Browne became a famous travel writer and most certainly influenced Clemens's western writing, especially his observations about the West—its land and culture. In the third installment of "A Peep at Washoe," in February 1861, for example, Browne begins the article by describing the land and the weather of Nevada Territory: "As ill-luck would have it, a perfect hurricane swept through the anon from Gold Hill; sometimes in gusts so sudden and violent that it was utterly impossible to make an inch of headway."[25] It is clear that Browne's description of Nevada in the winter influenced Clemens's description of a stagecoach ride two years later in January 1863, published in the *Placer Weekly Courier*. In "A Big Thing in Washoe City" "The Reliable" of the *Enterprise* writes that the "wind blew such a hurricane that the coach drifted sideways from one toll road to another, and sometimes utterly refused to mind her helm. It is a fearful thing to be at sea in a stage coach."[26] Browne, like Clemens two years later, transitions from accounts of the land and weather to details and illustrations that support how and in what ways the land and weather affect people—men in the West.

One illustration, "Snow Slide," printed in February 1861, which appeared in the final article in the series, offers a depiction of Clemens's masculine, dangerous landscape.[27] Here, a scene of a man and five "pack mules, tumbling fifteen hundred feet down the side of a mountain," out of control, in what appears to be a position of distress for all six poor devils, poses a threat for women and men alike.[28] For if a skilled miner can fall to his peril, all the more so can a green woman. Clemens's assessment of the West, here, becomes complicated, however, for not only are the masculine terrain and desperadoes dangerous, but farther west than Nevada in California is "the Garden of Eden reproduced." Nevada is hell because of the landscape, first, and second because of the violence. His failure in silver mining also affected his view of Nevada and influenced his language about the Territory. His dream of success in Nevada hatched in the mines. When that failure came, Clemens did not see Nevada as a utopia. This realization unveiled the reality of the West hidden beneath the dream. And yet he seems to expect danger in Nevada and tries to stop his family from encountering this danger, though a year later, Clemens invited his ill sister to spend the summer at Lake Bigler, which he called "the Fountain of Youth."[29] Soon California too will disappoint Clemens, for it promised a place of paradise, escape, rejuvenation—a new prairie Eden. By appropriating "prairie Eden" to mean a place of perfection and harmony, he already seems to fear that this Eden must fall, as did the first, that sin and crime exist within the framework of the utopia, that women are in danger of temptation. Still, his time in California was ultimately a successful period for his career. He wrote and later published his first collection of short fiction, starring "The Celebrated Jumping Frog of Calav-

2. The Space Betwixt the Garden and the Devil   61

SNOW SLIDE.

"Snow Slide." Published in J. Ross Browne, "A Peep at Washoe" [Third Paper], February 1861, *Harper's New Monthly Magazine*, Vol. 22, No. 129, 289–290. J. Ross Browne was born in Ireland and immigrated to America as a child. In 1849 he arrived in California to report on the state's Constitutional Convention. Browne became a writer and artist and was especially known for his travel writing. He later worked for the Treasury Department.

eras County" (1867), and he compiled remembrances of many of his experiences about Nevada and California for his second travel book, *Roughing It* (1872). Finally, he left California on an assignment for the *Sacramento Union* to the Sandwich Islands, which also provided some of the material for *Roughing It*.

In the 1862 letter, however, Clemens continues to compare an early view of California with Nevada, drawing heavily on the image from

Harper's of a man and mules tumbling from a height of heaven or the Holy Land to the depths of hell:

> You want to know something about the route between California and Nevada Territory? Suppose you take my word for it, that it is exceedingly jolly.... Why bless you, there's *scenery* on that route. You can stand on some of those noble peaks and see Jerusalem and the Holy Land. And you can start a boulder, and watch send it tearing up the earth and crashing over trees—down—down—down—to the very devil, Madam.[30]

The contrast between the top of the Holy Land and the bottom of hell marks the beauty and the danger of the landscape and reiterates the unpleasant even worrisome quality of Nevada for Clemens. Even in *Roughing It* Twain's narrator discussed the "high and steep" mountains that in the spring invite "disastrous land-slides."[31] Perhaps a more complicated problem exists, though, than simply a fear for the safety of women. For in the next portion of the letter, Clemens writes, corrects and edits, his idea about gender concerns traveling by coach in Nevada. He plays with the man/woman and male/female binaries as a way to suggest that no one, no matter how masculine or courageous, would escape fear while traveling through the Territory's perilous landscape:

> And the way to make that journey is not by coach, because, in that case, be you ~~man~~ male or ~~woman~~, female, ~~male or fe~~ man or woman, you would be eternally scared to death, at the prospect of rolling down a mountain, and it would take up so much of your time to enjoy that sort of thing, you know, that you couldn't pay much attention to the scenery. But just take the steamer to Sacramento City ...[32]

Clemens's warning, at least in this one letter in 1862, unlike his brother's, focuses more on the dangerous landscape than on the unethical men who might take advantage of traveling women. The mountains, like men, are the enemies of "male or female." Clemens's reordering of the words man or woman with "male" or "female" also indicates his play with gendered discourse and the meanings these words deliver. No one is safe, no matter how masculine and brave the man or how feminine and pure the woman.

In *Roughing It*, Twain's narrator also distinguishes between "maleness" and "manliness." He uses the word "male" three times to indicate "male and female wearing-apparel, such as clothes and hats (or bonnets for women), to denote a "male emigrant," and to discuss lineage on the Sandwich Islands, whose native peoples determine royalty through the "female line," not from the "male line." Though he also frequently writes "man" to indicate a male human, Twain writes "manly" but once, to describe a "manly,

Top: "Outgoing and Incoming." Published in J. Ross Browne, "A Peep at Washoe" [Third Paper], February 1861, *Harper's New Monthly Magazine*. *Bottom:* "We Are Waiting for You." Published in J. Ross Browne, "A Peep at Washoe" [Second Paper], January 1861, *Harper's New Monthly Magazine*.

HOLDING ON TO IT.

"Holding On to It." Published in J. Ross Browne, "A Peep at Washoe" [Third Paper], February 1861, *Harper's New Monthly Magazine*.

splendid, determined fellow," who draws a revolver to threaten men who have laid claim to a mining lead. This "manly" fellow is courageous and bold, not just the bearer of "maleness." Men, especially within groups comprised only of males, tended to perform in different ways than groups of mixed gender. Or, to satisfy Orion's concern, men were dangerous when they had the clear advantage of power in a private, mobile, secluded, dark space such as a coach. Clemens, though, liked "hell" and the mischievous "devil," and he found ways to play within a dangerous western environment. At the time, however, Clemens was a bachelor. The absence of women to protect afforded him a certain amount of freedom that his brother did not experience, not even when waiting for his wife to arrive out West. The depiction of such men in Browne's "A Peep at Washoe" was not a positive one, however. According to the illustrations, men turn haggard in the climate and under difficult toil in the mines and mountains.[33] In addition, though men must fight the land and the weather, they must also fight

2. The Space Betwixt the Garden and the Devil

"A Question of Title." Published in J. Ross Browne, "A Peep at Washoe" [Second Paper], January 1861, *Harper's New Monthly Magazine*.

wolves[34] and even other men trying to claim what does not belong to them.[35]

Public Sentiments

Clemens continued to write about dangers in the region in his "public" accounts published in Nevada papers. In July 1862, in Esmeralda, Nevada

Territory, Clemens reported that two men were murdered "by the Indians at Rabbit Hole creek" while one of the men "made preparations to build, and was on his way to bring over his family."[36] Such news items were published and read in both Nevada and California because of the close proximity of the regions, but also because both areas relied heavily on transportation and delivery of supplies from overland coaches. Clemens's other public carp about the landscape, and not its peoples, finds additional support in an article he published in January 1863, in the *Placer Weekly Courier*, a weekly periodical printed in Forest Hill, California. At the time, Clemens was a reporter for the *Enterprise* and covered political events. That winter he traveled by stagecoach to Washoe City to attend an ovation to "receive" members of the Nevada delegation. While most readers would not equate snow with the hell of Nevada that Clemens had previously described, the "hell" here is not heat, but the journey.[37] According to Clemens, writing as the "The Reliable," "The wind blew such a hurricane that the coach drifted sideways from one toll road to another, and sometimes utterly refused to mind her helm. It is a fearful thing to be at sea in a stage coach."[38] In this passage he uses nautical terms to describe the terror experienced on the road in a coach—hurricane, helm, and at sea—which naturally enriches the contrast of the weather in this place he has built into hell. On this journey on the "sea" of Nevada, the coach was delayed by poor road conditions, the wind, and finally because of a broken wagon spring that required the coach to "lay up for repairs."[39] Though the heat and dust plagued emigrants and travelers in coaches during Nevada's hot months, heat and dust were preferable to "hurricanes" of snow. Snow and wind produced traveling delays and damages to coaches, and passengers struggled to stay warm.[40] On the same page on which "A Big Thing in Washoe City" appears in column one, numerous advertisements for "Fall and Winter Clothing and Dry Goods!" appear in column three. The cold of the winter created a fashion industry even in a primitive mining culture such as Nevada Territory. Prescott & Brother's sold, according to the ad copy, "Ladies' Cashmere, Worsted and Woolen Dress Goods; Ladies' Cloth Cloaks, of the Latest Styles.... Hoods, Sontags, Nubias, Polkas, and Scarfs." Men could purchase here "Fine Beaver Overcoats.... Calf Skin Dress Boots" and for the working miner, "Rubber Goods.—Rubber Boots, Pants and Coats." Clemens had worried about the cold and snow, but not for himself. In a previous letter, Clemens had advised his mother and sister to bring a couple of blankets to warm them during night desert travel.[41]

2. The Space Betwixt the Garden and the Devil   67

Because of delays caused by the weather, either the dirt and heat or the snow and cold, the real fear of violence—and the anticipation of receiving by coach loved ones, mail, or supplies—Clemens noted that the arrival of coaches in Nevada and California proved consistently exciting. San Francisco's *Daily Morning Call*, for example, listed in each paper the names of anyone who had arrived since the previous report. Though Clemens wrote often about these issues, he was not the only reporter in Nevada or California to write about the importance of travel and how it relates to relationships between men and women. "Time for Her to Come Home," published November 14, 1863, in the *Amador Weekly Ledger*, may have been written by William Wright, known in the press as "Dan De Quille,"[42] and Clemens's friend, roommate, and mentor at Virginia City's *Territorial Enterprise*. The sketch bears no signature, but the opening includes the introduction of "the humorous local editor of the Territorial Enterprise," which could either be Twain or De Quille.[43] Like Twain's letter and articles, De Quille's sketch informs his readers about women arriving in the West by coach and the anticipation that men develop while waiting for "their" women to arrive. He notes that when "stages arrive from California and depart thither, there is always a crowd about the various offices—some interested spectators, other mere loungers. Wives leaving to visit their friends and relatives in California have their 'uglier' halves to keep back. 'Uglies' get very tired of this, and very anxious for pretty halves to get back, so they are quite punctual in their visits to the stage offices about the time wifey is expected home." When the "wifey" does not return for too long, the "ugly" "gets wolfy."[44] Here, the women are the pretty, "tender things" for whom "uglies," await a safe return. When this timely return is delayed, for any of the common reasons such as weather or crime, the man becomes "wolfy," animalistic, primitive, and in need of various kinds of feminine influence and aid, including sexual gratification, to diminish the wolf within the man.

De Quille's use of wolfy signifies men as animals in the absence of women (sometimes morality or civilization or sophistication), and that these animalistic men are anxious to have their "tenders" returned to them. In the end, readers discover "the wifey" has been gone six months, and the stagecoach driver tells the "Ugly" that "it was d—d near time for her to be getting back," a comment meant to evoke the realization that wifey might not be coming back. If she survived the trip, she has been gone too long without sending a letter, and she might prefer living in California to living in Nevada. And, with another "wolfy." And yet, "wolfy" seems harmless compared with Clemens's "devils," either the mischievous or the dangerous variety. The "local editor" uses the diction "their uglier halves to keep them back" as if to note that the wolfy men are guarding their prettier halves from a better life in California and with better men. For Clemens, too, California offered a better life for women and eventually for him. In the spring of 1863 he vacationed in San Francisco, and in the spring of 1864 he moved to San Francisco, where he remained for the better part of the next two years and eventually found fame. Dan De Quille never became famous, at least not compared with Mark Twain's fame. De Quille stayed in Nevada, worked for the *Enterprise* until its publication ended in 1893, and was a popular journalist in the West for four decades. His most notable book was *The History of the Big Bonanza* (1876), a book about the people and places of Nevada during the silver mining booms.[45]

Like Twain and De Quille, Sam P. Davis analyzed western culture and delivered his "public" sentiments about crime to westerners. He left the Middle West for California and then arrived in Nevada in 1875. He first worked as a journalist for the *Virginia City Evening Chronicle* and four years later as a reporter for the *Carson City Morning Appeal*.[46] He wrote deep into convalescence, and edited and contributed to the *History of Nevada* (1913), which was published five years before he died. Davis wrote the eighth chapter of the history, "The Lawless Element," which describes the kinds of dangers Clemens wrote about in the early 1860s. Davis begins the chapter be describing robberies of stages:

> Nevada was not without this most undesirable element and, for a time, they held a reign of terror over the community. In the grand scramble of wealth in this new region the robbing of the Wells-Fargo stages became a recognized industry of that section. The long distances between stations opened a most inviting field for the enterprise and daring of highwaymen.[47]

Though Davis portrays stage robberies as common and expected within a culture scrambling for wealth, he later notes that most highwaymen robbed stages of their gold bullion, and often left the passengers unmolested. According to this account, a wealthy company like Wells-Fargo was in more danger than its passengers, at least concerning highway robbery. Women passengers, though, still needed to fear male passengers as if they were the unseen devil lurking just beyond the light. Davis reports on the "grand scramble of wealth," which indicates that wealth was unevenly distributed, even in the West. Some possessed it, and others did not. But the possibility existed for enterprising men to escape this disparity through hard work or crime, a variation of the hard work western ethic that attracted emigrants from the East like Clemens and William Wright. Orion's fear, too, about devils dwelling in the dark of stages reflects his personal, and a larger cultural, anxiety, that women outside the domestic space and beyond the protection of their men, could expect beastly men to take advantage of this helpless situation. Such fear illustrates a real concern but also one designed to maintain certain gender roles for married women, and in some cases single women, in a highly masculine culture.

A Public Politic: Sentiments from California

Before moving to California in 1864, Clemens had been traveling in Nevada Territory and California for two years. In 1862, his correspondences had little to do with the war and everything to do with the hope that a man in the West could someday receive his family by coach, unmolested, to live with him in a new prairie paradise. The arrival of people, supplies, and mail symbolized this hope, not the fear of devils raiding the wagons. These fears and hopes would soon be supplanted by his real concerns about the effects of the war in the West. Rather than writing about the weather, in the summer and fall of 1864, Clemens reported for the *Daily Morning Call*, a pro–Union paper in a pro–Union city, on numerous robberies and murders of stagecoach travelers and emigrants that he linked to "Secessionists" and "organized" bands of robbers under the command of commissioned officers "in the Confederate army."[48] These kinds of raids on overland coaches traveling long distances filled the pages of the *Call*, linking the political and economic concerns of the Far West to the states east of the Mississippi. In this summer, the Civil War raged, and political tension grew, leading up the presidential election. Though Clemens had tried to escape the war in Missouri, he and Californians witnessed violence in the countryside and in the metropolis that reporters such as Clemens attributed to politics and the war.

In the summer of 1864, the Civil War and the presidential election affected the growth of violence in California and the West. During this time when Clemens worked for the *Call* and lived in the metropolis, he often wrote about his travels to be published in other newspapers, but he also wrote about stagecoach traffic and the violence associated with this traffic in greater frequency than he had in Nevada. His hopeful tone from

1862 appears to have diminished in his California reporting. At the *Enterprise*, Clemens had shared the editorial duties with Dan De Quille, among other reporters in Virginia City, but at the *Call* Clemens was the only local reporter for most of his four months on staff.[49] He considered this confining work to be "fearful drudgery, soulless drudgery," though he certainly infused a great deal of style, humor, and caustic wit into his often anonymous and short news items.[50] For these four months, he rarely left the city, considered giving up newspaper reporting, and in the final month took a pay cut from forty dollars a week to twenty-five dollars so he would have to endure fewer hours of "soulless drudgery."[51] In the fall, he lost his job at the *Call*. At the end of 1864, he finally escaped the metropolis and stayed the next three months "in some of the played-out mining camps of Tuolumne and Calaveras counties."[52] But his anonymous, or short, "drudgery" allowed Clemens to play with language and topic; it also enabled him to discuss publicly political matters inflamed by the Civil War.

While working for the *Call*, Samuel Clemens, now known as Mark Twain but often writing anonymously, wrote a "public" tone and judgment about crime performed on stagecoaches on journeys of great distances and between cities reflected his "tendency to link city crimes to the countryside raids of secessionist guerrillas."[53] The "Letter from Mark Twain" from September 1863, provides evidence for a shift in tone and concern with crime linked to the Civil War. Thus, comparing articles published during the same month in different newspapers is necessary to support the claim that Twain's reports from the *Call* "tell us much about the environment Clemens worked in and the variety of demands made upon him by his job."[54] The more complicated claim: Twain's reports on stagecoach travel in 1862 in Nevada focused more on men and women in conflict with the region itself because he did not begin reporting as much about the national and regional political dramas until the summer of 1864 when the Civil War appeared with greater urgency in San Francisco. In California, his reports did employ gendered discourse, but they also relied on sensational political messages intended for a region divided by the war.

The shift to California from Nevada marks a variety of modifications for Mark Twain's writing career, including his interest in and judgment of crime in the city compared with crime in the countryside, even though during 1864 he still published articles and letters in Nevada while working fulltime in California. Twain was not alone in reporting on such matters. Like De Quille and Davis, other reporters wrote articles, similar to Twain's, that reflected the discomfort or danger with travel in the West. One such letter, written on July 3, 1864, from San Francisco was published in Virginia City's *Union*, a competing newspaper with Twain's *Enterprise*. The letter titled "Our Traveler's Letters," signed "Marshall," who according to Twain's narrator in *Roughing It* was "the reporter of the other paper,"[55] or the *Union*, begins by describing a journey that nearly "everybody in Nevada" has taken across the Sierra Nevadas, which this time "was unusually monotonous." Accordingly, Marshall notes, "there is not much to say about it. We left Virginia on the Pioneer stage."[56] Though the trip to Placerville passed without incident and no danger befell him or his fellow travelers on any part of the trip, the worst of the journey was the leg between Placerville and Folsom. The overnight stagecoach was "dreadfully full, so full as to put the idea of sleeping out of the question, and rattled and bounced over the stony road, pitching into each other bodily," and arriving at daybreak in "complete silence and exhaustion."[57]

As bad as the ride was, the hands of "devils in the dark" did not grope Marshall and his fellow passengers. Nor were they robbed. Though this stagecoach ride was uncomfortable, a much worse event occurred along the same route just four days prior. On June 30, 1864, "six armed and masked men stopped the Pioneer stage from Virginia." They claimed to be "southern gentlemen," who were Confederate guerrillas. They robbed the coach of "seven sacks of bullion and two thousand dollars in gold coin being shipped by Wells, Fargo & Company."[58] This is the same route and stage that Clemens took the previous year with a chatty driver, many times since, and four days later when Marshall traveled this route without any trouble other than exhaustion. But Marshall did not write that letter for San Francisco readers. He wrote it for Virginia City readers, for whom he did not link crimes along the stagecoach routes to city crimes in San Francisco as Twain sometimes posed.

On July 9, Twain used the knowledge of the robbery of the Pioneer stage as connecting and contextual detail for a city crime. That evening a man named William Johnson attempted to burgle "a fancy goods importing house." Officers discovered a hidden bag intended for Johnson's accomplices, whom Twain calls "confederates," to retrieve the bag "containing fifteen pistols, five bowie-knives and two pairs of bullet moulds."[59] Twain closes the article, not by reporting these kinds of facts or even giving a humorous or horrific account of the capture. Instead, he politicizes the event, claiming that it "is probable this gang is the same that were concerned in the recent attempted safe robberies." Twain connected these two stories by making a case that secessionist fervor was alive in California.

He considered the city crime "significant, taken in connection with matters transpiring in the interior of the State, that the purpose of these scoundrels," according to the biased reporter, was to leave behind the valuable jewelry and use the weapons to arm themselves.[60] These "scoundrels" represented a different kind of man than the devils lurking about Nevada. The scoundrels Twain politicized.

Although these devils were dangerous, they were only connected to a war by journalistic judgment. Nor were the men cowards. Though this story does not contain an explicit criticism of men's masculinity, Twain does note the "vigilance of one of the clerks who slept in the store." These clerks confronted the burglar and yelled for an officer. The brave employee did not retreat. The burglar, however, ran, tried to escape, and once captured, admitted to having accomplices and gave the officers the name of at least one of the accomplices. The word "vigilance" here is important, not only for Twain's meaning, but for delivering a message to his readers. Those living in the metropolis of San Francisco were urged to be vigilant against secessionists and their pro–southern ideologies.

Clemens had concerns about such matters as early as April 1862. That month he wrote a letter to his brother discussing a boundary dispute between the governments of California and Nevada Territory that involved "secessionists."[61] In May 1864, Clemens wrote a letter to his mother and sister that mentions Reuel Colt Gridley, a schoolmate from Hannibal, whom Clemens calls "a Copperhead, or as he calls himself, 'Union to the backbone, but a Copperhead in sympathies.'"[62] Supposedly, Gridley raised a great deal of funds "in the process 'becoming from a positive secessionist an ardent Unionist.'"[63] These funds form only a portion of the story about Sanitary Funds in Nevada Territory, which, according to Clemens, were a waste of money, "a bully opportunity of giving away their money." These "sanitary" organizations gave relief to wounded Union soldiers. Part of this story also appears in chapter 45 of *Roughing It*. But these letters were Clemens's personal sentiments, whereas the article about the vigilant clerk was published in a newspaper. In those letters to his mother and sister, Clemens inserted no trepidation about the impending war or criminals trying to affect fear in pro–Union cities and territories. His dread was for the safety and comfort of his family, which the "devils" and "hell" might influence.

Later in July, Twain wrote another article for the *Call* alerting his readers to stage robbers linked to "Secessionists." A reporter for Nevada's Gold Hill *News* named Albert S. Evans published a correspondence for

2. The Space Betwixt the Garden and the Devil 73

San Francisco readers offering his opinion that matched Twain's. Evans, also known as Fitz Smythe, cautioned readers that there "is little doubt, none I might say, that we are threatened with civil war in California, and must be on our guard to put down with a strong hand the first demonstration made by the enemies of our country."[64] Twain published his article "A Stage Robber Amongst Us" two days before Smythe published his. This story offers additional details about the "Placerville stage-robbers," who attacked the Pioneer stage on June 30. One criminal survived the capture, and two of his companions were killed. The survivor confessed "that he belonged to an organized band of robbers, under the command of Ingram, who held a Captain's commission in the Confederate army," and who said his gang was "armed and equipped by Secessionists." Twain closes the article that helps spread the fear of secessionists in the countryside and in the metropolis and need for vigilance with a jab at the criminal: "He says he is only nineteen years old; but to a disinterested spectator he looks older by two or three years."[65] Twain is neither "disinterested" nor a mere "spectator." His ironic "public" tone here mocks the cowardice and ignorance of the robber, a move that reduces some of the paranoia that he, and Smythe, helped spread.

Moreover, Marshall failed, or refused, to mention such violence, fear, or need for vigilance when he traveled on July 3 on the very routes in danger of robbery and in the very stage line that was robbed four days earlier. Of course, the benign letter devoid of fear or violence was published in Virginia City, and not by Twain, and these articles about confederate forces invading the California countryside and metropolis were Twain's, published in San Francisco. Even so, Twain's appropriation of local and regional violence to link criminals to a larger national political conversation appeared in the California press, for readers interested in such affairs. Twain certainly had been interested in these affairs since at least 1862. After a bitter boundary dispute between the governments of California and Nevada Territory had erupted, Orion worked to legislate the dispute for the next two years. In 1862, California secessionists became violent. Returning to the letter to his brother in April that year, Clemens mentioned "Secessionists" in California who had staged "secessionist demonstrations in Aurora." Clemens also notes that the California military had confiscated the weapons of the Unionists who formed a home guard called the Esmeralda Rifles. Clemens was a pro–Union supporter of the Esmeralda Rifles who were vigilant to support the cause and opposed to secessionists in California. The home guard did eventually prevail, with help from pro–Union officers in the California military. When Clemens wrote the letter, however, he worried that the secessionists would win.[66]

Henry Nash Smith has noted that during Twain's time in Nevada Territory he was not "interested in national politics, despite the fact that the momentous issues of the Civil War filled the Nevada newspapers and lay just beneath the surface of everyday life in the Territory."[67] According to Smith, Virginia City residents and firemen suppressed pro–Confederate sentiments, which likely left little need for a satirical news reports to do this work. During this period in Twain's career, Smith notes that Twain was more interested initially in mining wealth and then, after failing in mining, in leading a life of leisure and entertaining writing.[68] Smith cites as evidence Clemens's letter to his sister Pamela on March 18, 1864, when he temporarily replaced Joe Goodman as the editor of the *Enterprise*: "Joe Goodman is gone to the Sandwich Islands. I stipulated, when I took his place, that I should never be expected to write editorials about politics or eastern news. I take no sort of interest in those matters."[69] Smith uses the word "national" when describing Clemens's disinterest in politics, but Clemens only uses the more general "politics." He, however, does use the word "eastern" to describe news, which may be analogous with, or similar to, national news, but certainly not a marker for national politics. Smith largely applies only a "personal" sentiment as evidence for a larger discussion about Clemens's multiple voices, while other "public" sources might complicate Twain's western writing or scholarly opinions about it. Certainly, Clemens admits to having "no sort of interest" in "politics or eastern news," but the "public" sources often refute this claim.

Furthermore, Clemens had covered politics for the newspaper since 1862 when he "talked Goodman into sending him back to Carson City to cover the second territorial legislature."[70] At this time, Clemens may have wanted to cover the political scene because his brother Orion was the acting governor of Nevada Territory. Clemens covered the legislature and political events for a region rich in silver and land and important within the larger national debate between North and South. The West was supposed to offer regeneration and rejuvenation for emigrants but also for a nation. Clemens, however, like many western emigrants, had attempted to escape the war. The war followed them West. But like many men, Clemens hoped to find a prairie Eden when he arrived. Instead, he found violence. In 1862, Clemens was clearly concerned with violence incited by the war. He wrote about the activities of secessionists, Copperheads, and Unionists in both in his journalism and in his letters. In a letter that men-

2. The Space Betwixt the Garden and the Devil 75

tioned his friend Gridley's transformation from a "positive secessionist to an argent Unionist," however, Clemens does not draw attention to the fact that both men were originally Missouri military men who had sided with the Confederacy. Of course, both men underwent transformations, which Clemens certainly established in the press in 1864. Even though Clemens had briefly served in the Marion Rangers in Missouri, a band of militia volunteers, when he wrote for the pro–Lincoln paper San Francisco's *Daily Morning Call*, Clemens called southern sympathizers not the euphemistic "Rangers" or volunteers, but "confederates," a "gang," or "Secessionists."

Only a few months after he wrote the letter to his sister, Clemens published articles such as "A Stage Robber Amongst Us" in San Francisco's *Call* that did not avoid political language or topics. Clemens applied the term, "secessionist" or "secesh," to coach robbers that he, and other reporters, criminalized in the press for displaying southern sympathies in a pro–Union California and Nevada Territory. San Francisco in particular was a political city in the West. In the summer of 1864, authorities arrested San Franciscans for treason; brawls started because of political demonstrations and meetings for the advocacy of Lincoln's reelection, and the press "cautioned against shadowy conspiratorial organizations such as The Golden Circle, The Loyal Leaguers, and The Knights of the Columbian Star."[71] The Knights of the Golden Circle was "founded in the mid–1850s to promote a 'golden circle' of slave states from the American South through Mexico and Central America to the rim of South America, curving northward again through the West Indies to close the circle at Key West."[72] Union Leagues and Loyal Leagues were formed "by businessmen and professional men of substance and influence" to fight the copperhead influence of "vast secret societies such as the Knights of the golden Circle and Order of the American Knights."[73] These events produced the background against which Mark Twain, and other reporters, recognized violence connected with the war. It is no surprise, then, that Twain wrote about such violence with judgment against a pro-southern or secessionist activities. Perhaps, though, Henry Nash Smith was correct, for the journalist did seem to become more political once he lived and wrote in California. Violence was of special note in San Francisco, the largest, most populated city west of St. Louis, Missouri,[74] and a place that was supposed to be a metropolis of hope for Clemens and other emigrants.

In August, Twain wrote two additional sensational stories of note for the *Call* that combined his political assessments while judging men because of how they performed masculinity. These reports include stagecoach robberies linked to secessionists and descriptions of these corrupt men attacking women in hacks within the city. In his "More Stage Robbers and Their Confederates Captured," published on August 3, Twain calls the capture of more criminals a "splendid haul of Placerville stage robbers," who are mostly farmers and "are all Constitutional Democrats."[75] Like the other stories, these two connect stagecoach robberies to secessionist fervor and southern sympathy. Twain accuses the robbers of raising "men for the Confederate service, and they were to furnish themselves with equipments and supplies by guerrilla practice on the highway."[76] He describes these men as "well-to-do farmers," who are well connected and aided by "many prominent citizens," which certainly supported the notion in San Francisco's press and local rumor that secret societies and secessionists were active and influential in the city. However, these stories also reflect the cowardice of male criminals and the rare mention of women. As he did on July 20, he undercuts the danger presented by such robbers by attacking their dedication to fight, and their willingness to carry through with secessionist plans, in the face of capture and arrest. Twain asserts that the "rumor prevalent here yesterday, that there was a terrific fight in San Jose the night before, with the stage robbers, was groundless; there was no fight." In this case, the absence of a fight represents both a gendered act and a political one.

Part of the reason for this fight, in addition to the gang's cowardice, was the overwhelming force raised by the military. The colonel telegraphed and received additional ammunition, and the local militia was raised, to fight the robbers. Twain makes clear that no such trouble arose. The gang was easily captured, and "[n]o blood was spilled in arresting the robber gang."[77] This story provided Twain with no opportunity to mix his "horrors and his general information together" the way the stagecoach driver had done the previous year, which had entertained Twain on the Pioneer stage.[78] But this story did allow for Twain's subtle use of judgment, for the robbers seem incapable of producing the kind of violence that Twain actually admired in some men and rejected in others. Skullduggery, even more than the threat of political violence, irritated Twain. According to Lawrence I. Berkove, Twain, as part of a movement of writers in the West Berkove calls Sagebrushers, "had a high regard for *manliness*," and praised "honor, virtue, and fair play."[79] Robbers so easily captured displayed no manliness, and Twain certainly found no honor, virtue, or fair play in their actions.

2. The Space Betwixt the Garden and the Devil 77

On August 27, Twain concluded his series on the San Jose robberies with the publication of "Arrest of Another of the Robbing Gang." Authorities made the final arrest "without difficulty" of the conspirator and "well-to-do stock-raiser" named Hall. The wealthy accessory confessed to his role, gave the arresting sheriff "a good deal of information in regard and to the combination of robbing gangs." Twain lumps Hall in with the other "well-to-do" farmers and confederate sympathizers, for the journalist calls their actions "schemes of robbing." Hall, and the rest of the robbers, "is a Secessionist, and both he and his wife admitted that all were bound to each other by horrid oaths to revenge any punishment inflicted on them."[80] Though this closing portrays Hall and the rest of the gang as vengeful and dedicated to a cause, all of the robbers, including Hall, surrendered without a fight, shed no blood, nor promoted the cause of the Confederacy. These men were also wealthy, which must have been an additional cause for Twain's disdain. He wrote the phrase "well-to-do" to describe these farmers and stock-raisers, and these men, according to the journalist, were connected to "prominent citizens." Twain, and writers in Nevada, cultivated distaste for the wealthy and powerful men who "subverted the law ... and did not refrain from using intimidation or force to achieve their ends."[81]

While these statements are general and concern Clemens's time in Nevada Territory, they are also true for his journalism in California. These wealthy, yet cowardly, secessionists intimidated Californians, but Clemens humiliated, or humanized, these criminals by writing about their easy capture, their baseless threats, and their preying upon vulnerable and isolated stagecoaches. The little detail about Hall as an ordinary, though wealthy, family man, with three children and a wife who conspired with him represents Twain's final jab. Hall's wife was not a vulnerable woman traveling alone. These men were not beasts, infernal "devils," or even just warriors for a cause. Hall's wife was a wealthy family woman with influence and security. The men were prominent men, easily captured, though they did torment travelers in the West. Mark Twain judged these men, and their politics, with a combination of dismissal and disdain. After all, the robbers did not prey on the individual, or especially on the individual woman. Instead, the gang robbed a Wells, Fargo and Company's stage.

For the "public" Twain, the robbing of the rich by the rich did not draw his fury in the same way unscrupulous hack drivers abusing women did. Berkove explains that this "unbridled capitalism" in the West defied the personal moralities of Twain and his fellow journalists. These wealthy men, though not secessionists or even devils, were beasts, for they infected an entire region with a "might makes right" philosophy that Twain mocked in his writing, such as "Arrest of Another of the Robbing Gang." Perhaps a more accurate way to describe Clemens's political writing is that in Nevada most of his political comments were "personal sentiments." In California, he developed these sentiments into the "public" variety for his editors and readership in San Francisco that supported the Union.

These reports combined his beliefs with the facts, as did his letters. In this way, his personal and public "voices" reflect his literary functions. We see one kind of personal performance in his letters, in which he is a son and brother, concerned for the safety of the women in his life. In his journalism, his performative voice still warns women and men readers, but the public sentiment also echoes his personal ideas and what Glenn Hendler calls Twain's "audience-oriented subjectivity." Hendler's phrase describes the role of public sentiment as transferred to readers through literature. He applies this term to Twain's writing in multiple works, especially in *Huckleberry Finn* and *Tom Sawyer*. Twain's sensational writing, like any discourse, delivered meaning within a particular context in the West, one that combined violence of men and violence of landscape, to illustrate his young view of the West—at first a masculine place of adventure and danger for women, and then as a violently political space dangerous for either sex, especially during the movement of people and goods across the West.

Like J. Ross Browne, Clemens developed a style that assessed the land and judged its inhabitants. His news reports, and those of his contemporaries, offer a literary version of historical events. In the summer of 1864, Twain witnessed and reported on a great many of these cases of violence related to political turmoil. Twain continued to write political reports late into summer and early fall. Many of these report on the demonstrations, meetings, and parades, some of which ended in violence.[82] On July 26 Twain reported in the *Call* the arrest and imprisonment in Alcatraz of California's ex-governor's brother for speaking in public to counsel "armed resistance to the draft, and insinuated that force would have to be resorted to by Democrats if they wished to vote at the next general election."[83] This was the city that housed societies such as The Knights of the Golden Circle. This was a western metropolis that knew conflict between the Constitutional Union Party and Copperheads. San Francisco, however, was also a city with pro–Lincoln newspapers, such as the *Call*, whose owners and editors "thought that most Democrats were more apt to sacrifice prin-

2. The Space Betwixt the Garden and the Devil   79

ciple in order to compromise with the Confederacy than to push on to a final military victory."[84] So by the time readers on July 26 had digested Twain's column on page two about "Treasonable Utterances," they had certainly already read the "Telegraphic Summary" on the front page.

This "overland dispatch, entitled "The Movement in Favor of Peace," delivers the story of a peace commission in Niagara Falls, which was led by Lincoln's newly "authorized" Horace Greeley. On behalf of the president, Greeley led the talks with "commissioners of the Rebel Government," at first "with the view of pacificating [sic] the country on a basis satisfactory to both North and South." Greeley's position, and that of Lincoln, was bold:

> The answer of the President through Greeley, insisted on the full and complete restoration of the Union in all its territorial integrity, the abandonment of slavery in the seceded States, under conditions which should, while respecting the property and rights of all loyal men, afford ample security against another war in the interest of slavery.[85]

This political turmoil did not inhabit Twain's imaginative space when on December 12, 1863, he wrote about Horace Greeley's stagecoach ride out West. That remembrance in Nevada's Virginia City *Territorial Enterprise*, largely invented, emphasized Twain's romantic ideas about the West, some of which he later helped dispel and others he perpetrated, with *Roughing It*. Though he no longer lived in the West when he published accounts of stagecoach travel and crime in *Roughing It*, Americans hoping to emigrate West certainly would have noted Twain's retelling of the violence on the plains. Western emigration had actually increased since Clemens and his brother had arrived in Nevada Territory in 1861. For example, the population of Storey County, Nevada Territory, grew from 3,016 in 1860 to 11,319 in 1870. By 1875, it had nearly doubled.[86] Because of the national interest in the West, either based on romance or reality, Twain incorporated into his journalism entertaining yet stern warnings for a readership in a city of conflict and peril. For Twain, San Francisco, like the Occidental Hotel where Twain stayed when he arrived in the metropolis, at first seemed shiny and comfortable. He called the hotel "Heaven on the half shell."[87] The crime and politics in the city, however, created for Twain and his readers a reality far more earthly. In this reality, devils tempted Twain and his readers. Though they sometimes dwelled in heaven, in the summer of 1864 they all lived in hell.

3

Exposing Hackmen and Demoralizers: Mark Twain's Punishment of Metropolitan Beasts, 1864

> *"Girls.—Some one out West boldly declares that girls will differ, and that furthermore, as proof, one of them lately broke her neck in trying to escape being kissed, while he knows a great many of them ready to break their necks to get kissed. True, every word of it."*[1]

The "obscene-picture epidemic," as Mark Twain called it, had swept across San Francisco all summer long. Men, women, boys, and girls were infected. Many like Charles Mayer, the "victim" in "Another Victim," had "probably become demoralized by the prevailing" epidemic. Mayer was eventually arrested "for exposing his person,"[2] certainly to a woman and in public. Pages two and three of the San Francisco *Daily Morning Call*, July 26, 1864, contain Mark Twain's numerous local correspondences—almost all of which contained details about murders and murderers, a second article in a series condemning hack drivers and highlighting the rape charge raised against one hackman, trials in the police court, men accidently wounded in a variety fashions, including being run over by an omnibus, and other twenty-word pieces reporting on crimes and misdemeanors.

But four connected and sensational articles appeared in these local columns that detailed criminal activity with lewd or obscene merchandise that led to the corruption of a few men and many women. It was an epidemic. Twain wrote all of the pieces in the local column that day. For

3. Exposing Hackmen and Demoralizers 81

nearly four months, he wrote, often anonymously, for the paper as its full-time local reporter. These articles showcase scoundrels and rapists, including drivers of hacks, who abused women. Viewed in concert, such reports show bad men acting badly. Twain used these daily columns to illuminate perilous places for women to dwell or travel in the metropolis. He also judged as a beast a man unwilling to apply morality and ethics to his treatment of women. These immoral men who wasted energy, opportunity, and victimized women appear in Twain's local columns as actors within a sensational journalistic discourse that problematizes Twain's view of masculinity and the regenerative and redemptive image of the West.

Mark Twain's full-time reporting for the *Call* from June to October 1864 delivered much disdain for men who took advantage of women, specifically for "demoralizing" men and for hack drivers. According to Twain, "demoralizers" tempted younger men, women, and girls to engage in immoral activities such as the spread of pornographic images and prostitution. Twain used this word "to demoralize" in its archaic sense, to corrupt. Hackmen also lured women into corruption, but through force—cheating them out of money or assaulting and raping them. Unlike his articles about stage robberies in the countryside, the *Call* articles about city crimes never accuse city hack drivers of being "secessionists" or "commissioned" Confederate officers. Like his appraisal on the larger landscape when viewing stage travel, however, he wrote stories about hacks, hackmen, or violence in hacks as judgments on the land of California, particularly the metropolis of San Francisco where hackmen worked.

Twain's literary disdain for male criminals and defense of "innocent" women further advances his contradictory verdict of justice and gender in the West. In these San Francisco articles, Twain parts ways with antebellum sensational writers who assigned social inequality as a reason for crime. Instead, Twain views male criminals as less than men, worthy of the punishment they were not legally receiving, or receiving with too little severity. While he supports courageous men enforcing the law and criticizes those in defiance as beasts and cowards, a more subversive judgment of women remains a secondary, yet curious, concern. Male rapists and "demoralizers" Twain mocked, for they had assaulted and "ruined" women. But some women Twain judged as imposters, as women willing to appear chaste in court after they had participated in the immoral or illegal behaviors for which Twain had eviscerated men. In all of these instances, Twain does not advance an anti-gallows sentiment and instead considers the individual and social consequences of men's moral and physical abuses of women, and some women's immoral influence on men, and the need to punish these criminals.

This chapter is concerned with two kinds of male criminals: the first involves hack drivers, whom Twain judged for being dishonest, especially to women fares, reckless drivers that even interrupted funeral processions, and at their worst, rapists who used their private, mobile spaces, neither exactly public or domestic, to assault and rape women. The second group of men was not comprised of hackmen, though they might have used hacks to escape public scrutiny and then hide in private rooms downtown. Nevertheless, these men, like the worst of the hackmen, lured women to hidden spaces to abuse them sexually or to turn them to a life of prostitution. The "scoundrels" and "beasts," as Twain called them, were not noble or masculine men who rallied against social injustice, as did Officer Blitz and Judge Shepheard. Blitz and Shepheard attempted to punish and remove under the force of law these criminals from society. Still, in the cases of crimes inflicted on both traditional and subversive women by men in San Francisco, Twain judged the criminals as cowards, beasts, or devoid of masculine morality and assigned a certain amount of agency to women who participated in, or advanced, immorality in the city. He offered no sympathy, however, for women who contributed to their own physical and moral demise. Twain tried to enact social change by warning readers about the metropolis of San Francisco, which allowed men to lurk within the corners of man's constructed spaces as beasts, ruffians, and bullies and to devour the women unable to escape the clutches of the beast. These scoundrels and beasts contributed to the fall of California's Eden and created a conflicted space unable to fulfill the dream of westward expansion, especially for Twain, even as the Civil War raged a thousand miles to the east. But in San Francisco, Twain exposed and punished male criminals, not as a detective such as Officer Blitz or as a judge such as Shepheard, but as a journalist.[3]

According to Michael Schudson, journalism can satisfy one of two models—"the ideal of the 'story' and the ideal of 'information.'"[4] The first ideal, as argued by George Herbert Mead, offers information but also entertains the reader. The news in this model satisfies a kind of storytelling, one small item at a time. Schudson explains this model as acting "as a guide to living not so much by providing facts as by selecting them and framing them."[5] The second ideal, advanced by Walter Benjamin, regards journalism simply as information, unframed and without context. Schudson views this "informational ideal" of news as being concerned "with fairness, objectivity, scrupulous dispassion."[6] In 1864, Twain labored under the burden to deliver information. He also played with humor and used figurative language to entertain his readers. With these stories, then, Twain participated in acts of judgment that began with journalistic exposure and ended with legal judgment. Even if the criminal were found not guilty or released with little discipline, Twain used the pages of the newspaper to punish these men and to offer his readers "a guide to living."[7] Such a method followed in the tradition of sensational journalism and fiction born in antebellum America that was produced and consumed in 1860s America and England.

Sensation in the City

Sensational writing set on the frontier and in cities influenced Twain's western journalism and his writing about the West. Journalists and fiction writers, such as George Lippard and George Thompson, wrote numerous stories involving the seduction and rape of women, which had infected cities such as Boston, Philadelphia, and New York for three decades. Even sensational novelists, such as Lippard, ripped headlines and stories from the local newspapers as inspiration for the novel. David S. Reynolds has argued that Lippard used this technique to craft a unified discourse in his sensational and popular novel *The Quaker City* (1845), which is largely concerned with the seduction, demoralization, and rape of women. In fact, Lippard based one of the plot lines on a famous seduction and murder case of 1843 starring a Philadelphia man who murdered his sister's "seducer" but was acquitted in court. Reynolds suggests that "Lippard invites us to 'glance at the contents of a newspaper' to learn the fates of the other characters." These character resolutions occur within the novel that "resolves itself into a series of sensational headlines and news reports."[8]

In *The Quaker City* Lippard reinforces traditional gender roles, and perhaps Twain does not diverge from this model when, in his journalism, he warns women of the dangerous men lurking in San Francisco. Though some women attracted Twain's criticisms for acting like the very "demoralizing" men he tried to expose for "innocent" female readers. In a similar fashion, Lippard's novel contains subversive women who are not victims but agents in the demoralization of men. For example, Dora Livingstone, one of Lippard's subversive women, attempts to cross class boundaries by using her sexuality to seduce wealthy men. Perhaps, too, Twain did not always subvert traditional gender roles in his novels, which is one point Susan K. Harris has argued in her discussion of Twain's stagnant view on gender in *The Gilded Age*.[9] But certainly Clemens had read Lippard's 1847 fictionalized account of Washington, for he mentioned Lippard and his book in an 1853 letter to his brother. Reynolds cites as evidence a letter written by a then seventeen-year-old Samuel Clemens: "Geo. Lippard, in his 'Legends of Washington and his Generals,' has rendered the Wissahickon sacred in my eyes, and I shall make that trip,—as well as one to Germantown, soon."[10] Reynolds then wonders if Lippard's "romantic portrayal of the Wissahickon River" might have influenced "Twain's later romanticization of the Mississippi."[11] And, perhaps, Clemens had read Lippard's most famous sensational novel, *The Quaker City*. Reynolds notes that in 1869 Twain named his "ship of fools in *Innocents Abroad*" *The Quaker City*.[12] Furthermore, the style and technique that Lippard used to write *The Quaker City* might have "piqued" Clemens's "imagination: the use of vernacular language; the depiction of human savagery in Devil-Bug (who anticipates the cruel Pap in *Huckleberry Finn*); the cynical view of conventional society."[13]

While these aspects of Lippard's novel may or may not have influenced Twain's writing, a larger, perhaps more interesting, question, bursts forth from reading this paragraph: How and in what ways did Twain's western journalism display a tradition of didactic, sensational writing, which he exploited in his journalism and even in his headlines? Like Reynolds's short investigation of Lippard's influence on Twain, this essay traces Twain's sensational literary lineage by illustrating a discourse of violence prevalent in his western writing—a style and topic that had dominated American journalism and fiction for twenty years. Such writers, including Twain, justified their application of violence by claiming to report facts, "information," and the "awful realities" of the day. In addition to style and topic, sensational literature, including Twain's journalism, flourished within a marketplace in which publishers and editors advertised and published journalism and fiction for regional, national, and international audiences familiar with and devoted to sensational writing and writers.

Like Lippard two decades earlier who wrote "city sketches and courtroom accounts" for the Philadelphia penny paper, the *Spirit of the Times*,[14] in 1864 Twain became a city reporter in San Francisco. Here, he began crafting sensational headlines and news reports about "Lewd Merchandise," men "Vending Obscene Pictures," the alleged rape of a woman in

"Concerning Hackmen," and "Another Obscene Picture Knave Captured—He Solicits the Custom of School Girls." These headlines could have easily appeared in Lippard's sensational novel. Toward the end of the novel, newsboys shout the most recent headline concerning the outcome one of the prominent female characters: "The seduction of Mary Arlington with a portr-a-i-t! Daily Black Mail—only one cent!"[15] According to Michael Denning, Lippard's headlines reflect the actual news of the day. His novels, and dime novels in general, were often plotted with generous use of actual events from newspapers.[16] Lippard had learned how to craft sensational stories and headlines when he was a young reporter. Twain followed a similar path. Like headlines in Lippard's sensational novel that create a unity of theme similar to the stories printed in a single newspaper on a specific day, Twain's newspaper writing also reflects the violence of the day that appeared in one issue. In San Francisco he exposed the hidden dangers in hacks, cribs, and alleys of the western metropolis.

A "Story" of Hackmen: "Information" on Beasts in the Space Betwixt

San Francisco provided a new city for the continued growth of Mark Twain as a writer of sensational news reports. In 1862, when Samuel Clemens had deserted the war, and his brother had become the secretary to territorial governor, Clemens and Orion had offered more personal concerns for their female family members traveling West. Clemens had warned his mother and sister against stage travel, as had Orion warned his wife. But living in San Francisco two years later, Clemens had reason to fear for the safety of his mother and sister, even if they arrived safely in California, the "Garden of Eden reproduced."[17] In fact, other women also had reason for concern. In an article dated June 12, 1864, and titled "Beasts in the Semblance of Men," Twain wrote about one of the seduction and rape cases polluting the city. While many such stories exist, of which Twain wrote at least twelve,[18] this one in particular exhibits Twain's use of sensational, violent language to describe the masculine abuses of a woman. His judgment assaults men, who are actually not men but "beasts." These men are animals, monsters given over to an inhuman form, as depicted in an 1864 report from the *Call* titled "Beasts in the Semblance of Men":

> A private examination was held in the Police Court yesterday, which revealed a shocking criminality that, for baseness, bestiality, and degradation, can scarcely

be conceived. Teresa Ford, a young woman of prepossessing appearance, swore that a few nights ago she was standing on the sidewalk conversing with a person on the corner of Dupont street and St. Mark's Place, when a hack stopped opposite to her, and three men came from it, and, seizing her with force, carried her to the hack, and putting her inside, fastened the door, and took her to the Abbey, where James McKenna and Peter Tully got inside, and Tully forcibly held her down while McKenna, the hack driver, outraged her person. Then McKenna got out, and Tully forcibly outraged her in a similar manner, and during her struggles nearly bit a piece of flesh out of one of her fingers, which caused such excessive pain that she fainted away, and lay unconscious for some time. When she had somewhat recovered her senses, she found that her dress had been torn from her person, no clothing on but her chemise—the hack windows broken and both her dress and chemise were spotted with blood.[19]

Twain begins the article by calling the men "Beasts," who act with "baseness, bestiality, and degradation." These beasts used the interior of the hack to take turns raping Ford. During the struggle for her life, one of the animals bit a piece of her hand away. The result: a raped, nearly naked Teresa Ford, unconscious inside the hack, whose driver and accomplices took her home and dropped her off as if they had done nothing more than fulfill the duties of a driver. To further introduce his outrage for the male criminals and his sympathy for the female victim, Twain notes that Ford's clothes were also "spotted with blood," a literal description of the result of violence, but also a figurative reference to her virginal degradation.

Because of the increasing population and urban density in San Francisco, hacks became popular, which then created problems with traffic and crime about which Twain selected to write in the *Daily Morning Call*.[20] Neither the climate nor the landscape, or the threat of injury or robbery in the countryside, provided danger for the women in San Francisco. Danger existed in a transitional space, and a transient one, where men could partner to perform rapid and violent acts against women, hidden, confined inside the hack but also inside the metropolis. The other heinous possibility for crime existed because of the city and its density—men could "seize" an innocent woman while standing on a "sidewalk conversing with a person." Though Ford was not alone, the beasts did not fear witnesses or acts of defense from others waiting near the street. They acted with precision, and in combination, with a swift exit from the hack and with an even swifter abduction that Twain calls "seizing her with force, carried her to the hack, and putting her inside, fastened the door," and whisked away the victim. Their baseness was bold, for they knew that they could escape within the city.

Though Twain notes this terrible situation for Ford the victim, later in the letter Twain mentions that during the court proceedings, "Miss Ford, who it appeared was a girl of previous loose habits, acknowledged that she had been drinking during the night, but swore positively that McKenna was in the hack and had been guilty of outrageous violence."[21] No evidence exists within the letter, or the court case, that influences a reader to suspect Ford of promiscuous behavior, and Twain the reporter notes that the judge defended Ford's rights: He "stated that the base and disgusting venality that had been forcibly committed by the defendants upon a defenseless woman, who, whether degraded or not, was entitled to the protection of the law."[22] Twain could have included this description of Ford as a "girl of previous loose habits" for a variety of reasons, including the statistical fact that single women in mining towns and cities, even in a metropolis such as San Francisco, were often domestic servants or sometimes prostitutes and more available to receive a man's abuse. Perhaps she was once a prostitute but no longer. But by the end of the article, his discourse suggests that he maintains the innocence of Ford—a woman abused, raped, bloodied, all at the hands of pusillanimous men. Twain might also have questioned Ford's moral position within the community as a way to illustrate her experience with crime, which would support the idea that even a woman with street intelligence can be abused. This crime then informs female readers to be wary of men, for if a woman of knowledge can fall prey to these criminals, innocent women are in special danger.

This argument seems viable, considering Twain wrote an article one month later, titled "Rape," which accuses the victim, Miss Margaret McQuinn, of being "supernaturally green" and therefore not being prepared to watch for the snares of rapists.[23] This article, like "Beasts," reflects Twain's disgust with the inefficient legal system. Twain seems to prefer that individuals take precaution and not depend on the courts to protect women, for he admits that there "is charge of this kind brought against some hackman or other about once every five or six months, and it is fully time an example were made that would forever put a stop to such villany [sic] on their part."[24] His discourse produces both caution and sarcasm, for certainly one charge "every five or six months" hardly constitutes an epidemic of crime. In fact, he wrote a dozen such stories while he reported for the *Call*. The supernaturally green victim of this alleged rape, one Miss Margaret McQuinn, accused another hack driver, Barney Gillan, of the crime that infested the metropolis every few months, and yet the crimes still occurred. The end of the Ford article supports this idea and Twain's frustration with the court system designed by men, for men, to uphold economic and political pursuits that almost wholly excluded women. In the Ford rape case, the beasts were found guilty only of assault, which seems mild for a rape case: "The Judge," Twain wrote, "found Tully and McKenna guilty of a criminal assault, and would sentence them on Monday, and should meanwhile require bail from both of them to a heavy amount."[25] It is apparent, too, that Twain expects the criminals to be free on bail and most likely back to driving a hack in the near future. This cynicism, of course, was supported with the additional rape allegations against hack drivers one month after he had called men of their profession "beasts."

The July 23 article "Rape," is the first of three that follows the court case brought against the hack driver, Barney Gillan, by Miss Margaret McQuinn, the "supernaturally green" emigrant from New Hampshire. Though in the first article Twain does not yet know the case will be discharged, he already suspects that McQuinn has put herself in a precarious position, and that she may responsible for welcoming Gillan's advances. So Twain's judgment here is less about criminal men and more about women's need to be vigilant against such men. McQuinn, though, seemed an unlikely target. The "large and strongly built" McQuinn, "about thirty years of age," stated in court that in the past few days, "three different hackmen have endeavored to entrap her."[26] Twain notes that the woman is inexperienced in the West, newly emigrated from New Hampshire. He also comments on her physical appearance, for she is large and powerful and too old to be so green and so helpless. Finally, even though Twain does not doubt the potential criminality of hack drivers, by including the victim's three claims of the same sort within a few days' time allows him to undercut the validity of the claim. Even if McQuinn has perjured herself in court, Twain does not diminish the need to make an example of hackmen "that would forever put a stop to such villany on their part."[27]

This particular court case did not end with a conviction that might stop such villainy, however. In this case, neither the hackman nor the woman was innocent. Though not all women were in danger at all times, the article does offer a more realistic and complicated view of life in the city. Perhaps Twain, in the first article, was wrong to assume that men were to blame and that women were victims. During the proceedings, McQuinn admitted to joining Gillan in the Portsmouth Hotel, where they spent the night together. Twain notes that "the lady did enter her protest" when Gillan began to take "undue liberties with her," and yet she remained at the hotel. Twain sarcastically describes McQuinn here as not green but

3. Exposing Hackmen and Demoralizers   89

too free with men and too welcoming of physical attention, only, perhaps, to accuse them of taking undue liberties. The article ends with marked irony, as McQuinn "sought a refuge and assuaged her grief that night at the Portsmouth Hotel, in the embraces of a benevolent person with whom she had met for the first time that day. He protected her injured innocence until seven o'clock the next morning, when she sallied forth to seek another protector. The case was discharged."[28]

Though in this series of articles, and in many others, Twain mocks men, here he scorns instead the woman whom he had defended in the second article as "a defenceless [sic] young woman, thirty-five years of age," who had been raped by Barney Gillan. The defenseless woman had proved quite cable of manipulating the legal system, and, to some degree, Twain's opinion of her and of Gillan. When judging McQuinn as a woman of ill repute, he was also assigning to her a certain amount of agency that reformers fighting for women's rights and suffrage tried to advance. Twain, though, was not a reformer, and he was less concerned about McQuinn's rights and more occupied with notions of eviscerating her in print. And yet, according to Twain, the beasts were worse than the women.

Because so many instances of criminal hackmen filled the pages of the *Call*, it must have been easy to believe any allegation brought against one in their fraternity. It must have been especially standard, given the conditions of crime in the city and inside hacks, to believe a woman's allegations. Twain crafted a story, though news, about two types of people—hackman as criminal and woman as victim. In these sensational and connected stories, Twain wrote with a persuasive, yet biased, style that automatically allowed readers to view Gillan as a rapist and McQuinn as a victim—until the end of the third article. Here, the reporter makes clear the circumstances of McQuinn's accusations and the character of the young woman. Twain withholds, however, a clear vindication for the hackman. Twain gives Gillan nothing more than one phrase: "The case was discharged." No apology, no positive portrayal of Gillan. Twain made clear in his journalism that he disliked hackman, that he distrusted them, and even that he thought they often escaped the punishment that they deserved. This tone is also clear at the end of "Concerning Hackmen," the second article in the "Rape" series. Twain ends this article with sarcasm, and perhaps with a sexual overtone, admitting that the court "will probably make him sweat" for his crimes, rather than being punished.[29] At the time, Twain wanted hack drivers to be punished, and he had taken that task upon himself by writing about so many cases concerning hack drivers.

Such judgments allowed Twain to fulfill the "aesthetic function" of a newspaper.[30] Even though he was harsh in his tone and unapologetic for writing about the guilt of a man not yet found guilty under the force of law, Twain offered his readers a "story" view of the facts. His journalism framed the events and assigned meaning to them without rendering the "news" items with dispassionate discourse. The aesthetic, then, provides the tone, the style, the story. The facts are nearly insignificant. After all, Twain was not a detective who solved crimes. He was a journalist who exposed men. Even a woman such as McQuinn needed to be exposed.

Blitz and Shepheard: A "Story" of Bravery and the Law

Twain was not a particularly brave or confrontational man in the West. But he was influential. He had the power of the press. In his four months as the only local reporter for the *Call*, he wrote at least twelve articles that illustrate his disdain for hackmen, his desire to see them punished, and his appreciation for law enforcement officers appointed to deter criminal behavior and to arrest offensive hack drivers. These articles create a kind of twelve-part "story" more than they represent twelve disparate items with "information." With his words, Twain not only reported on cultural events, but he persuaded readers to view these events in a certain way, within a certain context. In the case of hacks, Twain warned that they were dangerous because unscrupulous beasts posing as men controlled these hacks. To combat these acts of "baseness, bestiality, and degradation," the city needed a strong man, a man of legal and ethical force, to hunt down these hackman and make them behave more like men.[31]

Officer Bernard S. Blitz was Twain's man. His name reoccurred in many of these articles as a hero tracking hackmen and making them pay for their crimes. In 1865, more than a year after quitting the *Call*, Twain praised Blitz as an officer "doing more justice to the position than any eighteen men in San Francisco,"[32] and continued to laud the officer as a detective who "can hunt down a transgressing hack driver by some peculiarity in the style of his blasphemy."[33] During the summer of 1864, Twain also respected Blitz. Twain notes at the end of "Beasts in the Semblance of Men" that Blitz was the investigating officer. In "Rape," Twain mentions Blitz as the officer "whose duty it is to attend to the followers of that occupation [hack drivers], deputed to ferret out the criminal and arrest him, which he did."[34] But in the second article in the series, "Concerning Hackmen," Twain sarcastically calls him "Signor Blitz," who, along with "the Police Court, and the Board of Supervisors, all put together, have not been able to keep the hackmen straight."[35]

The alleged rape of McQuinn and the hackman Gillan do not appear until the end of the article, as if to make an emotional appeal to readers about the dangers lurking inside hacks. The rest of the article delivers details about a new city ordinance meant to reduce the possibility of hackmen "extorting money from passengers." Apparently, drivers often worked in pairs. One driver would trade hacks with another driver at a stop en route, and upon arriving at the destination, the new driver would feign ignorance about the original agreement between fare and driver for the cost of the taxi. The new ordinance required a license for drivers, which was to be displayed so that fares could identify the driver.[36] These minor offenses, compared with assault and rape, drew the ire of Twain, and he certainly thought Blitz, whose only job was to be the watcher of hackmen, should stop any and all offenses. For this reason, articles about Blitz tracking and punishing hackmen serve two purposes—to expose the unscrupulous and dangerous hackmen and to promote the heroism of Blitz. Twain portrayed him as a heroic but "small man" that despite his stature filled the roles of "eighteen men."[37]

This new ordinance must have been difficult to enforce, for Twain once again published a warning for his readers to look for hackmen's licenses, and a threat to hackmen who chose not to display them. His short article, which appeared on August 6 and titled "Attention, Hackmen," advised readers, notably hack drivers, that "all runners, hackmen, etc., must wear upon their hats a badge denoting their licenses, in compliance with an Ordinance of the Board of Supervisors to that effect. Disobedience of this order will entail heavy penalties upon the offender."[38] Another item, published the same day on the following page offers the account of an additional hackman who violated the new ordinance. This driver "found himself charged with, and convicted by his own confession of a violation of the city ordinance concerning licenses, and ordered into custody until he should give bail in the sum of twenty dollars for his appearance this morning for sentence."[39] A third article published on August 6 also includes Officer Blitz. Though we do not know the occupation of the man Blitz arrested "for stealing a lady's watch, which may be worth six bits, perhaps, if they succeed in making the gold plating stay on it and find out how to start her up and make her go,"[40] we know that Blitz, whose job was to hunt hackmen, made the arrest. More importantly, though, Twain continued to laud Blitz in the press and to denigrate hackmen and other petty criminals who steal watches that appear to be worth just "six bits" and might not even keep time. The next day, Twain reported that four hackmen were "arrested for violating the order to travel with a badge denoting their occupation attached to their hats."[41] Though these crimes are petty, and not as sensational or horrific as rape, the purpose of these articles, as much as exposing hackmen as "labricks," was to advertise the success of Blitz and to establish the city as a safe space. In this case, then, Twain's promotion of Blitz illustrates the usefulness of a moral, law enforcer over the beastliness of immoral men abusing women.

And yet, Twain thought Blitz was the only officer making an effort to enact change among the ranks of hackmen, and these articles published in July, August, and September certainly advertise him as a lone hero. Even in a June 28 article, Twain praises Blitz, this time for arresting two hackmen. The first, Thomas Phelan, for "driving through a Masonic funeral procession on Sunday, and striking one of the gentlemen composing it." Blitz arrested the second hackman "for using obscene and insulting language towards a gentleman who declined to employ him."[42] Though these crimes are not violent, they are crimes against what Twain would consider better judgment. As if to scold the drivers, he follows the arrest report with advice for hackmen, who "are in the habit of violating the law." Twain believes that Officer Blitz will arrest offensive hack drivers: "It would be well for hackmen to conduct themselves properly and with due attention to the proprieties of life for the present, as it is Blitz's especial business to look after them, and he manifests a disposition to do it."[43]

Other officers, at least to Twain, were unequal to the task. On Wednesday, August 18, he published an article that condemns both hack drivers and officers, not for drivers' involvement in crimes against women or for officers' neglect in punishing the drivers, but for the course and "insolent" behavior of hackmen.[44] Twain narrates a third-person experience of "a gentleman of this city" who "concluded business duties" at "half-past twelve o'clock on Tuesday night." The gentleman entered the street, where "he was assailed with insolent language by two or three hackmen ... one of whom ... followed him some distance with bullying insolence." The gentleman questioned the hackman. At this point Twain shifts the discourse so that the hackman becomes a "ruffian," with "bullying" behavior, whose language is "insolent."[45] It is clear that Twain is trying to criminalize the driver. It is also apparent that the drivers dislike this gentleman and have waited outside of his place of business, or have taken the opportunity, since they were parked outside the building, to accost the gentleman for a particular reason. That reason: the gentleman was a newspaper reporter, and none other than Twain himself.[46] The hackman, now labeled a criminal, moved toward the gentleman: "The ruffian thrust his hands into his over-coat pocket, as if to take out a weapon, and bellowed out at the same time: 'B-a-h; go to h—l, you d—d hog!'" This scare caused Twain to seek "a police officer not far distant, who, however, paid no attention."[47] In this scene, the police officer is little better than the ruffian.

Twain, however, had the power of his pen and could attack (and did) these hackmen in the popular press. At the end of this article, it seems clear that the hackmen have harassed Twain in retaliation for his vehement writing against them in June and July in the newspaper.[48] Because Twain was the sole local reporter, he was recognizable, especially because he left the office at night on foot after finishing his work. Four days prior, a group of hack drivers published a "card" in the newspaper that "vindicated the respectable character of their fraternity, stating that newspaper reporters took every occasion to heap opprobrium upon them."[49] When writing about the threatening and insolent behavior, Twain is referring to that defense published a few days before his altercation with these hackmen. Their words of damnation and insult that would send this "damned" journalist "hog" to hell gives Twain more ammunition for his reporting cannon. Since hackmen wanted to be known as respectable, a claim that would help their business, and published that defense in the *Call*, Twain now had the opportunity to close the article with a retort: "If this is a feature of their respectability, they cannot find fault with members of the press and others for speaking of them only as ruffians and bullies."[50]

Even though Blitz and other officers made numerous arrests, hackmen continued to defraud their fares. In the last article concerning hackmen that Twain published during these three months, between June 12 and September 22, the journalist reported that a group of drunken men agreed to terms with a hack driver, violated those terms, and then kept the driver "waiting there a couple of hours." The driver then "demanded five dollars for his trouble, and forced them to pay it." Once these details came out in court, "Judge Shepheard said that hackmen in general have a bad reputation for fair dealing with their customers, but he could not see that in this instance the defendant had demanded any more than his just rights, and dismissed the case."[51] Twain must have reluctantly written those final words, "dismissed the case," for in every other article about hackmen, he used vehemence and humor to abuse their kind and noted in each case that these men were arrested, were made to pay, or found guilty in court—except in two instances.

The most recent instance occurred on August 18, which Twain used to craft a response to those hackmen who treated him with "bullying insolence," those hackmen Twain called "ruffians and bullies" who escaped that night the concern of a police officer less able than Blitz. The more disconcerting instance in which a hackmen "case was discharged" concluded the "Rape" sequence of the three stories concerned with hack driver Barney Gillan. In "End of the Rape Case," Twain turned his attention from attacking Gillan and instead chastised Miss Margaret McQuinn for being of loose moral character. Twain closed this article and the "Trial of the Hackman" with the simple diction that both cases were dismissed or discharged. Though Twain might have been disappointed in July that he had been wrong about a detested hackman—a beast, ruffian, and bully—and that one of his kind was found not guilty, perhaps in November Twain found a modicum of pleasure in the pages of the *Call* if he happened to read the November 5, 1864, issue. Though he was no longer a local reporter for the paper, one item might have caught his interest. Barney Gillan, though not guilty of the rape of Miss Margaret McQuinn, robbed a man and was once again standing trial for his crimes.[52]

City of Obscenity: A New(s) "Story"

On July 23, the same day Twain began writing about the Gillan "Rape" case, Twain started a series of local columns about men who "demoralized" young women, sold "lewd" merchandise, and vended "obscene pictures." Though these stories do not contain hacks, hackmen, or crimes perpetrated against women inside of hacks, when read alongside the hackman rape stories, this second series of columns enriches our understanding of the dangerous western culture for women and Twain's sensational method to expose criminals. Comparing these columns also allows us to witness an unfolding of Twain's disdain for these beasts' "villanous [sic] transactions" with women. Whether these "infamous" men and "miscreants" lured women into their hacks or into their private rooms, these men deserved severe punishment, and Twain relished inserting this opinion into these anonymous, local columns. And though the word hack does not appear

3. Exposing Hackmen and Demoralizers   95

in these articles, the girls were transported from streets outside of their schools to rooms of men downtown, certainly within hacks. Even though hackmen are not directly responsible for this series of crimes, men took advantage of schoolgirls because of the secrecy and seclusion of spaces within the metropolis, in this case Twain's San Francisco, rather than Lippard's labyrinthine Philadelphia.

The first of these articles, "Demoralizing Young Girls," ran the same day as "Rape." The men arrested for creating a "regular system of prostituting young girls" worked in pairs assigned by age. For example, George Lambertson "a full-grown man" bossed "a boy of fourteen" named Ralph Doyle, who distributed "obscene pictures" to young girls. These men manipulated pairs of boys, similar in age to the girls, who lured the girls aged "ten or twelve to fifteen," to private rooms downtown. Here the boys showed the girls "obscene books and pictures." Twain termed this process "their ruin," for somehow these vulnerable girls could be used as prostitutes. According to Doyle, many of the girls were "'baldheaded,'" that is, "unbonneted street girls." They probably had no means or support and were desperate. Doyle suggested that many of these girls "have done the seducing in most of the other cases, as they did in his."[53] Twain continues to support the notion that Doyle, like these young girls, is a victim. The "full-grown man" is the real monster, and Twain inserts his bias that "it is to be hoped that the law will be stretched to its utmost tension for the punishment of the men."[54] This passive construction is typical of newspaper reports. Dime novels of the day often followed the model of "'unauthored' discourse" as did journalism.[55] Twain's discourse also satisfies a particular judgment against the criminal, which therefore makes language both his "authored" judgment and his "unauthored" and "official" speak about these men. Doyle, though, was not the leader and "was the most innocent on the party," which is the reason Twain hopes that Doyle will not receive the severe punishment deserving of a full-grown man, which, according to Twain's metaphor about stretching the law "to its utmost tension," includes hanging.

While chastising the men and protecting young Doyle, Twain did not forget about the plight of the girls. Twain laments the girls' situations, noting that "there are *thirty* names of debauched young girls on the list [emphasis original]." One of these girls has received the worst of Lambertson's abuses. Twain explains that this girl is "a poor orphan girl of fifteen has become *enceinte* [emphasis original]."[56] She has become pregnant by Lambertson, who "in the hope of escaping the penitentiary," has given to her all of his property in the city. This tactic was unsuccessful, however, for the next day Twain reported in his aptly titled column, "A Merited Penalty," that Lambertson, "who was arrested for infamous demoralizing practices with young school girls," whom Twain also called a "miscreant," received in police court "the heaviest penalty prescribed by the law for his crime." That penalty included "three months in the County Jail" and "a fine of five hundred dollars."[57]

Though Lambertson's punishment must have pleased Twain, although the punishment was less severe than hanging, two days later he had reason to be cynical that criminals would continue to commit beastly acts, even though officers continued to arrest and cage these beasts. On July 26 Twain wrote two additional locals about immoral men luring women with obscene pictures and merchandise. These items appeared the same day as Twain's "Concerning Hackmen," the second report in the Gillan rape series in which Twain lamented how little punishment Gillan would likely receive for his crime—"they will probably make him sweat for it." This lamentation appears on page three, one column over from "Lewd Merchandise." Twain's short item names two men, the first arrested "for selling French playing cards which show obscene pictures when held up to the light," and the second, "snatched, for the fourth time, for importing and selling all manner of pictured obscenity. The work of grabbing these fellows still goes on with unabated zeal."[58] Arresting so many criminals in the city created a great deal of work for officers, but Twain notes here that one of the men had been arrested three previous times for the same offense. Another item of note—the obscene pictures appeared on French playing cards, which, by American standards, at least as reflected by Twain's conservative sensibilities, must have seemed risqué.

A similarly themed story, the second criminal offense for obscenity on which Twain reported that day, appeared on the previous page under the title "Vending Obscene Pictures." Twain withholds all judgment of the criminal in this story, for the man, Jean Rosseau, "whose name and idiom are very French."[59] By marking the man and his lewd merchandise as French, Twain plays into the idea that all things French carried a certain kind of meaning that might be construed by Americans in the West in negative ways. In this obscenity case, though Jean Rosseau was arrested for exhibiting plates painted with "obscene" images in his store, Rosseau claimed that these plates were fine art in France, and "that the pictures were purely classical, at least histrionic." Judge Shepheard disagreed with this assertion, however, stating that though the pictures "might agree with

French ideas of morality, the stricter regime in the United Sates would condemn them." The judge ordered the pictures to be destroyed and for Rosseau "to appear for sentence."[60] The judgment caused the defendant consternation, and he requested an appeal. Twain ends the article with the wry declaration that Rosseau "may go farther and fare worse,"[61] not because Twain has also condemned Rosseau, but because the reporter knows how many obscenity charges filled Judge Shepheard's police court. Like the frequency of charges filed against hackmen, even Gillan, whose story appeared the same day, most readers and editors of the paper would have already found guilt in a "vender" of obscenity. Unlike the Gillan case that caused Twain to doubt the hackman could receive a strict penalty, at the end of the Rosseau piece, Twain seems resigned to the fact that Rosseau will be found guilty, even if he appeals. Judge Shepheard disapproved of Rosseau's behavior and thought the man was guilty. Twain assumed that appealing the case might bring Rosseau more pain under the force of law and "fare worse." This Jean Rosseau article, however, published on July 26 was the second article that Twain published in as many days about a man named Jean Rosseau.

On July 24, when Twain delivered his satisfaction for the punishment of Lambertson for demoralizing young girls in "A Merited Penalty," Twain offered an additional judgment for such men, including the additional Jean Rosseau. In "Obscene-Picture Dealers," the reporter notes that three more men were arrested on obscenity charges. But, here again, these men are not men but instead beasts: "Three of these cattle were arrested yesterday: Jean Rosseau, John Doe and Joseph Isaacs." Though we read no more about the arrest or sentencing of Rosseau, we do see his name appear again two days later when a Rosseau was arrested for displaying obscene French plates. It is likely that these men share only a name and not an identity, for they appear to be of disparate social classes, and Twain did not mention any connection with the first crime when he wrote the second article just two days after the first. Ironically, on July 26, a third Jean Rosseau was charged with the misdemeanor of petty larceny.[62]

More than likely, when Twain wrote in the second article that his "name and idiom are very French," the reporter was playing with the coincidence of a common French name of three men charged with crimes so soon after the other, even though petty larceny is dissimilar from the other crimes. In addition, those risqué French playing cards from another column must have increased Twain's pleasure when noting how "very French" all of these obscenities appeared to be in America. Still, though Twain does not mention Rosseau again as one of the three "cows," nor does the reporter mock the name for being French, Twain does deride "John Doe" as a coward for hiding behind his pseudonym—an ironic turn, considering Samuel Clemens wrote under various pseudonyms for most of his adult life. And he wrote anonymously for most of his reports on crime in the *Call*. Twain must have wanted to report Doe's actual name, for the reporter closes the article by sacrificing his desire because he has been ordered to do so, probably by Judge Shepheard. Though Twain is unable to release the criminal's name, he can instead unleash a certain power over the criminal—the power of the reporter to offer judgment against these men and to deride these beasts, cows, miscreants, and hackmen. Twain offers a final judgment, in addition to the legal one administered by Shepheard: "We allow 'John Doe' to enjoy his fictitious name by special request, accompanied by solemn assurances from the leading spirit of the newly inaugurated crusade against this class, that he is an angel. We do it under protest."[63] His protest here serves as his way to confront justice without physical confrontation. Twain's power did not surface in the courtroom with Judge Shepheard. The reporter's power came later, in an office, recording details and facts, and crafting a sensational consideration of what he thought about those details and facts.

A Unity of Date: A "Story" or "Information"

Though these violent crimes—crimes against women's bodies, and crimes that attacked the moral fortitude of San Francisco's thriving society—are significant and horrific and in many ways offer small items of "story," they might seem less culturally significant when compared with events, or "information," that affected the national culture. While Twain railed against hackmen rapists, men who dealt in obscene pictures, scoundrels who turned "unbonneted" girls into prostitutes and impregnated orphans, and played with the names of three arrested Jean Rosseaus, the Civil War's influence swept across the nation and the western territories. In July in Virginia, Union and Confederate forces clashed in the Petersburg campaign. These concerns rarely invaded Twain's sensational items about local crime. For certain, Twain's twenty- to thirty-word local items illustrate his, and the local readers', concerns for safety, morality, gender roles, and the explosion of a new city whose laws are not always readily enforced. But on the front page of the July 26 issue of the *Daily Morning Call*, every article reflects at least one aspect of the war or its effects. Twain wrote none of these items. Most are summaries from telegraphic news items or regular correspondences from reporters living in other cities. Twain had served in such a capacity for the *Call* in 1863 while living in Virginia City, but even then he did not report on national stories disconnected from local life in Nevada Territory.

One of the notable July 26 articles on page one bears significance, even though the article contains no information about demoralizing men or hackmen.[64] The article comes from St. Louis, a city important for the idea of the West, for, at the time, it was the largest city west of the Mississippi. The culture of St. Louis was unlike San Francisco's, however. The gateway city, whose arch would be built one hundred years later, was a Confederate city on the western boundaries of the Upper South, whereas, San Francisco enjoyed a culture sympathetic to the Union. The correspondent's writing in "Our St. Louis Letter" for San Francisco readers also displays a pro–Union tone, published in a pro–Union newspaper, and focuses on an issue the rest of the paper that day seems to reflect: women should not cross certain boundaries, physical or ideological. Twain's items teach women that they should not trust men, should not enter into a hack alone, should not allow a man to show her obscene photos, should not travel to a private room with a man. In the case of McQuinn, at least according to Twain, a woman should not accuse a man of rape when she has willingly placed herself within a private room with numerous men and allowed these men entrance to her private intimacies. In letters to his family and in his fiction, Twain often helped perpetrate the image of woman as victim. When McQuinn subverted his view of an emigrant woman as being "supernaturally green," he mocked her chastity and blamed her for the abuses a man like Gillan could manufacture.

Though the front page of the *Daily Morning Call* offered new "information" items about politics and the Civil War, even a story about women's subversive roles in the war, Twain continued to write sensational and short articles that mostly delivered what crimes had occurred that day and which criminals had been prosecuted in police court. These news items portrayed men upholding the law and order, especially Officer Blitz and Judge Shepheard, as heroic symbols for the law and masculinity. Men who lowered themselves to seducers of women deserved all of the retribution of the law. Even men who assaulted or threatened women received Twain's disdain. For example, in October 1864, once the "epidemic" had weakened, a drunkard named Benjamin Roderick was arrested for entering the home of Mary Roberts, where he threatened her life with a Bowie knife, assaulted her, and "smashed up all the furniture in her home."[65] Though Twain does not note Roberts's social position, it is clear that she lives alone. In the concluding article the following day, Twain's readers discovered that she escaped the grasp of her abuser through "interference of Providence." This divine salvation surprised Twain because once he, the reporter, saw Roberts, the victim, in court, he made assumptions about her based on "general appearance, and her known character and antecedents."[66] In other words, Twain thought Roberts was a prostitute. Even though he saw Roberts as a "bad" woman, not an angel, in the "devil's territory, he thought Roberts deserved justice. He thought that Roderick deserved "to be punished" for assaulting Roberts "with a deadly weapon," for "malicious mischief," and "for breaking furniture that did not belong to him."[67] Though the man was bad, Twain did not heap abuses on him as the reporter had against the male criminals in the obscenity cases.

The warning for women here is more specific. Twain seems to expect that single women, whose appearance and character suggest that they are subversive, perhaps "immoral" themselves, will receive the abuses of unscrupulous men, drunkards, and men of violent character who smash women's furniture. Twain ends Roderick's list of violence with the destruction of the furniture, which, according to Twain, received the worst of Roderick's outburst. At the end of the article, in fact, Twain satirically laments that Roberts's body was not destroyed in the manner of the furniture. Twain realizes that he could have had a more interesting article to write if Roderick would have murdered Roberts.

This realization marked the difference between Twain the journalist and Twain the fiction writer. A novelist, working through the performative narrator, has full control over his material. A journalist must adhere to the facts. Twain, however, not only reports the facts but also weaves a narrative within his news items. Even though the news is supposed to deliver information, Twain's "news" advances a more personal admission in the closing lines of the article: Had Roderick killed the woman, he "might have made a good sensation item for the newspapers, and he carelessly threw that opportunity away also. Roderick is a useless incumbrance [sic], any way you take him."[68] The male abuser, in this case, is not a beast or a ruffian. He is a useless thing, a simple nuisance, incapable of providing the reporter with a sensational story that his readers could devour.

Twain did not necessarily avoid writing about more "important" national issues, such as the war, though he had often avoided the war and

3. Exposing Hackmen and Demoralizers

the politics surrounding the war when he traveled to Nevada Territory with his brother. Even if Twain had not yet developed a profound interest in national politics,[69] Twain did write about "Secessionist" activities in the countryside of California and Nevada, which illustrates his judgment about the division of the country during the war. But during this period in Twain's career, he wrote mostly about crime and issues related to the West, and specifically to San Francisco. These crimes drew Twain's attention. Indeed, this was his job. He was not paid to write about national events, even if he were interested in them. Events in Nevada never seemed mundane to the young reporter. Twain enjoyed being a reporter for the *Enterprise*. Yet he despised his job for the *Daily Morning Call* in 1864.

The position he held in San Francisco, however, influenced the ways in which he wrote and how he reported on mundane daily events. What he called the "fearful drudgery, soulless drudgery"[70] of writing for the *Call* caused him to insert sensation and violent details, which appear even in the ways he constructed headlines. He wrote twenty or more locals for publication each day, except for Mondays when the *Call* did not publish an issue, and these small items required a great deal of leg work. On July 26, when so much news about the war filled the front page, Twain was relegated to writing about "Stolen Merchandise," "Gambling Cases Dismissed," "Bail Forfeited," "Contempt of Court," "A Contraband Transaction," in addition to the numerous items about obscene merchandise sales or the lewd behavior of men, and finally the continued story about the much despised hack drivers, "Concerning Hackmen." This work may have been drudgery for Twain, but it served a social purpose, beyond Twain and because of Twain. Beyond Twain's influence, according to Branch, "the 1864 *Call* printed city news that today often seems unusually trivial, but we must remember that in those days the only outlet for community news of gossipy or sensational kind was the local column."[71] This was Twain's realm. He wrote about the trivial and the sensational.

These local columns were not actually trivial, however, though they certainly were sensational. Twain used his style and his power as a reporter to reflect social trends and anxieties, but he also judged them, assigned meaning to these events. At the time, "political issues" and "inflammatory social problems" were "controversial questions debated on the editorial pages."[72] Twain used the local columns to introduce doubt about the safety of women in the metropolis. He subverted the image of the strong male whose success in the West was based on power rather than morality. Dangers for women and immoral male behavior appear in Twain's columns as markers for a problematic application of westward expansion escape from the war, and the designs of a new Eden reproduced in the American West. Though his tone is often satirical and humorous in these locals, Twain is not necessarily happy—with his job or with the region. So when we read words in a local column that blame a man's behavior, exposing his genitals to women in public, on the "prevailing obscene-picture epidemic," we see two kinds of discourse packed into Twain's locals. First, the story relates fact. He published four locals about obscenity cases on July 26, and numerous others that summer. He also published twelve articles about hackmen's crimes, four of which dealt explicitly with the assault and rape of women. Though McQuinn, one alleged rape victim, proved to be a participant in her abuses, she nevertheless was part of a culture that involved men taking advantage of women. So, with so many cases that summer about the sexual abuses of women, perhaps there was an epidemic.

The second kind of discourse is a subversion of masculinity and western male identity. One popular myth of the West narrates stories of strong men making a new life for themselves, if they are strong enough to claim the land and its resources. This kind of discourse is present in Frederick Jackson Turner's frontier thesis (1893) and Theodore Roosevelt's four volumes of *Winning of the West* (1889–1896). Richard Slotkin has explained how the American West became a literal and ideological space that represented these conquering ideals of the American spirit—"capitalist competition, of supply and demand, of Social Darwinian 'survival of the fittest' as a rationale for social order, and of 'Manifest Destiny.'"[73] Twain sometimes advanced this narrative in his letters, journalism, and even in *Roughing It* (1872). But the more subversive quality of the West, advanced by Twain the reporter in these locals, is the cowardice and wasted energy of men. Twain seems exasperated by such men's actions. In "Another Victim," Twain nearly sighs between the words when he writes that this man who exposed himself to women in public had "probably become demoralized by the prevailing obscene-picture epidemic." In another article three days later, Twain called the epidemic an "obscene picture tempest."[74] The infection spread by the obscene had become a turbulent storm pounding to a "fury" the citizens of San Francisco. But perhaps it was too easy to blame "obscene" pictures for the acts of men.

The longer local, "Demoralizing Young Girls," published on July 23, starred the infamous "miscreant" Lambertson, who prostituted young girls, impregnated an orphan, and misguided the young Ralph Doyle. These men, under the leadership of Lambertson, "made use of the boys to decoy the girls to their rooms, where their run was effected. These rooms were well stocked with obscene books and pictures."[75] The pictures did not cause the ruin of the girls. The men's influence, or threats, or abuses, and social and economic functions of class caused girls to become prostitutes. The images and books may have normalized sexuality for young, influential boys and girls, but such images should have had less influence on men and women. These obscenity cases, however, certainly reflected the cultural anxiety about the demoralizing force of sexual content and especially about the power men had over women and children. While Twain's tone in "Another Victim" might suggest that he is ironically calling the male exposing his genitals a victim, Twain does not diminish the victimhood of young boys and girls under the influence of "miscreants" and "scoundrels" willfully causing the ruin of youth, especially young women.

Providing a view of July 26 as reported in the *Call* allows us to see two kinds of unity—the unity of date that each newspaper delivers, even if the articles are disconnected, and the unity of theme. A larger view of theme might suggest that on this mid-summer day in 1864, ordinary events occurred—mines gained value, emigrants arrived in the West, battles were fought in Virginia, men murdered and raped his fellow humans in San Francisco, and the courts handed down various judgments against these criminals. But with so many articles about women crossing social boundaries or becoming the victims of men who crossed social boundaries to abuse women, more important is how Twain, and then his readers, viewed crime associated with gender norms. Even if these norms appear to be conservative, sometimes the newspaper printed humorous pieces unrelated to crime that subverted such traditional roles. He explored in these sensational news items the causes for rapes, assaults, and public genital exposure. Often, especially in the series of cases about girls with obscene books and images or in the cases about unscrupulous hackmen, Twain judged the male criminals and found them guilty in the press before Judge Shepheard had ruled against these men. Even if Shepheard found them guilty in police court, Twain's job was to make sure his readers knew of the crimes, the criminals, and the punishments. Twain believed that men posed a social threat to women in San Francisco, and he took seriously his job to warn readers, especially women.

Unfortunately for the victims, but fortunately for the sensational writer, Mark Twain, the obscenity "epidemic" of June and July continued into August. By connecting these obscenity cases that summer, Twain reported on the social situation in the city, but he also helped construct and perpetuate the epidemic. These sensational headlines grabbed the attention of readers. The last of these stories concludes the series with Twain's assessment of the man involved and of the epidemic caused by such men. In this August 6 story, Twain reports that a "scoundrel named George R. Powers has been detected in the obscene book and trade and captured." Twain later calls Powers "the thoughtless numbskull," and then finishes the article with the assessment "that a whole school might be corrupted by the circulation among them of a single column of the lecherous trash dealt in by Mr. Powers."[76] Though Powers, and his kind, such as Lambertson, is a scoundrel, a knave, and a numbskull for distributing "lecherous trash," Twain, too, helped distribute sensational news—violence, sex, blood, and excitement—to his readers each day in the columns that he wrote.

Furthermore, the newspaper depended on this unity to provide readers with a cohesive view of San Francisco each day. The newspaper, unlike any other literary format in Twain's career or any other format within a culture, for that matter, weaves events into a unified message built on a simple idea—the date. Benedict Anderson calls this disjointed unity among stories and ideas within one paper an "imagined linkage."[77] While the date provides the connection, the "relationship between the newspaper, as a form of book, and the market" forms the more lasting social and economic reason for a narrative with multiple plots, characters, and resolutions to be printed and sold. According to Anderson, the newspaper is an "'extreme form' of the book" in that the newspaper was the most sold printed commodity.[78] Because the *Call*, and Twain's writing within it, was popular in San Francisco, its columns added to this unity each time Twain reported on the crime in the city and on the men committing these crimes.

Its publication date and its city unified the *Call*. Though a newspaper "combines stories by sheer juxtaposition," readers in one city, in this case San Francisco, devoured local, sensational stories relevant for their daily lives.[79] Twain's San Francisco journalism lacked plot, but by writing multiple stories about male beasts and "demoralizers" for a single issue of the paper, Twain created a kind of narrative about a city and its people. Even if women spies captured in St. Louis was a bigger national story, hackmen cheats and rapists that turned girls into prostitutes or nearly corrupted an entire school were more important local stories for San Franciscans in their daily lives—in school, or waiting on busy street corners, or traveling within the city. George Lippard, the journalist and fiction writer, had cautioned readers in Philadelphia about such dangers two decades earlier,

3. Exposing Hackmen and Demoralizers

and Twain, the journalist, continued in this sensational tradition in the 1860s. Something insidious slithered between the lines of Twain's columns that showed his disdain for men who abused women. These men, especially in the West, were supposed to be hard working, heroic, and self-reliant. If they, like Twain, failed to find fortunes in the mines or in business, they could reinvent themselves. As men. Not as beasts or scoundrels.

Twain's letters and journalism, like the antebellum writers who published violent accounts of crimes in periodicals, critique social abuses of multiple kinds, but for him the seduction, assault, and rape of women symbolized the decay of the new Garden of Eden and the possibility of a western utopia. The West was supposed to offer an outlet for Americans crushed within the walls of the eastern metropolis, a place that George Lippard judged as dangerous for women. Crimes against women in California, however, mark the West as a fallen Eden, and yet the hellish Nevada landscape offered wealth and adventure for men and women strong enough to harness its danger for personal regeneration. Perhaps Twain found both in the West—a time of regeneration and success as a writer but whose time in the West was temporary. While writing in the West, and even later in life, he wrote about these adventurous men and women. They often became items of satire, humor, or even moral judgment, but some crimes, such as rape and the assault of women, received a separate kind of literary treatment. The Teresa Ford case in "Beasts in the Semblance of Men" delivers more than any other Twain's judgment of men and women when men become degraded monsters and women become abused victims. Twain introduces no humor into the descriptions of a bloody and raped Ford, and he offers no satirized view of violence against western women. Though Twain offers no details about Teresa Ford's origins, she appears to be a western woman who feels comfortable standing and conversing on the streets without the aid or protection of men.

In the "Rape" series of articles, however, Miss Margaret McQuinn does not ultimately represent a green, naïve band of weak, feminized metropolis dwellers unable to navigate the rough and masculine West. Initially, she appears to be innocent, but upon further examination, Twain decides that she is a different kind of woman—a participant in her own demise and perhaps in the demise of a region. Certainly, her behavior has caused Twain to doubt her purity. But McQuinn's performance also encouraged Twain to see her as an agent. The women of the West symbolize a kind of complicated Eden—women who know the danger that exists but choose to dwell within the corrupt space and thrive. The danger, then, is not being too naïve to recognize danger. The peril lies in plain site for these women of knowledge who illustrate more than any other class of women the fallen circumstances of Eden. The men who abuse these women are not green or experienced, eastern or western. They are degradations of the land and culture that cannot offer a paradise for women because it cannot offer a place of rejuvenation and utopia for men, either.

On the pages of the *Call* women were not always portrayed as victims, even if these portraits were small, insignificant, and humorous—words that mark a situation dissimilar from McQuinn's. I return here to the anonymous piece from "Dispatches by the State Line," printed on the first page of the *Call*, January 3, 1864, during a year when so much horror invaded San Francisco and haunted women. In this piece, girls are not victims. They are agents, self-aware, playful, even tormenters of men:

> Girls.—Some one out West boldly declares that girls will differ, and that furthermore, as proof, one of them lately broke her neck in trying to escape being kissed, while he knows a great many of them ready to break their necks to get kissed. True, every word of it.[80]

In the West, it seems, not only men carried the burden of one of two kinds of masculinity—strong, courageous pioneers capable of protecting their bodies, interests, and family, or beastly male ruffians willing to take what does not belong to them, which included other men's wealth or the lives and bodies of weaker men and women. To read "Girls" alongside news items that deliver violence of men against women illustrates Twain's contradictory view of women in the West. She did not have to be a prostitute, a green woman from the East, or a young schoolgirl to offer a split image—on one side a victim, and on the other an agent.

Such a method appears in Lippard's *Quaker City*, for Dora Livingstone, a prominent middle-class woman, attempts to become an elite woman by using her sexuality to seduce wealthy men. Her discontent causes her to display great agency, and yet her power comes from her sexual influence, not from her hard work ethic or because of her role as a mother. Subversive women, like Dora Livingstone, existed in the press in the West two decades later. Twain considered Miss Margaret McQuinn to be a type of "Dora," who in Twain's writing became a literary "Laura," a woman of agency and a seducer of men. McQuinn, like Adah Isaacs Menken, performed masculine qualities that Twain found distasteful in his writing. In "Facts and Fancies," a page four anecdotal section of the *Call*, a short piece appeared on July 26 that supports this more complicated interpretation of gender norms. "—Among the prisoners brought from

3. Exposing Hackmen and Demoralizers   107

General Grant's army the White House recently, was a woman—a coursefeatured Amazon—who was in charge of a Rebel battery when she was captured, and had on a United States officer's uniform."[81] But these women who crossed the gender line were not the women Twain commonly wrote about during the summer of 1864. His articles were not warnings for men to beware of women or "Girls" of the West that tease unsuspecting men or of an "Amazon" posing as a male officer. Instead, Mark Twain's critiques of crime and criminals warned women about the beasts within hacks or the ruffians in the shadows of the city's hidden spaces, which was also the goal, in many instances, of sensational writers publishing in antebellum periodicals. The destruction of the female in the West, whether commuting between local destinations within the metropolis or being abused by men in private rooms, displays the unraveling of the possibility of the utopia, the "Garden of Eden reproduced."

If Twain's journalism reflected such degradation in the West, while delivering facts, perhaps it combined both ideals of "story" and "information."[82] On the one hand, the series of news items about hackmen or "demoralizers" certainly included a series of sensational stories over the course of days, which could have been the journalist's way to provide "a guide to living not so much by providing facts as by selecting them and framing them."[83] On the other hand, news items such as "Stolen Merchandise," "Gambling Cases Dismissed," "Bail Forfeited," "Contempt of Court," "A Contraband Transaction" could reflect the objective and dispassionate "informational ideal."[84] Which "ideal" did Twain espouse? Twain's journalism exposed male criminals lurking in the metropolis, which served to caution his readers of these dangers. Furthermore, these exposures eventually led to a public understanding of crime and punishment in which both writer and reader participated. When criminals received little, or no, punishment, Twain eviscerated these men on the pages of the newspaper. Sometimes, Twain included women in this group of miscreants. Even using linguistic markers of judgment, such as "beasts," "thoughtless numbskull," or "scoundrel," and building sensational news stories starring these criminals, provides evidence that Twain was not an objective or dispassionate journalist. On the contrary, he exposed and punished male hackmen and criminals such as Barney Gillan and Lambertson, and he praised Officer Blitz and Judge Shepheard. His insistence on taking facts and making a story, even at the expense of those facts, marked Twain as journalist concerned with informing and entertaining his readers and judging his beasts, even if the beasts he initially hunted turned out to be women.

At the beginning of the next decade, Twain became a resident of New York. Twain and his wife and children moved to Buffalo and then Connecticut, and returned to Quarry Farm, outside of Elmira, each summer to live with Olivia's family and so Twain could write. His life became more domestic, though no less interesting than his bachelor days in the West. It was New York, in 1871, where Mark Twain began petitioning with sensational, satirical discourse his readership to care, to feel, and finally to consider the brutality of state execution and the corruption of justice in the New York Supreme Court located in Elmira. Though in San Francisco Twain had attacked the local and state governments for allowing the beasts to prey on the innocent, now he turned his attention to beasts that punished the guilty with capital punishment.

4

Between Law and Outlaw: Mark Twain's Anti-Gallows Sentiment, 1861–1872

> *"I am happy in an opportunity to bear my testimony against Capital Punishment.... Punishment is justly inflicted by human power, with a twofold purpose: first, for the protection of society, and, secondly, for the restoration of the offender. Now it seems to me clear, that, in our general age and country, the taking of human life is not necessary to the protection of society, while it reduces the period of reformation to a narrow, fleeting span. If not necessary, it cannot come within the province of self-defence, and is unjustifiable."*—Charles Sumner, "Against Capital Punishment. Letter to a Committee of the Massachusetts Legislature," February 12, 1855
>
> *"Show me the law. Does it exist? If it exists, some learned Senator can point it out. But, while Senators fail to point out any law sanctioning such a procedure, I point out an immortal text in the Constitution of the United States, borrowed from the Magna Charta, which is difficult to disobey: "No person shall be held to answer for a capital or otherwise infamous crime, unless on a presentment or indictment of a Grand Jury ... nor be deprived of life, liberty, or property, without due process of law."*—Charles Sumner, "Power of the Senate to Imprison Recusant Witnesses," May 18, 1871[1]
>
> *"I do not love the law. And besides, there are many young lawyers here, and I am too generous to allow the glare from my lamp of genius to dim the feeble lustre of their two-penny dips."*—Samuel Clemens, Letter to Jane Lampton Clemens, October 26, 1861, Carson City, Nevada

In 1871, as Mark Twain finished revising *Roughing It* in Elmira, New York, Massachusetts senator Charles Sumner was fighting for the rights of prisoners and battling President Grant in Congress over the annexation of the Dominican Republic. Sometime that year or the next, Twain and Sumner agreed to appear in a "great lecture-jubilee" with notable reformers, speakers, and writers, including Ralph Waldo Emerson, Wendell Phillips, Bret Harte, Frederick Douglass, and Anna Dickinson, among many others.[2] This lecture never occurred. Charles Sumner died in 1874 after decades of crusading for equality for black Americans and for the abolition of capital punishment, and between 1871 and 1874, Twain engaged in an incredibly busy period. He wrote *Roughing It* (1872), *The Gilded Age* (1873), began work on *Tom Sawyer* (1876), and traveled to Europe for business. During the spring of 1871, Twain also became fascinated with the corruption of New York Supreme Court cases that would eventually influence his critique of this system of justice in *The Gilded Age*. One death-penalty case in particular attracted Twain's ire. Edward Howard Rulloff (also spelled Ruloff), convicted burglar and murderer, appeared before the New York Supreme Court, where testimonies "revealed his thirty years of crime, including the murder of his own wife and child, all of which was widely reported in the newspapers."[3] In addition to the sensational printed accounts of his crimes, newspapers printed items about the paradoxical character of Rulloff—a criminal and a scholar. His 1871 biography, *The Man of Two Lives*, described his murderous inclinations and his academic pursuits, including medicine, law, and philology. In numerous contemporary images he appears at study in a prison cell or even in an act of murder with a weapon that evokes the scholarly murderer. For example, though in 1870 he shot and killed an employee of a dry goods store named Frederick Merrick, in 1844 Rulloff had bludgeoned his daughter and wife to death with a pestle, a tool designed to aid in the preparation of medicine and not an instrument of death.[4]

Though he lacked professional qualifications, Rulloff was a renaissance man and often provided a social good with his teaching, which newspapers, including the *New-York Tribune*, noted as an important consideration when sentencing a person to death. Perhaps a criminal could serve his community, if he were qualified in various subjects and disciplines and able to share his knowledge, rather than be executed and serve no one. In this way, journalists participated in a common utilitarian argument against the death penalty.[5] James Fenimore Cooper, whose literature Twain had

Opposite: "Life, trial, and execution of Edward H. Ruloff: perpetrator of eight murders, numerous burglaries, and other crimes; who was recently hanged at Binghamton, N.Y...." (courtesy Fenimore Art Museum), "Murder Pamphlet Collection," 1871. Edward Howard Rulloff (also spelled Ruloff), convicted burglar and murderer, appeared before the New York Supreme Court where he was sentenced to death in 1871. But he was also accomplished in multiple academic pursuits, including medicine, law, and philology.

HE ATTEMPTED TO TAKE THE CHILD AWAY FROM HER. SHE CLUNG TO IT. IN HIS PASSION HE STRUCK HER WITH A PESTLE OVER THE LEFT TEMPLE. THE BLOW BROKE HER SKULL, AND SHE FELL WITH THE CHILD IN HER ARMS.—PAGE 46.

Er versuchte, das Kind von ihr fortzunehmen. Sie hielt es fest. In seiner Wuth schlug er sie mit einer Mörserkeule in die linke Schläfe. Der Schlag brach die Hirnschale, und sie sank nieder, mit dem Kinde im Arme.—Seite 46.

read, makes a similar argument in *The Ways of the Hour* (1850). In a conversation about execution, Counselor Dunscomb and Mrs. Horton agree that hanging is a useless act. Mrs. Horton states that the "country hangs a body to reform a body; and what good can that do when a body is dead?" The counselor agrees with the woman and adds that a "hanged body is certainly an unreformed body; and, as you say, it is quite useless to hang in order to reform." Like Twain, Cooper believed that courts were corrupt, and that through his literature he could "draw attention of the reader to some of the social evils that beset us."[6] George Lippard's *Quaker City* (1845) also satirically critiqued capital punishment. Devil-Bug, one of the novel's villain's, cheers when he sees the gallows and says, "Hurrah! The gallows is livin' yet! Hurrah!" The same year Lippard's novel appeared, 1845, Walt Whitman, writing journalism as Walter Whitman, published in the *Democratic Review* "Revenge and Requital. A Tale of a Murderer Escaped" and "A Dialogue." The closing line of "Revenge and Requital" directly asserts the author's intention when narrating the outcome of the murderer: "Some of my readers may, perhaps, think that he ought to have been hung at the time of his crime. I must be pardoned if I think differently."[7] In 1846, he published "Hurrah for Hanging!" in the Brooklyn *Daily Eagle*. The title, even the use of the exclamation point, echoes Devil-Bug's words in Lippard's novel.[8]

On April 29, 1871, Mark Twain wrote a satirical letter, in the lineage of Lippard and Whitman's satires and in the vein of his own early sensation hoaxes he had written in Nevada and California for the past ten years. All of these pieces had questioned the justice enacted by a group of fallible humans, whether the group was sanctioned by the law or operated outside of it. In the West, Twain had been skeptical of lynch mobs. In New York, he doubted the ability of juries, courts, and governments to be just. Twain included an explanatory letter with the April letter to Whitelaw Reid, editor of the *New-York Tribune*, commenting on the injustice in the courts and Rulloff's impending execution that would deprive a community of such a man's academic service: "Sir: I believe in capital punishment. I believe that when a murder has been done it should be answered for with blood.... The fact that the death law is rendered almost inoperative by its very severity does not alter my belief in its righteousness."[9]

Twain's literary western persona was caught between law and outlaw, for though Twain often supported the rights of the individual against the brutalizing power of the group, including the law, Twain wrote about masculine, heroic outlaws, criminals, and murderers as symbols for personal justice when he finds group (legal and extra-legal) justice distasteful and unjust. Viewing Twain's depictions of three such men—Edward Howard Rulloff, and Joseph A. Slade and Captain Ned Blakely from *Roughing It*, two heroic criminals who have entered into Twain's mythic storytelling – illustrates the tension between Twain's distrust of governments that execute criminals and his admiration of strong, yet flawed "desperadoes," who perform extra-legal execution upon men who have broken the law of the land or the laws of morality and ethics.[10] These case studies also illustrate Twain's rhetorical strategies that relied on the "feeling" of his readers. He wanted for these criminals, these "desperadoes," redemption, not retribution. Sources from this period include the letters, journalism, and book-length works of Samuel Clemens, beginning with his journey to Nevada in 1861, as portrayed in *Roughing It*, which began as a series of collected, previously published newspaper clippings, and ending with the publication of *Roughing It* in 1872. Finally, by reading *Roughing It* against the contemporary legal discourse of Massachusetts senator Charles Sumner, letters written to Twain by the Wisconsin senator and reformer Marvin Henry Bovee, Twain's un-mailed "responses" to these letters, and journalism written by Twain in the 1860s and 1870s, we see a more complicated perspective about Twain's published, unpublished, and often contradictory views of legal and extra-legal execution. Twain's views on punishment *were* complicated and sometimes contradictory, but his anti-gallows discourse followed in the tradition of antebellum reformers petitioning for the abolition of the death penalty (and prison reform, women's suffrage, and the abolition of slavery, among others). While Twain's views about capital punishment were not unique, he did carry the discussion into his western writing and his writing just after he left the West, which continued the exposure about social issues made by reformers two and three decades before. Northeastern executions caused men such as Charles Spear, editor of *Prisoner's Friend*, the leading mid-nineteenth century American periodical dedicated to prison reform and the abolition of capital punishment, to criticize the State's right to kill.[11]

Edward Howard Rulloff: Twain's Sydney Carton

In the opening paragraph of the letter about Rulloff, Twain's sarcasm about the uselessness and ineffectiveness of capital punishment signals the satirical nature of the letter, a response to an opinion of Rulloff published in the *Tribune*, which Twain hoped Reid would publish and that

New Yorkers would read. Like his sensation hoaxes, however, this piece's tone is serious, which counteracts the irony—the death penalty is ineffective, but supposedly Twain supports it. He continues with an explanation of his purpose for writing the letter:

> I am not sorry that Rulloff is to be hanged, but I am sincerely sorry that he himself has made it necessary that his vast capabilities for usefulness should be lost to the world. In this, mine & the public's is a common regret.... What miracles this murderer might have wrought, & what luster he might have shed upon his country if he had not put a forfeit upon his life so foolishly! But what if the law could be satisfied, & the gifted criminal still be saved. If a life be offered up on the gallows to atone for the murder Rulloff did, will that suffice? If so.... I will instantly bring forward a man, who, in the interests of learning & science, will *take Rulloff's crime upon himself, & submit to be hanged in Rulloff's place*. I can, & will do this thing; & I propose this matter, & make this offer in good faith. You know me, & know my address.[12]

As if the reporting of Rulloff's crimes, intellect, and sentencing were not sensational enough, Twain has created an alternate resolution[13] for a criminal that readers have encountered in literature, most recently in Charles Dickens's *A Tale of Two Cities* (1859), when Sydney Carton sacrifices his own life to save Charles Darnay. In fact, the *Tribune* published Twain's satirical letter on May 3, 1871, under the title "A Substitu[t]e for Rulloff. Have we a Sydney Carton among us?"[14] Similar situations in which characters offer to sacrifice themselves for others appear in James Fenimore Cooper's *The Spy* (1821) and in Shakespeare's *Measure for Measure* (1604). Twain, of course, had read works by Dickens, Cooper, and Shakespeare. Public executions spawn conversation, as do murders, but so does heroism. Twain has offered to supply the state of New York with a life "to atone for the murder Rulloff did," an actual Charles Darnay, perhaps even Twain himself. Twain's accompanying letter to Reid explains his "bully" article and what he hopes it will accomplish if Reid decides to print it:

> I have written this thing for an *object*—which is, to make people *talk* about & look at, & presently ENTERTAIN the idea of commuting Rulloff's penalty.
> The last paragraph (as magnificently absurd as it is,) is what I depend on to start the *talk* at every breakfast table in the land—& then the talk will drift into all the different ramifications of this case & first thing they know, they will discover that regret is growing up in their souls that the man is going to be hung. If the *talk* gets started once, that is sufficient—they'll *all* talk, pretty soon, & then the *acting* will come easily & naturally.[15]

Twain's explicit hope is that people will change their minds about Rulloff, and, perhaps, the governor, the people's elected conscience, will commute Rulloff's execution. It in not clear if some readers misread Twain's satire for sincerity. Probably, some did. However, the Rulloff case provided enough interest from readers to warrant at least nine stories to be published about the legal case. These items appeared in papers in New York and Washington. By May 18, when Rulloff was executed, readers had digested the facts and opinions of the case, including the *New-York Tribune's* opposition to the death penalty just days before Twain wrote his satirical letter. Though Twain does not actually expect a real Sydney Carton to sacrifice his life in place of Rulloff's, the writer uses his one tool, written expression in the form of satire and sensationalism, to affect some social change.

Even before Twain emigrated to Nevada Territory as the secretary for his brother Orion, newly appointed Secretary to the governor of Nevada Territory, Twain was intrigued with law and its application—just and unjust. After all, he had grown up around law and punishment. Twain's father, John Marshall Clemens, had practiced law in Tennessee before moving the family to Florida, Missouri. Here, Clemens became a judge of the Monroe County court. A year later, in 1839, the Clemens family moved to Hannibal, where Judge Clemens served as justice of the peace.[16] Still, Twain's view of hanging is complicated, for he offers conflicting perspectives about execution in his early writing. In 1871, as Twain reflected on the events from the previous decade—silver mining, his writing career, his brother, politics, his friends, the West, coyotes, and Goshoot Indians—he was also thinking about hanging. Two specific events from Twain's childhood experiences with his father influenced episodes in Twain's books. In *Innocents Abroad* (1869), Twain relates how in 1843 he saw a corpse of a murder victim in his father's law office. A second story inspired the Colonel Sherburn murder of Boggs in *Huckleberry Finn* (1884). Judge Clemens took depositions in the murder case of Sam Smarr by William Owsley in 1845.[17] At the time, he recalled stories about criminals in Nevada, California, and Montana—their crimes and their punishment. Twain, and his personas and narrators, hoped to entertain, but, with his brand of sensationalism, he also desired for the people to "talk" so they will act, a desire he expressed in his letter about Rulloff. Twain possibly even considered dedicating *Roughing It* to Edward H. Rulloff. This information is contained in a letter, dated May 15, 1871, to Elisha Bliss, Jr. (president of the American Publishing Company, which published all of Twain's major books between 1869 and 1880). Just two weeks after writing his letter to Whitelaw Reid, Twain submitted this dedication for Bliss to read:

> This Book is Dedicated: Not on account of respect for his memory, for it merits little respect; not on account of sympathy with him, for his bloody deed placed

him without the pale of sympathy, strictly speaking: but out of mere humane commiseration for him in that it was his misfortune to live in a dark age that knew not the beneficent Insanity Plea."[18]

Though Twain openly condemned capital punishment in 1871, his western literature often condones frontier justice, including gun fights, duels, and vigilante hangings. The previous chapter illustrated Twain's support of extra-legal justice or for criminals to be punished beyond the court when the judge fails to level punishment.

In many published responses to justice, Twain's discourse swings from the idolization of men, such as Joseph A. Slade, a gunslinger who straddled a nearly invisible line between desperado and vigilante, and the condemnation for New York state governor, John Thompson Hoffman. He refused the final appeal to commute Edward Howard Rulloff's execution. In a letter to the *Tribune*, Twain argues that Rulloff should not be executed, though he should be imprisoned, because he possesses "one of the most marvelous intellects that any age has produced."[19] In other words, Rulloff is valuable to society and could be used, somehow, for the betterment of society, which in the case of Rulloff was Twain's utilitarian argument. In various stages of his life and career, Twain respected courageous men who subverted social conventions and offered social value, even if these men were flawed and violent. Clemens did not advance such a utilitarian argument in the case of Jack McNabb. Clemens considered McNabb a nuisance, though "a notorious desperado." Twain's "use" of Rulloff as a sympathetic figure to illuminate the flawed system of legal execution provides a mode of discourse analysis to extract additional contemporary arguments about punishment. Though Twain used Rulloff as a symbol for a useful human and as a victim of a useless punishment, Twain built on this utilitarian argument as he crafted the episodes that contain Blakeley and Slade in *Roughing It*. These men, though useful, were also bold and violent, but they were particularly masculine and western. According to Twain's narrator in *Roughing It*, in the West a useful man must also perform manliness, which is one aspect of the desperado persona.

Jack Slade: The "most dangerous and the most valuable citizen"

Joseph A. Slade, also known as J.A. or Jack—a man made for adventure, a man of impulse or genius, a socially useful man—captured Samuel

4. Between Law and Outlaw 117

Clemens's admiration and fear sometime during his migration to Nevada in 1861 and held it, at least, until he finished *Roughing It* in 1871. While Slade (the man), and Clemens's relationship with and opinion of Slade, may not have been the only influence on Clemens's developing ideas about justice during his time in the West, Slade does serve as a symbol, albeit a paradoxical one.[20] He was a contradiction, as were other men in the West, who for Clemens symbolized a kind of tragic hero—not entirely good or evil, who acted in vile ways but had purpose. When considered among other masculine and sometimes criminal influences on Clemens—Rulloff, Ned Blakely, McNabb—Slade represents a prominent one, for he was one of the first such influences on a young Clemens. Though Twain certainly exaggerated the importance of his initial meeting with Slade while traveling West with Orion, Twain appropriated men, and their actual lives, as symbols for justice. The actual Slade Twain may have never included in *Roughing It*. The mythic man, Twain's creation, served as an illustration for Twain's criticisms about extra-legal hanging, as Rulloff had been for legal hanging.

According to the work's narrator, a constructed persona of "Mark Twain," Slade is "a man whose heart and hands and soul were steeped in the blood of offenders against his dignity; a man who awfully avenged all injuries, affronts, insults or slights, of whatever kin—on the spot if he could, years afterward if lack of earlier opportunity compelled it ... hate tortured him day and night till vengeance appeased—and not an ordinary vengeance either, but his enemy's absolute death."[21] This ruthlessness made Slade a feared man, but also a respected one. People in Illinois first came to fear Slade after he killed a "white man" and then battled and killed "Indians" while avoiding the legal justice system. For this reason, Twain advanced his utilitarian argument for the salvation of Slade. Because of his reputation, Slade became a division agent for the Central Overland Company protecting coaches from other outlaws attempting to steal the mail, horses, and cargo of the coaches and to rob their passengers. Company officials thought these criminals might fear Slade as the greater desperado and avoid any contacts with the coaches such a man, such a legend, protected. On Clemens's way out West, and once he lived there, he became fascinated with such stories of the desperado Slade—stories of his murders, his justified executions, and eventually his own execution on the gallows of a vigilance committee. And yet the narrator notes that Slade is "the most dangerous and the most valuable citizen that inhabited the savage fastnesses of the mountains."[22]

As Richard Slotkin has noted, the "creation" of the West was related to political and economic needs of the Northeast in antebellum and Civil War America. Eastern politicians and businessmen relied on the availability of land and resources, even at the expense of the region and its peoples.[23] For this reason, law increased as capitalism spread. Men like Slade took advantage of a business-like Overland that relied on the wealth from the East, including transportation of goods, mail, and emigrants. Yet while Twain and his circle often ridiculed these companies for being run by greedy, selfish men, there is a certain necessity in the distribution of goods, and people, to the territory that required so many of both commodities, goods and men, in order to extract silver from the mines. But the literary Slade is not content to kill solely for the benefit of his employer, which might benefit society, and begins murdering outlaws who molest emigrants. It seems that his desire for justice and his thirst for blood intermingle to produce a kind of agent-criminal. His role as hired, legal killer does not seem to match his desire for justice, or greatness, or murderous ambition—all of which report only to Slade, not to the Central Overland Company.

Through Twain's mythologized accounts of the desperado, Slade becomes something beyond a killer. Slade surpasses even his legal boundaries. He becomes "supreme judge in his district, and he was jury and executioner likewise" and with "his own hands" hangs two thieves.[24] Slade's killing, here, is an execution on makeshift gallows, and the narrator uses legal diction to express this frontier courtroom scene. Such mockery of the legal justice system also introduces onto the frontier a certain amount of prolonged torture. A just or righteous kill for the frontiersman is one that eliminates the criminal who directly reduces one's ability to pursue life, liberty, and happiness (wealth) in a swift, and precise manner. Slade, though he often kills with a single revolver shot, also tends to prolong the death of his victims, including "nipping" with his revolver the flesh or a finger, or hacking body parts with his knife.[25] After an altercation with his superintendent, Jules Beni, that left Slade nearly dead from shotgun wounds, Slade hunted down Beni a year later and killed the superintendent. Slade also cut off both of Beni's ears, just as he had promised the former boss—a sensational act of retribution and dominance.[26] Twain's narrator seems to recognize the brutality of these actions, not as heroic or understandable, but as acts of a useful man on the frontier. Still, Twain's romanticized view of a man who employs an excess of violence seems out of place. Twain did not avoid, overlook, or diminish Slade's violent acts, so, perhaps the writer's appreciation of the criminal is generated in Slade's ability and desire to defend his "dignity," to avenge "all injuries, affronts, insults or slights, or whatever kind."[27] When Twain was young and living in the West, he respected men who displayed such manliness, especially performed by strong men willing to display individual acts of power.[28] Sometimes, as in the case of Slade, such a man crossed the line between honorable and dishonorable and was willing to mutilate lesser men to prove a point.

Mutilation, though, was a common practice among gangs, vigilantes, and even legalized Rangers, the most famous of whom was Captain Harry Love, the California Ranger who in 1853 captured and decapitated Joaquin Murieta, California's "notorious bandit."[29] Slade's participation in a kind of execution made popular by the state is no less torturous, as he eventually discovers at his own public hanging. The process is slow. First, he must fashion a make-shift gallows, commonly assembled by using combinations of convenient items—horse, rope, tree, crates or dry-goods boxes, corrals, beams, and gate posts—which construction the victim (or criminal, depending on which side the rhetoric falls) witnesses. Second, the victim must be fitted with a noose upon the "platform," where he might perform the pantomime of masculinity and either "die game" or die cowardly. Third, the platform is knocked from underneath the hanging man, and there he dangles until he dies from a broken neck or from suffocation. Twain's narrator does not record Slade's victims' responses. Rather, the narrator devotes a great deal of space to describing the actions of Slade. Slade is fulfilling his contract as a division agent, and though he is involved in extra-legal justice as a kind of vigilante against the criminals of his own kind, his murders eliminate crime that reduces the profits of the Central Overland Company. Eventually, however, Slade's crimes inflict too much damage to go overlooked, and he is captured by a vigilance committee in Montana (Idaho Territory) and hanged in the courtroom of the frontier. In other words, once his violent acts caused his usefulness to wane, the Central Overland Company chose profits over a man.

Twain, however, profited (in a literary sense) by using the exploits of Slade to prove a point about crime and punishment when the criminal was worth admiring. Perhaps this was the case with the fictitious Sherburn, a character Twain crafted from the memories of brave yet criminal men. Twain's views of such criminals and vigilantes range from admiration to pity. The narrator of *Roughing It* mentions many of Slade's criminal and extra-legal exploits the narrator hears from westerners and that he reads in a "bloodthirstily interesting little Montana book," *The Vigilantes of Montana*, written by historian Thomas J. Dimsdale.[30] In *Roughing It*, one relevant discussion is the position of the gallows on the western frontier and the shadow it casts on the developing western societies. Though Twain's style mixes admiration for Slade with the sensation and entertainment of murder, the narrator takes a moment to speak on the social problem of crime and punishment, while using Dimsdale's view of Slade and the vigilantes who hanged the desperado as examples. In fact, Dimsdale suggests that the vigilantes "had freed the country from highwaymen and murderers to a great extent, and they determined that in the absence of the regular civil authority they would establish a People's Court, where all offenders should be tried by a judge and jury."[31] The vigilantes have provided the West with an alternative to legal justice, but Dimsdale values their violent acts within the vast western landscape. Dimsdale, of course, was not the only voice of approval for vigilantism. Citizens of Nevada Territory, Idaho Territory, and California, for example, tolerated vigilance committees in the 1860s and '70s when and where law enforcement was already prevalent.[32] In these cases, citizens acted when they believed the law had not.

Such is the case in Slade's hanging. Dimsdale goes on to record that at Slade's execution the "doomed man had so exhausted himself by tears, prayers and lamentations, that he had scarcely strength left to stand under the fatal beam. He repeatedly exclaimed, 'My God! Must I die/Oh, my dear wife!'"[33] This fearful display progresses in front of a crowd of Slade's friends and family, miners, vigilance committee members, citizens, an actual judge, Judge Davis, and, perhaps, other criminals and desperados. The spectacle of public execution was intended to deter men from performing future crimes.[34] According to Dimsdale, many people express emotions that match Slade's, and yet Slade is depicted as a coward at the moment of his death. Twain's narrator argues against Dimsdale's view that the vigilantes are heroes, even images of justice in a land without much legal justice, and with Dimsdale's bias against Slade. Twain's narrator does not agree that Slade actually deserves to be hanged. The frontier law of *lex talionis* (an eye for an eye) would suggest that he does, for he has maimed, robbed, murdered, and hanged men. Slade's regret at his own hanging does not negate the need for punishment, but it might illustrate the brutal effect public execution has on citizens who have been brutalized by the man under the gallows. Of course, the effect on the criminal Slade is also a consideration. The gallows reduce him to a weeping figure of pathos rather than a brave and murderous man. And yet such a combination of fearful and fearless emotions, according to Twain's narrator, marks Slade as a "true desperado." Slade is "gifted with splendid courage, and yet he will take the most infamous advantage of his enemy." He will fight "until he is shot all to pieces, and yet when he is under the gallows and helpless he will cry and plead like a child."[35] To Twain's narrator, these qualities made Slade human, a man, a "true desperado." To Dimsdale, these qualities made Slade a true coward.

The narrator's view of Slade is a sympathetic one, for the writer has met Slade, has heard stories of Slade's exploits, has taken part in the legend of Slade, and now defends the courage of Slade: "Words are cheap, and it is easy to call Slade a coward (all executed men who do not 'die game' are promptly called cowards by unreflecting people) ... never offering to hide or fly, Slade showed that he was a man of peerless bravery. No coward would dare that."[36] The narrator suggests that though Slade does not die game, according to Dimsdale's narrative, and weeps and asks for his wife at the gallows, Slade is no coward. The desperado could have escaped, hidden, or had his men cut him down or shoot him at the gallows, and, yet, Slade stands on the platform and displays human emotion, which, to the narrator, illustrates bravery, not fear. Twain's narrator begins to question here what is courage or cowardice. Cowardice at the gallows, it seems, is a pantomime of masculinity. Cowardice is not manly because it is not human. It is not human because it is performed upon the stage of execution and requires no truth, no "moral courage." Of course, all bravado is staged, whether such bravery is performed in battle, retribution, protection, or at the gallows.

Twain was particularly critical of Dimsdale's opinions about Slade's cowardice. Twain's opposition probably had as much to do with his mythologized account of Slade and the friendship with Slade as with Twain's position on human emotion. But the writer is concerned with this particular performance and emotion and poses the question: If Slade did not lack moral courage, what quality did he lack? The narrator's Slade, and the actual overland agent, fought advantaged enemies, endured wounds, killed true criminals, and even warned his "enemies that he would kill them whenever or wherever he came across them next."[37] If these qualities make Slade a hero, though a corrupted one and possessor of moral courage, then perhaps Twain's early view of justice is flawed. Certainly, Slade is a charismatic, even romantic, character feared and admired by many, including Twain. But Slade is also a criminal and a murderer. In this sketch, Twain's narrator does not agree, fully at least, with Slade's punishment, for the writer defends the desperado's honor.

Twain appeals to the reader to humanize Slade as a victim and not as a murderer who deserves to be hanged. Twain accomplishes this humanization by reporting on, or by giving, the "affect" of Slade's sentimental "act." This rhetorical technique became popular in the 1840s when temperance societies, such as the Washingtonian Temperance Society, staged performances of inebriates whose tears and sentimental displays allowed the audience to sympathize with drunkards and criminals.[38] Though Slade did appear on the stage of makeshift gallows, he also performs on the stage of Twain's pages. His literary representation as a murderer relies on a defiance of allowing readers to see Slade as a guilty man. Instead, this masculine, useful man, though a "badman," is nothing less than a pitiful human on the gallows. This literary transformation allows for readers to see, to "feel," that Slade could be redeemed.[39]

The narrative, however, does invite a conversation about Twain's contradictory views of frontier justice and legal justice, and who deserves such punishments. Though Twain's narrator often praises criminals and desperados for taking justice into their own hands, he rarely compliments the courts for enacting lawful justice. While discussing Slade's usefulness as a harbinger of fear for less noble criminals, the narrator frequently mentions Professor Dimsdale's "bloodthirstily interesting" accounts of executions at the gallows of Montana's vigilantes. According to the narrator, the book serves "as a specimen of how the people of the frontier deal with criminals when the courts of law prove inefficient."[40] When such people of the frontier grow impatient with the courts' lack of progress, or when the courts and justice system cannot or will not protect the people, the people find swift forms of extra-legal justice most effective. One goal of a vigilance committee is to terrorize—the isolated criminal element if possible, but the entire society, if necessary. If the terror of the vigilance committee is greater than the terror of the criminals and bands of desperadoes, then vigilance committees wield excessive power.

This power often transforms the vigilance committees into bands of criminals, themselves, but, according to Dimsdale, the public execution of Slade at the hands of the vigilance committee seemed to produce only positive effects on the mountain community, at least for that moment. "The execution of Slade had a most wonderful effect upon society. Henceforth, all knew that no one man could domineer or rule over the community. Reason and civilization then drove brute force from Montana."[41]

4. Between Law and Outlaw   123

Certainly, Dimsdale romanticizes the violence of vigilance committees and views them as champions of justice. Because they execute Slade, his singular brute force is no longer a social problem, but other criminals exist; in fact, the vigilance committee has become a terrible force that works outside the bounds of the law. Though Dimsdale wrote specifically about the Montana Vigilantes, vigilance committees existed in numerous regions in the West in the 1860s and 1870s. The committee in San Francisco, for example, was more localized around this one city. The Montana Vigilantes and vigilance committees in Nevada mining towns such as Virginia City and Gold Hill covered larger territories. Nevada and Montana were not yet states in 1864 when vigilantes executed Slade. Nevada was a territory, and parts of Montana comprised Idaho Territory. Furthermore, Slade's criminal exploits and business affairs extended into multiple territories and regions, which is why Twain discusses Slade and the vigilantes in relation to life in Nevada Territory. In this way, Twain conflated the extra-legal response to discuss the heroic and useful qualities of Slade. Still, if Twain's narrator is correct, and Dimsdale's romantic view is accurate, if the most valuable and feared citizen in the land can be captured and executed (and turned into a weeping "coward"), then one noble criminal stands little chance against the greater, terrorizing power of the vigilance committee. Such a realization, then, allows Twain to romanticize Slade and thus create an image of a relatable criminal man that Twain would write about in journalism or create in fiction over the next several decades.

What matters to Twain, a decade after meeting Slade, is the man's surprising demeanor. Twain's narrator portrays this murderer as "friendly," "gentle spoken," and "pleasant," which is a surprising combination of descriptions for a man who, according to the narrator, has killed twenty-six men.[42] And yet, Slade is recognizable as human, a man, when he weeps at the gallows where vigilantes summarily hang him. For though in these scenes Twain tries to redeem Slade and exploit his social value, citizens and emigrants who had experienced violence at the hands, knife, or gun barrel of Slade might have considered him less useful and more harmful, as did Dimsdale. Dimsdale continues to praise the vigilance committee for its duty and benefit to society and not for its terrorizing power: "When the stern Goddess spoke not, the doom was unpronounced, and the criminal remained at large. [The vigilance committee] acted for the public good, and when examples were made, it was because the safety of the community demanded a warning to the lawless and the desperate, that might neither be despised nor soon forgotten."[43] Twain's narrator does not seem to place the same amount of praise on the gallows of the vigilance committee when he describes Slade's final moments. The writer calls Slade a "true desperado," "gifted with splendid courage," and "a man of peerless bravery."[44] He singles out the rogue criminal that the vigilance committee has killed as an example for other rogues, for he admires the rogue, the solitary, strong hero. But this rogue, too, has summarily hanged men, not to instruct so much as to fulfill his drives for violence and power and, eventually, to serve the purposes of the Central Overland Company. The importance of Slade was tied to the importance of an overland transportation company. In 1862, the transcontinental railroad had not reached Virginia City, Nevada, where Twain wrote. It would be a decade until this line connected the towns of Gold Hill and Virginia City to Reno, the state capital.[45] At the time, the Central Overland Company and other overland lines delivered news, supplies, workers, and emigrants to the Comstock. In 1864, mines in the region produced nearly sixteen million dollars in silver bullion.[46] With so much at stake—silver, land, supplies, and people—Central Overland found value in a man like Slade who could reduce crime and increase their profits.

Because he wanted to redeem Slade, Twain dedicated two chapters of *Roughing It* to the life and death of Slade, which Twain finished writing in March 1871.[47] He wrote these chapters not only as sensational entertainment and as illustrations of life in the West in the 1860s but as a kind of eulogy for a man he barely knew but respected, even though Slade was a "desperado." Though an earlier chapter includes Clemens's judgmental responses to crimes performed by Jack McNabb, "a notorious desperado," and Jack Williams, "a highwayman and a desperado," the analysis in this chapter complicates Mark Twain's more complimentary, more romanticized use of the term "desperado." Clemens certainly considered Slade a desperado and referred to him as such in a letter to Orion, dated March 10, 1871. At the time, Clemens was working on the manuscript for *Roughing It*, and he solicited his brother's help in remembering any details about meeting Slade on their journey West. Clemens ends the letter with this request: "Please sit down right away & torture your memory & write down in minute [detail] every fact & [exploit] in the desperado Slade's life that we heard on the Overland—& also describe his appearance & conversation as we saw him at Rocky Ridge station at breakfast. I want to make up a telling chapter from it for the book."[48] Here, Clemens seems to be using the term desperado as a factual state of being rather than as a marker for a certain kind of man—bad or a robber. Furthermore, even in Clemens's early 1861 account of Nevada in a letter to his mother, he lists "desperadoes" as one of the inhabitants of the region. He writes that "Nevada [Territory] is fabulously rich in gold, silver, copper, lead, coal, iron, quicksilver, marble, granite, chalk, slate, plaster of Paris (gypsum), thieves, murderers, desperadoes, ladies, children, lawyers, Christians, gamblers, Indians, Chinamen, Spaniards, sharpers, cuyotes (pronounced ki-yo-ties), preachers, poets and jackass-rabbits."[49] The list includes "thieves" and "murderers" and then "desperadoes," which reveals a twenty-five-year-old Sam's distinction among criminals, especially the kind he would judge when writing about Jack McNabb or Jack Williams, and the kind he would romanticize when writing about Slade.

In September 1870, while working on these two chapters, Clemens wrote a letter to postmaster of Virginia City, Idaho Territory (which became Montana), and requested any newspaper articles or notices of Slade's crimes or executions that might have survived. Clemens wanted to use this material to help him fill out the details of Slade's life. But, like his letter to Whitelaw Reid of the *Tribune* the following April in which he admits that he hopes "to make people *talk* about & look at, & presently ENTERTAIN the idea of commuting Rulloff's penalty," Clemens explains to the postmaster that he hopes to redeem Slade's reputation:

> Dear Sir:
> Four or five years ago a̶ righteous Vigilance Committee in your city hanged a casual acquaintance of mine named Slade, along with twelve other prominent citizens whom I only knew by reputation. Slade was a "section-agent" at Rocky Ridge station in the Rocky Mountains when I crossed the plains in the Overland stage ten years ago, & I took breakfast with him & survived.
> Now I am writing a book (MS. to be delivered to publisher Jan. 1), & as the Overland journey has made six chapters of it thus far & promises to make six or eight more, I thought I would just rescue my late friend Slade from oblivion & set a sympathetic public to weeping for him.
> N̶ Such a humanized fragment of the original ł Devil could not & *did* not go out of the world without considerable newspaper eclat, in the shape of biographical notices, particulars of his execution, etc., & the object of this letter is to beg of you to ask some one connected with your city papers to send me a Virginia City newspaper of that day if it can be done without mutilating a file.[50]

As if to support the view that vigilance committees in the West enacted "righteous" justice, Clemens opens the letter by using this word, which appears in his correction, to describe the extra-legal committee that condemned and hanged Slade. Clemens did not think the vigilance committee righteous, for he wanted to "set a sympathetic public to weeping for him."

Joseph A. Slade was in fact summarily hanged by a vigilance committee on March 10, 1864, less than three years after Clemens had first met and dined with Slade on the journey to Nevada Territory with his brother Orion in August 1861. Though Clemens barely knew Slade, Clemens found the desperado's life and death compelling. Clemens respected the usefulness of Slade, as he did Rulloff's, but Clemens also found in Slade a brave man worthy of a literary treatment that would "rescue" Clemens's "friend." Slade had not the opportunity to receive legal justice and instead had endured extra-legal justice on the gallows of a vigilance committee. The community in Virginia City, Idaho Territory, apparently found Slade to be much less sympathetic than had Clemens and celebrated the man's summary execution.

Two days after Slade's lynching, an article appeared in *The Youth's Companion* with a purpose to redeem the citizens for lynching Slade, as opposed to redeeming Slade, as Twain tried to do in *Roughing It*. In the 1870s, Clemens contributed to this magazine, which promoted morality to youth. The article about Slade begins with a definition of lynching and then a defense of the act, in the case of Slade's lynching:

> "Lynching." This term is applied to the infliction of punishment by persons who are not officers of the law, and therefore have no legal right to perform such an act. It designates a very dangerous assumption of power, which should never be indulged in unless men are without a civil government, and are forced by self-preservation to take the law into their own hands.[51]

This article, not unlike Twain's writing about Slade, tries to assign meaning to an act of violence. Its writer, like Twain, also prescribes a reasonable explanation for extra-legal justice, what Twain's narrator in *Roughing It* would mark as "how the people of the frontier deal with criminals when the courts of law prove inefficient." Clemens was not always opposed to frontier justice, but he did oppose it when his friend Slade was its victim. The writer of "Lynching" explains the term, its uses, and that Slade recently was lynched. The writer goes on to quote an account printed in the *Rocky Mountain News*:

> At 3.40 P.M. a company of about three hundred armed men marched through Jackson Street, and halted directly in front of the place in which Slade was.... Slade was arrested and conducted to a ravine at the edge of the street, where there stood before him a newly erected gallows. He was made to mount the stand.... His legs trembled, his face was pale and his whole frame shook.[52]

The language here is not metered for a young readership, and yet the diction still judges and assigns meaning. According to the reporter of "a paper published near the tragedy," when an army of citizens approached Slade, they "arrested" him, though they had no force of law behind their arrest. These citizens arrested Slade before "other warrants could be drawn," after others were destroyed when citizens "threatened vengeance against the court" trying to suppress mob violence and execute the law.[53] The article also represents Slade as a coward, an opinion Thomas J. Dimsdale had tried to advance. Twain tried to subvert Dimsdale's view. Twain's two chapters, he hoped, would serve as redemption for the brave man and as a rebuttal to Dimsdale's "history."

In the "Prefatory" to *Roughing It,* Twain makes clear that he is not writing a history: "This book is merely a personal narrative and not a pretentious history or a philosophical book."[54] In the Slade chapters, however, Twain is writing a vindication. In the case of Slade, Twain was opposed to the ideas of lynch mobs and vigilance committees, even juries—groups that judged an individual life, especially in the summary hanging of Slade. Even before the Montana Vigilance Committee of the 1860s hanged Slade, California had known the rise of vigilance committees, including the Los Angeles Vigilance Committee (1850) and San Francisco's Committee of Vigilance (1851 and 1856), and Clemens noted the idea of vigilance committees in his Nevada journalism. In the case of Slade, the vigilance committee represented an unnecessary and overwhelming display of extralegal force. Slade was the victim. Twain did not always express these sentiments for desperados or judgment against vigilance committees, however.

In 1863, one year before Slade was hanged, Clemens wrote for Virginia City's *Territorial Enterprise* but also served as the Nevada correspondent for San Francisco's *Daily Morning Call.* On September 3, Twain wrote an article about the local violence in Virginia City, Nevada, for the consumption of his California readers. This article, unlike the letter he wrote about Slade or Rulloff, does not depict a murderer as heroic, as socially valuable, or worthy of redemption. Instead, Twain displays disdain for a criminal not brought to justice:

> This afternoon, Jack McNabb, a notorious desperado, shot at a negro. He was not arrested. Afterwards, he created a disturbance, and Officers Watson and Birdsall tried to arrest him, when he shot Birdsall in the breast, and a special officer, named Burns, in the arm. Birdsall is not expected to live till morning. The people wanted to hang McNabb, but were prevented by the officers. Gen. Van Bokkelen, Territorial Provost-Marshal, asserted his authority, guarded the jail, and closed the saloons and stores. The city is infested with thieves, assassins and incendiaries. There is some little talk of a Vigilance Committee.[55]

In this news item, Twain withholds judgment against the possibility of a vigilance committee. He seems outraged that legal justice was not satisfied after McNabb had shot at an innocent man. Not until the criminal "created a disturbance" did officers arrest him. Had the desperado been arrested for shooting "at a negro," McNabb could not have created a disturbance that led to the murder of a police officer. All of these actions caused a lynch mob to form in order to deal extra-legal justice in the absence of the legal variety. The officers prevented the summary hanging, but the people continued to talk about forming a vigilance committee. Clemens might have supported such a hanging in this situation. After all, he included McNabb in the fraternity of "thieves, assassins and incendiaries" that infested the city. Twain never used such diction to describe Slade. In fact, Twain's diction when describing Slade's execution separated him from the infestation of criminals like McNabb. Slade's ability to weep at the gallows illustrates his emotional response to injustice, which Twain's narrator calls "moral courage." Slade is a moral man—a man Clemens would later call a "friend." McNabb is unlike Slade, however, for he is like a bug infesting the good places in the city. A man like this, as opposed to Slade, is the kind Twain's narrator in *Roughing It* called a "notorious coward," a "chicken-livered poltroon," and "course, brutal, degraded."[56] In the "dispatch" from Nevada, Twain is not trying to redeem McNabb. Clemens noted in his letter to the postmaster, however, that he did want to redeem or "rescue" Slade. Clemens, the journalist, is reporting the news, yes, but with judgment against a kind of man—a coward, an insect, a "notorious" desperado worthy of death. Slade is a brave, useful man, worthy of redemption.

Certainly, contradictions exist in Clemens's opinions of these two desperadoes, but Twain romanticized Slade. They had met at stage-station on Clemens's trip out West. At the time, he was in his mid-twenties and had heard of Slade. As Clemens sat down to eat breakfast, someone addressed the man at the head of the table as Slade. Clemens responded with fear and admiration: "Never youth stared and shivered as I did when I heard them call him Slade!"[57] By the time Clemens the journalist wrote about McNabb, the writer had reported on numerous murders and murderers. A man such McNabb did not capture Clemens's attention or cause him to stare and shiver. McNabb had shot at "a negro," an innocent man. Clemens did not find this act brave or romantic. The criminal also had shot two police officers trying to restore order. McNabb, then, was one of many "thieves, assassins and incendiaries." Slade was "pleasant," "friendly," and "gentle-spoken," all markers for a man telling stories and being "polite."[58] Even if Slade were a murderer, he was a man of refined behavior. McNabb possessed no such qualities. Though Slade had cried, thus betraying the masculine expectations of a writer like Dimsdale, Slade was worthy of redemption. McNabb, however "manly" he might have acted, did not possess the kind of true "moral courage" that Twain's narrator had found in Slade.

As a young western journalist in the 1860s and while writing *Roughing It* a few years later, Mark Twain believed that one ethical man, a man of quality, could serve justice better than could a flawed jury or a legislature or a vigilance committee or mob. He had witnessed evidence in action for this argument in the stories of Slade and Rulloff, but also as a boy in Missouri. In a posthumous work, Twain recounts the influences that led to his belief about one useful man, even a badman, being worth more than the meat hanging on a makeshift gallows, advertising the force of extralegal justice. In "The United States of Lyncherdom" (1901), Twain remembers how in Missouri, as a boy, he once "saw a brave gentleman deride and insult" a lynch mob until the mob retreated; in Nevada, Twain "saw a noted desperado make two hundred men sit still" until he "gave them permission to retire," and even a strong man can "rob a whole passenger train by himself" if he is "plucky" enough.[59] Here, Twain understands the power one courageous man can wield over a mob of bloodthirsty cowards. One man can be moral. According to Twain, a mob of men cannot. Twain has faith that the "Moral Sense teaches us what is right, and how to avoid it—when unpopular."[60] For Twain, one problem with legal and extra-legal execution is the fallibility of man, especially when groups of men make decisions for a society. The man being executed could have social value, as Twain believed Rulloff possessed. But, if the solution to crime lies at the feet of one moral, brave man, rather than at the base of the legal gallows, we must find such men who will stand between a mob and the accused. Twain provided that voice for Rulloff, for Twain brought attention to the legal case and, he hoped, sympathy for this man among his readers.

In the case of lynching, Twain supposed that stationing "a brave man in each affected community to encourage, support, and bring to light the deep disapproval of lynching hidden in the secret places of its heart" might be the remedy. In both cases, Twain thought appealing to the emotions of people could be the "remedy."[61] Unlike the young, sensational, western journalist forty years earlier, however, the twentieth-century Twain has started to lose his faith in humanity. In 1901, when Twain wrote "The United States of Lyncherdom," Leon Czolgosz had just assassinated President McKinley. Czolgosz was soon thereafter electrocuted. A year before, King Umberto I of Italy had been assassinated. And though lynching in the United States had decreased from 230 in 1892 (the worst year for lynching) to 115 in 1900, lynching increased by fifteen in 1901.[62] For these reasons, in 1901 he argues for the abolition of execution through singular illustrations of moral and ethical behaviors in an essay he never published. Ironically, he worried that redeeming the victims of southern lynching would alienate him from his friends and family in the South, though he never fretted that redeeming a "victim" Slade, or Rulloff, would jeopardize his friendships in the West or in New York. The problem for Clemens existed in his roots. He was a southerner who often championed the rights of individuals, even ones as flawed as Slade or Rulloff, even as humorously flawed as Tom and Huck. In "Lyncherdom," however, Twain fears that "upon reflection, the scheme will not work. There are not enough morally brave men in stock."[63] Twain never found out. He lacked the "moral courage" to publish the essay in his lifetime. But perhaps Twain had reason to be skeptical. Joseph A. Slade, both murderer and man of value and "moral courage," was extra-legally hanged on March 10, 1864. Edward Howard Rulloff, the scholar whom Twain satirically argued could better serve society through his research and scholarship from inside a prison cell, was legally hanged on May 18, 1871.

Captain Ned Blakely: Judge of a "very extraordinary trial and execution"

Throughout his writing career, Mark Twain offered many conflicted views about execution. McNabb and Slade committed the same crimes, but one was worthy to hang, the other had reason to live. In at least two instances, *Roughing It* uses the lives of murderers to present these kinds of contradictory views of the gallows—when they are valuable and useful, who should administer such punishment, and which is more just, the single executioner, such as Slade, or the group, such as a vigilance committee or a court. Slade's story offers one example of a criminal who also deters crime on the frontier, as much as his story serves "as a specimen of how the people of the frontier deal with criminals when the courts of law prove inefficient." A second example also focuses on a romantic, rogue criminal, Captain Ned Blakely, whose story further illustrates, according to Twain's narrator, how justice might be achieved when the courts of law prove inefficient. The narrator makes certain to explain that he does not believe that justice exists in a court of law or wisdom within the American jury system. When describing the early society of Virginia City, Nevada, he mentions the cemetery, which is occupied by the first twenty-six murdered men of the mining town. Their murderers were never punished, and the narrator blames Alfred the Great, the ninth-century Anglo-Saxon king, for inventing trial by jury, a flawed system of justice. The narrator remarks that the king "was not aware that in the nineteenth century the condition of things would be so entirely changed that unless he rose from the grave and altered the jury plan to meet the emergency, it would prove the most ingenious and infallible agency for defeating justice that human wisdom could contrive."[64] The narrator distrusts the current jury system because a man who possesses knowledge of the case, the affair, or the crime may not serve on the jury. According to the narrator, with modern communication technologies—"telegraphs and newspapers"—the only people left without knowledge of a legal case in a localized area are "fools and rascals, because the system rigidly excludes honest men and men of brains."[65] If the system of justice supplied by the state proves inefficient, or, more specifically, incapable of executing ethical decisions, based upon evidence deliberated by men of logical reasoning, then only a single, ethical man can dispatch justice. The narrator does not wish to disband the legislature, but wants "to tamper with the jury law."[66] His reason—he cannot trust ignorant men, unread men, "fools and rascals" to decide a man's punishment, especially execution. The narrator would rather trust honest, intelligent men, but because his every attempt "to save the country 'misses fire,'"[67] he offers for support of his plea to reform the jury system a "very extraordinary trial and execution" concerning a man Twain respects—Captain Ned Blakely.[68]

Though Ned Blakely shares a few traits with Slade—tough, independent, masculine, privileges his own sense of justice, and mixes elements of the desperado with the honest business man—Captain Blakely does not seek to break the law, kill for pleasure, or terrorize societies with his brutality. The sailor, unlike Slade, is not the type to start a fight, but both men certainly will finish one. And, finishing a deed another man began is exactly the kind of story Twain's narrator offers as support for his point that personal justice is superior to legal justice. On a voyage to the Chincha Islands off the coast of Peru to export guano (for the manufacturing of gunpowder), Blakely is confronted by Bill Noakes, a mate aboard another ship. Noakes fancies himself "the best man on the islands" and hopes to prove it to Blakely.[69] Twice the sailors fight, and twice Blakely bests Noakes and then throws him overboard. Because Noakes's ego is battered, as is his face, he shoots and kills Blakely's friend, his "negro mate" and "his pet."[70] Blakely wastes no time capturing Noakes and holds him prisoner aboard Blakely's ship. When the other ships' captains at port realize what has happened, and that Blakely intends to hang Noakes, the captains convince Blakely to create a makeshift court with a jury. Blakely argues that everyone knows that Noakes is guilty; therefore, a trial is a mockery of justice.

Apparently, Blakely is in danger of being tried for murder by American courts if he hangs a man without a proper trial. This situation offers no logic, according to Blakely, nor to the narrator, for any logical man could see the crime, identify the criminal, and execute justice. The trial by jury could only interrupt such logic and introduce doubt into the execution of justice. Eventually, though, the makeshift jury finds Noakes guilty and appoints a sheriff to hang the murderer. Blakely's wrath is so great that the jury allows him the satisfaction of fashioning a noose from a halter hung in a tree. Here, at the gallows, Blakely reads four chapters from the Bible and offers the final words before the execution: "There. Four chapters. There's few that would have took the pains with you that I have."[71] Blakely's pains include cultivating patience for a system that seems to lack justice, arguing with captains trying to impose a sense of a law on a lawless man, and, most importantly, losing his friend, "mate," and "pet" because an ignorant, arrogant man could not accept that he was not the best man in the islands. Blakely's desire to hang his man is pure *lex talionis*. Such swift justice, according to Twain's narrator, is an example of "simplicity and primitiveness itself," the kind Californians could admire when "inflicted" in the West and elsewhere, and, in fact, the kind of justice that Twain respected.[72]

Simple, primitive justice relies on how one man applies these codes. Though Twain's narrator considers Blakely honorable, the narrator does not indicate that Blakely should have waited for a jury to decide the fate of another man. For this reason, as an example of swift justice when the courts prove ineffective, the story of Captain Ned Blakely is flawed. Though Twain's narrator admires Blakely for getting his man, and for distrusting the jury system, the narrator admits that the Chincha Islands possessed "no courts and no officers; there was no government."[73] Without any legal justice system on the islands, one might expect a criminal to be subject to the laws of the controlling land—Peru. Though Peru controlled the Chincha Islands, Spain did not yet recognize Peru's independence. And, because the vessels were American, as well as the crew, it is unclear which country's laws might take precedent. Of course, Twain's narrator has made clear that the jury system is subject to the decisions of ignorant, dishonest men, but the narrator does not suggest what might happen if a man, such as Captain Ned Blakely, were not an honest, informed man. The narrator does not consider what might happen if Blakely executes extra-legal justice and hangs the wrong man. Without such a line of reasoning, Twain's narrator executes false logic—if the murders of the original twenty-six victims in Virginia City's graveyard have gone unpunished because of one jury's poor decision (or the decisions of a small sample of juries), then all juries must have the potential to be incapable of executing the proper decision. The narrator is discounting one of the features of a jury—that no one man has the power to decide a person's fate. But incapable men of a jury have lied about knowing no facts of a case and are mocking justice by claiming to have formed no opinions about a case, is the system of trial by jury a system unable to consistently execute justice? Clearly, Twain's narrator thinks so. He would prefer to leave justice in the hands of the honest and just individual.

Twain's narrator uses the hangings of Bill Noakes and Slade to support opposing ideas. Though both men are murderers, Noakes deserves to be hanged and Slade does not. Noakes, on the one hand, is an arrogant man who seems to possess little redeeming value. His main narrative purpose is to illustrate how a coward and a murderer should be treated when the courts prove ineffective. Captain Ned Blakely, on the other hand, is the infamous man, the star of this sensational sketch. He is an example of an honest man seeking justice in a system that is unjust. Noakes is the criminal, Blakely the hero. Slade is a more complicated character than either Noakes or Blakely, for Slade is "the most dangerous and the most valuable citizen" in the territory.[74] Slade is a division agent, employed to protect the Overland Company's profits. He is a vigilante, too, hunting fellow badmen for crimes similar to his own. First, of course, he is a murderer, but Twain's narrator tries to protect Slade's image by suggesting that Slade is trying to bring about a "wholesome change" by killing men that make the world "the richer for their loss."[75] Even after casting a shadow of fear across the frontier, and after beating a man in his band of vigilantes or desperadoes, depending upon ones perspective, Slade still influences such a man to the point that he weeps as Slade awaits his death at the gallows.[76]

Because Slade is useful, feared, admired, and brave (even though he weeps and shows fear at the gallows—both of which Twain uses to show the humanity of Slade rather than his cowardice), witnesses actually care that Slade is being executed, and they are conflicted with feelings of sadness for the execution of a human and with feelings of justice for the hanging of a deserving criminal. No one, however, seems to lament Noakes's hanging. The captains disapprove of Blakely hanging Noakes and suggest that Blakely should allow a form of legal justice to run its course, not because they are trying to save Noakes, but because they fear Blakely would incur the wrath of the courts in America for having "murdered" Noakes on an American vessel. No one weeps for Noakes, even though, like Slade, Noakes is guilty of his crimes.

Guilt does not seem to affect Twain's narrator's view of hanging. At the end of "Chapter XI," the narrator discusses Slade's moral courage, his sense of ethics in warning "his most ruffianly enemies that he would kill them whenever or wherever he came across them next!" and Slade is "a man of peerless bravery."[77] The narrator offers no such commentary for Noakes's character. At the end of "Chapter LI," the narrator's commentary focuses on simple and primitive justice and how Californians admire such justice. The tones of these endings differ so greatly as to suggest that Twain's narrator is using the stories of Slade and of Noakes to support differing ideas about justice. Specifically, legal hanging is subject to the decision of an ignorant, incapable jury that knows nothing of the case or facts, and extra-legal hanging is subject to the honor of one wronged man, who knows the facts and cares whole-heartedly about justice. In "The United States of Lyncherdom," however, Twain worries that the just actions of one brave man trying to suppress acts of violence like lynching will never work. His ideas about lynching in the South not representing justice but instead fear and retribution contradict his support for Noakes's lynching. These cases differ, though, for a southern-lynching victim's only crime might have been being a race different from those in power. Blakely has determined, through an extra-legal proceeding, that his victim has killed a man, and ironically, a black man. In the cases of Slade and Noakes, however, Twain's narrator reports elements of legal and extra-legal hanging. Slade is brought to justice by a vigilance committee, tried on the frontier, and hanged on makeshift gallows. Similarly, an actual court does not try Noakes. A band of ship captains appoint a jury, try him, and then allow a private citizen who has entered into the realm of vigilantism to hang Noakes. These cases, then, illustrate a conflation of legal justice and frontier justice, rather than a criticism of southern racism. In *Roughing It*, Twain is careful to write within a particular set of circumstances—manly and individual justice in the West—rather than attack a national and divisive problem such as racism.

The wry, satirical, sometimes condemning voice of the narrator in *Roughing It* is the carefully crafted product of Mark Twain, which is also the created literary persona of Samuel Clemens. Twain recalls events ten years earlier and shaping them to fit into a narrative structure. The narrative voice in "The United States of Lyncherdom" arrives toward the end of Clemens's life when he has witnessed racial violence and increased lynching. The shift in tone of these voices illustrates, among other ideas, the events to which Twain is responding. In 1901, Twain's essay reflected the national and international violence against powerful leaders and less powerful southern blacks. In 1871, Twain's anxieties about justice appear in both *Roughing It* and his journalism (and journalistic letters). The *Roughing It* narrative voice is quite similar to the voice Clemens uses in his letter writing intended for newspapers, such as the letter to the *Tribune* in which he argues for the commutation of Rulloff's death sentence. Clemens wrote these letters, and newspaper articles, in prose that compiles journalistic details with wry satire to encourage readers to think about issues such as lawful execution. Just as the narratives of Slade and Captain Ned Blakely, including Noakes, in *Roughing It* illustrate Twain's conflicted views of hanging, his newspaper letters and articles also reflect Clemens's differing views about criminals and their punishments. This journalism emphasizes the point that the courts are incapable of hanging the true criminals, but that true murderers certainly deserve to be hanged. For, in a more immediate sense, these writings are intended to be read weekly or daily, and the readers are citizens affected by crime. The tone of this journalism concerning Rulloff, then, functions like a wake-up call or a verbal battle for those who can make a difference in the local or regional communities. The sensational sketches, letters, and articles are often actually entertaining expressions of social reform.

Charles Sumner: Genuine Law and a "genuine signature"

On February 12, 1855, Massachusetts senator Charles Sumner offered his "testimony against Capital Punishment." In a letter he cited three reasons for the "prejudice in favor of the gallows": a desire for "vengeance, which surely does not properly belong to man," a fear that a "civilized community would be in peril, if life were not sometimes taken by the government," and finally a "blind obedience to the traditions of another age."[78] These "discreditable sources" illustrate how, according to Sumner, humans' fear causes them to act in unjust ways. The gallows represented for Senator Sumner the State's antiquated desire for retribution and deterrence that need not exist in his day. Sumner's positions about social justice, especially the abolition of slavery and abuses of power, were not always popular among his more conservative contemporaries. On May 22, 1856, just days after Charles Sumner delivered his "Crime Against Kansas" speech, South Carolina representative Preston Brooks caned Sumner and caused such injuries to the senator that he did not return to his duties until 1859, the same year Samuel Clemens earned his steamboat pilot license. Sumner opposed and often railed against social injustices, including slavery, and the decisions of men who advanced injustice through their use of power. In this speech delivered on May 19 and 20, Sumner stated that power "comes from the habit of power," and that power can be wielded through "a control of Public Opinion through venal pens and a prostituted press; an ability to subsidize crowds in every vocation of life,—the politician with his local importance, the lawyer with his subtle tongue, and even the authority of the judge on the bench."[79] In this passage, it is clear that Sumner took seriously the responsibility of those in power, whether these men controlled public opinion through the law or the press. Though Samuel Clemens was not yet a member of the western press in 1856, he soon would be, in 1862, when Sumner read a broadside that Clemens probably wrote, which criticized the Nevada Territorial government's use of power. Sumner did not know personally Mark Twain, but their circles of personal friends and professional acquaintances overlapped. On July 27, 1873, Twain wrote a letter to T. B. Pugh, a publisher, promoter, and manager, telling of his delay in London but his desire to appear in a "great lecture-jubilee" with notable reformers, speakers, and writers. Editors of the Mark Twain Papers have noted that the lecture probably never occurred, but a list of names for the lecture has survived:

> Under the first heading, entitled merely "The List," are twenty-six names, all of well-known lecturers, readers, or other performers—including Mark Twain himself, Charles Sumner, Wendell Phillips, Petroleum Nasby, Anna Dickinson, Josh Billings, Bret Harte, Frederick Douglass, Ralph Waldo Emerson, and three musical groups. Under a second heading, "*Invited*," are six more names—including John B. Gough, Henry Ward Beecher, and Henry Wadsworth Longfellow.

4. Between Law and Outlaw 137

The third heading, "*Present*," includes only "Gen. U.S. Grant & cabinet." The list cannot be dated with certainty, but must have been prepared between February 1871, when Harte arrived in the East, and March 1874, when Charles Sumner died.[80]

Sumner, a lawyer and senator from Boston, must have admired, or at least enjoyed, later in life Twain's satirical writing that displayed his passion for justice and ridicule for those opposed to its progress. Twain and Sumner each used their public positions to critique their respective societies and systems of justice.[81]

On July 20, 1863, Sumner presented to Harvard, where he graduated from college and then law school three decades prior, a broadside entitled "Annual Message of Captain Jim, Chief of Washoes, and Governor (de facto) of Nevada."[82] The document is unsigned, but it bears the trademark satirical style about a topic on which Clemens reported during 1862—the Nevada territorial legislature.[83] Though Samuel Clemens did not use the pen name Mark Twain until February 1863, in 1862, he often wrote anonymously or used various names such as the Reliable. During the fall of 1862, Clemens was the sole reporter for the *Enterprise* that covered the territorial legislature, which spanned November 11 to December 20.[84] This anonymous 1862 broadside, dated November 14, the Friday of the first week the legislature convened, is relevant within Twain's early western writing about legal and extra-legal punishment for one major reason: it offers a satirical judgment of the legal system that has reproduced murder as punishment for a convicted murderer. The writer argues that the "sentence of death" causes more harm than good because goodness must be achieved through justice, a utilitarian argument that Twain would take in 1871 when he supported the commutation of Rulloff's death sentence. Clemens's intended readership must have been impatient concerning the length of time the State took to hang a criminal, for the author cites law, specifically the writ of *supercedeas*, in order for the Supreme Court of the Territory to slow down and then suspend the local court's decision to execute a murderer in the first degree. What might have caught Sumner's eye was the broadside's other critique of justice—the rights of Americans regardless of race or sex. Sumner opposed slavery and all legal decisions that supported the institution, including fugitive slave laws and the Kansas-Nebraska Act. Moreover, the broadside's writer "recommends" the end to such legal acts against Americans. The writer asserts that he is against unequal treatment of black Americans and Native Americans. He states, "I hold that this usage of the barbarous ages should be forgotten, and this marked distinction between the races should be obliterated; and the black man, in every respect, should be entitled to fully enjoy all the rights, privileges and immunities, legal, social and political, of the white man."[85] Likely, this kind of discourse against legal, social, and political injustice attracted Sumner to the broadside, rather than its potential authorship.

In 1862, "Mark Twain" did not exist. Even in July 1863, when Sumner presented the document to Harvard, the name Mark Twain was only beginning to gain notoriety in the West. Though Sumner must have recognized the importance of this broadside's critique of injustice in the West in a time and region not yet known for producing a national protest discourse or social reform movements, Sumner probably did not recognize the potential significance of the broadside's author. The serious, New England, Harvard-educated lawyer and politician Charles Sumner may never have known that both he and Clemens narrowly escaped pistol duels, Sumner because he was not a Southern gentlemen and unequal to the possibility of Brooks's challenge, and Clemens because he and a friend fled on a stagecoach to San Francisco. In 1863, Sumner could not have known that the anonymous writer would later become connected with the social and political elite in New York and in the East, and that Clemens would become a personal friend of Frederick Douglass. Clemens later helped Douglass enter the world of politics.

Four years later, Twain would use the fame of Charles Sumner in a letter he published in the *Territorial Enterprise*. Like the anonymous broadside, Twain's letter attacked men in government. Twain was appalled by corrupt territorial delegates who forged signatures to charge mileage for invented travel. To prove how foolish these politicians were, Twain notes in his letter that he wrote "an order for four reams of fancy foolscap and got a blind lunatic to sign Charles Sumner's name to it (no man can counterfeit the genuine signature unless there is something awful the matter with him), and went up to the Senate and presented it. They said it would not do. I asked if they meant to insinuate anything against the soundness of the signature. They said no; they could see by the general horribleness of it that some member of Congress wrote it."[86] Here, Twain uses the fame of lawyer and politician Sumner to illustrate the corruption within the institution that Sumner tried to improve by supporting equality and ethics. Though Twain and the legislature and Twain's readership knew the name and reputation of Charles Sumner in 1867, did Sumner know Twain's name and reputation in 1863? Probably Sumner did not, but he did know the value of a western broadside that attacked the Territorial government. And the writer of the document was attacking the government of which his brother Orion, secretary to the governor, was a part. In fact, the writer recommends part of the penitentiary system be made "into a Lunatic Asylum, for the keeping and confinement of the members of the two lower branches of the Legislature; that their Governor be appointed warden of the institution, and the Secretary of the Territory door-keeper thereof."[87]

The satirical tone certainly sounds like Twain, especially when the writer appoints the governor as the "warden" of the asylum and the secretary, Clemens's brother, as "door-keeper." Though the broadside is large and contains much diction that challenges law and chastises the government for abusing its citizens, I include here the bulk of one long section that uses legal discourse, satire, and knowledge of territorial culture to both judge those in power and to argue for the improved power of the powerless. The writer begins this section by assessing the legal and social application of the death sentence. He refers to a specific murder case in which the jury found the man guilty of "murder in the first degree," was sentenced to die, but his death sentence was commuted when the Supreme Court issued a writ *supercedeas*, which invalidated the lower court's death sentence. This section begins, much like Twain's 1871 letter arguing for the commutation of Rulloff's death sentence, with an acknowledgment of a man's crime and then a satirical attack on the justice system. The writer states that the murderer would not have escaped the death sentence,

> had it not been for one of the judges of the Supreme Court of this Territory, who, in the exercise of his judicial functions, as the law provides he shall do, issued what is the right and privilege of every citizen, under our present judicial system, to have issued for the protection of life and liberty, and as a security against malfeasance in office, a writ of *supercedeas*, thereby hindering and preventing the immediate execution of this man.[88]

While the writer seems initially to agree with the issuing of the writ and calls the legal act "a security against malfeasance in office," the writer shifts into satire and attacks the potential argument that "preventing the immediate execution of this man" has corrupted the legal system This shift becomes apparent with the "recommendation" that follows:

> I would most earnestly recommend and seriously impress upon your deluded minds the paramount necessity of so amending the laws of this Territory, and disregarding the inalienable rights of our fellow-citizens, by expunging from your Statute Book, the wholesome and necessary writs of *Supercedeas* and *Habeas Corpus*, and all other legal proceedings now known to the law of the land ... and confer upon your worthy Chief Executive the untrammeled right

to hang whom he pleases, by the issuance simply of his proclamation to that effect. And henceforth care will be taken that such as incur his Excellency's displeasure will be hung first and tried in the Supreme Court six months or one year thereafter, as circumstances may direct. For, sirs, in the judgment of your Executive, it is far better that nine hundred and ninety-nine innocent parties should suffer the penalties and rigors of the laws, than that one criminal should escape.[89]

The writer has recommended that criminals "be hung first and tried" later, "six months or one year" later. Such action would diminish "the inalienable rights of our fellow-citizens" and give the ultimate power to destroy the lives of any citizens to the courts. This power, in fact, is what the anonymous writer feared the government already expressed, what the state of New York wielded when it executed Rulloff, and even what the people of Idaho Territory allowed to happen to Slade. If the state or group in power hangs first the convicted and tries him later, the state has acted with power worthy of disdain, horror, and satire. This satirical message to hang first and try later ends with the notion that "it is far better that nine hundred and ninety-nine innocent parties should suffer the penalties and rigors of the laws, than that one criminal should escape." Such a message inverts Lafayette's famous saying that appeared two decades earlier on the front page of Charles Spear's newspaper, *The Hangman*, soon renamed under a softer title, *The Prisoners' Friend*: "I shall ask for the Abolition of the Penalty of Death until I have the infallibility of Human Judgment demonstrated to me."[90]

Twain held a similar belief in his satirical letter to the *Tribune* arguing for the salvation of Rulloff. "The fact that in England the proportion of executions to condemnations is only one to 16, & in this country only one to 22, & in France only one to 38, does not shake my steadfast confidence in the propriety of retaining the death penalty. It is better to hang one murderer in 16, 22, or 38, than not to hang any at all."[91] The idea remains that the State hungers to hang someone, anyone, whether or not justice has been satisfied. Twain's satirical voice suggests that if critiquing power and men in power has taught Twain anything, his analysis has proved that execution impinges on the "inalienable rights of our fellow-citizens." Such an abuse of power Sumner argued against in May 1871 when he chastised the Senate for imprisoning two newspaper correspondents, without due process of law, for refusing to disclose their sources. In his speech to his colleagues, he asked, "where is the legal authority for the imprisonment of these witnesses? Only in mere inference, mere deduction,—the merest inference; but surely you will not take away the liberty of the citizen on any such shadowy, evanescent apology, which is no apology, but a sham, and nothing else."[92]

Whether Sumner criticized the State for wielding undue power to usurp the rights of citizens—black Americans or wrongly punished Americans—he considered excessive State power to be a "sham." For Twain, at least in the case of Rulloff, capital punishment represented the boldest kind of sham, especially because it represented the force of law. The execution of Slade illustrated how this sham could cast a shadow that allowed men and committees to function outside of the law but still within its darkened reach. Noakes's execution reflects how those in power represent the corruption of the law even when *lex talionis* justice seems to promote swift justice when the courts prove ineffective. These men, all hanged, denoted the destruction of human rights of Americans or the application of unjust power that Twain despised and wrote about in order to make his readers think and talk about the death penalty. Though the editors of the Mark Twain papers include no letters that Twain or Reid might have received from readers, Twain's letter appeared amidst a larger conversation in the press. Articles about Rulloff were published regularly throughout the first half of 1871 in newspapers in addition to the *New-York Tribune*. The New York *Times*, the Washington *Morning Chronicle*, and the new York *Herald* all ran stories about the man, his murder, and his execution. In 1871, Twain hoped his readers would "discover that regret is growing up in their souls" and help produce change in their culture. In 1862, the anonymous writer, yet to sign his pen name Mark Twain, hoped for something very similar to his more established future self. And, this hope that Twain shared with Sumner, likely caused Sumner to read the broadside and then donate it to the college that yielded his legal and political career.

Marvin Henry Bovee: A "bore" and an "inextinguishable dead beat"

Problems exist with stating that Mark Twain wrote in defense of the individual rights of man, or railed against the legal and political systems that suppressed these rights, or, specifically, that Twain deplored the death penalty and wrote articles that influenced citizens and politicians to fight for the abolition of the death penalty. These statements are true, but Clemens was not a political activist in the early 1860s when he covered the events of the Territorial legislature as a reporter for Virginia City's *Territorial Enterprise*. I cannot argue that Clemens's experiences or writing about those events had direct influences on the justice system or the government, but his writing must have influenced his readership. Mark Twain became one of the most famous living Americans in the second half of the nineteenth century, and readers of all classes and regions read his writing beyond his death in 1910.[93] Another problem is that Twain did not always support the civil liberties or write against the death penalty. For example, in 1868, he celebrated the hanging of John Millian for the murder of the famous Virginia City prostitute, Julia Bulette.[94] Additionally, Twain's fictional Hank Morgan in *A Connecticut Yankee in King Arthur's Court* (1889) electrocutes thousands of troops invading the castle. This problem of contradictory messages is compounded because Twain kept excellent records of his correspondences with famous people, politicians, family, friends, and fans, which in the case of two letters to follow, tells a different story than the letters he wrote in defense of Rulloff. These answered and unanswered letters often contain Twain's personal notes that allow us to read his thoughts that were not published in his books or journalism. Rather than supporting his anti-gallows views, these "personal" writings show, at the least, his ambivalence about a man supporting the abolition of capital punishment.

Two such unpublished notes exist that complicate my arguments and allow us to view Twain's humor, his disdain for one man who did fight for the abolition of the death penalty, and Twain's nearly throw-away view of capital punishment. Marvin Henry Bovee (1827–1888) wrote two letters to Mark Twain, both describing Bovee's views about the criminal justice system. Bovee was a Wisconsin farmer and one-term senator, who in 1853 introduced and helped pass legislation in Wisconsin that abolished the death penalty. His national campaign against capital punishment in 1859 influenced more moderate legislation concerning punishment in Minnesota, Iowa, Illinois, and New York. In 1870, Bovee published his anti-gallows appeal, *Christ and the Gallows, or Reasons for the Abolition of Capital Punishment*.[95] In the first letter, dated April 7, 1875, written on *New-York Tribune* stationary and mailed from New York, Bovee asks for Mark Twain's help to promote Bovee's lectures that denounce capital punishment.[96] Bovee claims to have delivered "six hundred lectures," and he tells Twain of his impending lecture in Boston "the early part of next week."[97] Twain did not respond to the letter, nor did he help Bovee advance the abolition of capital punishment in the way that Bovee had requested. Instead, Twain saved the letter and the envelope. On the outside of the letter he wrote: "From some bore who wants to destroy the death penalty—with an eye to his own future, doubtless."[98]

Ten months later, apparently, Bovee thought he might persuade Mark Twain to respond and petitioned Twain once more for help. On February 10, 1876, Bovee wrote a second letter and mailed it from Chicago to Twain. Bovee begins this one by stating his credentials as a public lecturer, this time by inflating the number of his lectures beyond the number he cited in the previous letter: "My Dear Mark: During the past twenty years I have delivered over 700 public lectures in all different states upon the subject of penal reform."[99] Though he reported ten months earlier to have delivered six hundred lectures, that number has rapidly grown by more than one hundred. Perhaps Twain found this braggadocios discourse distasteful, for once again, though Bovee wrote, "I shall be glad to have you help a little if you feel inclined," Twain did not respond. Perhaps Twain found in his file the 1875 letter and the envelope with the insult "from some bore," considered this new letter, and pondered what insult he might write on this envelope from Chicago. He probably huffed or smirked and then wrote on the envelope: "From that inextinguishable dead beat who has infested legislatures for 20 years trying to put an end to capital punishment. No answer."[100]

Just because Twain seemed to dislike Bovee does not mean that the two men disagreed on the subject of capital punishment. Perhaps, however, they disagreed on the methods to promote the cause to abolish the

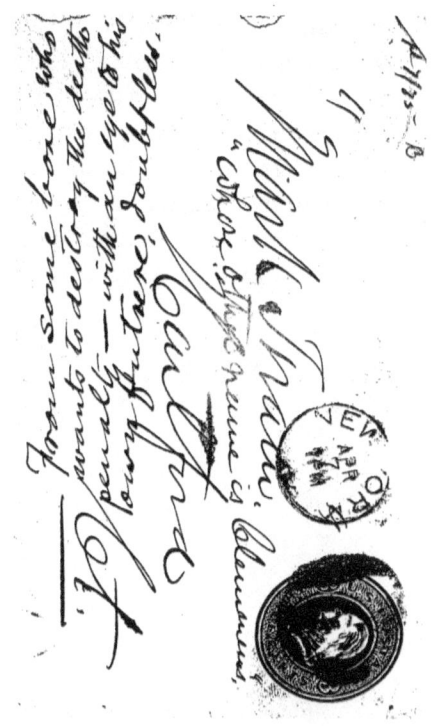

"Note on envelope of Bovee's letter to Twain," 7 April 1875 (courtesy the Mark Twain Papers, Bancroft Library). Marvin Henry Bovee was a Wisconsin farmer and one-term senator, who in 1853 introduced and helped pass legislation in Wisconsin that abolished the death penalty. His national campaign against capital punishment in 1859 influenced more moderate legislation concerning punishment in Minnesota, Iowa, Illinois, and New York.

punishment. Or, also likely, is Twain's dismissal of a man whose writing or lectures or personality Twain found abrasive. Twain's gripe with Bovee, then, might have more to do with the man, a reformer, than with Twain's view on capital punishment. Twain's dismissive personal notes written on Bovee's envelopes illustrate Twain's dismissal of Bovee and not necessarily ambivalence toward capital punishment. Certainly, Twain made clear in his journalism and in his fiction his position on execution—his sympathy for its victims, and the brutalizing force execution had on society.[101]

"Note on envelope of Bovee's letter to Twain," 10 February 1876 (courtesy the Mark Twain Papers, Bancroft Library).

Still, in the twenty-first century Mark Twain is not commonly known as an anti-gallows proponent, even though he often spoke his mind—and wrote it—concerning hanging in the 1860s and '70s. His journalism and fiction display this criticism, but his more personal notes like the ones he scribed on Bovee's envelopes and his letters also display his thoughts on execution and punishment. In a letter to his wife, Olivia, from London, dated September 25, 1872, the same year *Roughing It* was published, Twain mentions that he was supposed to have dined with Sir John Bennett, the sheriff of London, and the criminal judges at Newgate Prison. Twain might not have visited the prison on this trip, but he certainly visited the prison one year later.[102] According to a letter from Moncure Conway, a famous abolitionist who lived in England and Europe during and after the Civil War in order to spread the cause of abolitionism across the Atlantic, a prison guard and an American visitor shared a conversation about the Newgate Prison with "a remarkably intelligent American" man who had recently toured the prison. Apparently, the American man, according to the guard, "admired our arrangements exceedingly, only he thought we were too lenient." The American man complained that the American system of justice was also too lenient, for in America "we caught a rascal ... whom we ought immediately to have burned, and we only hung him. But we are coming to our senses, and are now making arrangements to burn certain men for whom the gallows is too good."[103] At the end of the anecdote, the guard tells the American woman that the "American gentleman" was Mark Twain. Conway reports that the "lady gave a smile of relief and went off."[104] This woman, like Twain's readers of the 1860s and '70s, smiled because Twain had mocked a social convention with humor, and rather than offending, which he often did, he created tension between the necessity to punish or redeem men like Rulloff, Slade, Blakely, and Noakes, and the horror, and absurdity, of capital punishment.

5

Laura: Mark Twain's Conflation of Gender Performance and Judgment, 1863–1873

When police entered the rented cottage of Julia Bulette, Virginia City, Nevada's most famous working-class prostitute, they discovered her fresh corpse in bed. Her throat, "lacerated with the marks of fingernails, and the blood-suffused and distorted countenance, together with the writhing position of the body, showed conclusive evidence of strangulation." Because "the back of her left hand was somewhat lacerated," officers speculated that Bulette had fought with courage and rigor "in the struggles to free herself from the grasp of the fiend who had her in his power."[1] She had last walked among the living on January 19, 1867, when a door attendant at Piper's Opera House denied the prostitute front-door entrance. Bulette refused to sit in the undesirable gallery and returned home, where Frenchman John Millian allegedly murdered her early the next morning. Mark Twain, Joseph T. Goodman, Dan De Quille, and other journalists for Virginia City's *Territorial Enterprise* had known Bulette. The murder of this marginalized woman outraged the community and Twain.[2] Before leaving Nevada for New York in 1868, Twain wrote a letter published in the *Chicago Republican*. For half of 1868, Twain was a correspondent for this weekly newspaper. He submitted letters to the paper from Nevada and from New York once he had left the West. During this period, he also wrote for San Francisco's *Alta California* and three papers in New York—*The Galaxy*, *Herald*, and *Times*. His eulogy in the *Chicago Republican* revealed his admiration for the prostitute and his disdain for her cowardly murderer, the man Twain "wanted to see hung."³ This letter, journalism from the 1860s, and *The Gilded Age*, inspired by his time in the West, illustrate Samuel Clemens's quarreling views of justice and gender that influenced the creation of *The Gilded Age's* Laura Hawkins. Interrogating these sources within one literary context advances a complicated reading of Twain's western writing, which reveals his literary attraction to women who challenged traditional sexual mores and "gender performances."⁴ After all, Julia Bulette was, and Laura Hawkins is, a prostitute.

Mark Twain wrote about women, their sexuality, and violence enacted on their bodies, even when he was a reporter for the *Call* in San Francisco. And yet, Twain did not always portray women as innocent. If Twain thought the female victim might have been naïve or culpable in her own "ruin," he included these opinions in his news items. Such tension is common in Twain's *Call's* 1864 pieces about rape, three of which starred Miss Margaret McQuinn. Though Twain rejected capital punishment and lynching, he sometimes supported personal extra-legal justice enacted by men such as J.A. Slade and Captain Blakely. Such a contradiction often existed because of how Twain viewed men and women. The previous chapter focused on Twain's writing about men whom Twain judged as useful criminals, even though they were violent "desperadoes," and their legal and extra-legal punishments. Twain's view of women and femininity, sometimes in relation to men and masculinity, receives attention that both complements and complicates the sources and their analyses related to legal and extra-legal punishment. For example, rarely have scholars discussed how a young Clemens watched and viewed subversive women—the prostitutes, murderesses, and stage performers. Scholars have mostly focused on Clemens's relationships with women after 1870, when he married Olivia Langdon. In addition, Laura Skandera Trombley and Ann M. Ryan have written much about Clemens's relationships with his daughters Susy, Clara, and Jean and the end of his life when he was old and lonely (after Livy's death in 1904)—which inspired his relationships with many different women—young girls in Twain's Angelfish club and Isabel Lyon, Clemens's secretary and "siren," whom Clara disliked.⁵

Mark Twain's western journalism and letters (when he lived in Nevada and California in his mid-twenties to early thirties) and *The Gilded Age* position the author's literary view of women in more complicated, sometimes conflicting, similar to his anti-gallows discourse when mythologizing or romanticizing men like Slade or Rulloff. Twain's early writing casts subversive women as performers of both masculine and feminine roles. These women, and their performances, finally conflated into one multi-vocal female character, *The Gilded Age's* Laura Hawkins. Or, to represent this lineage in reverse, Mark Twain had been thinking and writing about subversive women for ten years prior to creating Laura Hawkins. His inspection, judgment, and inscription of these western women are evident in his 1873 female creation.[6]

Because such an examination allows for a culminating view of Laura, situating Twain's western views of women and men who performed gender in nontraditional ways relies on a discourse of creating "Laura." Laura, then, becomes a developing, and finally a crowning, symbol for Twain's judgment that allows him to offer a literary verdict. In his journalism, Twain had rendered literary verdicts of male murderers for more than ten years. His assessment of John Millian, for example, appeared in the papers after Twain had witnessed the legal execution of Millian for the murder of Bulette. This letter, like his journalism, letters, and fiction in this chapter and the previous, illustrates Twain's disdain for men like Millian and a simultaneous valuing and devaluing of women in the West.

Though Twain initially judged women as victims in the masculine Trans-Mississippi West, he soon came to marvel at unconventional women whose sexualized and sensational gender performances both attracted and repulsed him. Because he reported on violent crimes against women for papers in Nevada and California, he had witnessed how men abused women's bodies. Much of his western journalism warned his female readers to avoid certain locations in the countryside and cities where men might prey on women. Subversive women, however, were not readers of Twain's reports that required his warnings and instead received both his literary admiration and judgments. This chapter examines three cases of socially deviant women through the lens of Twain's early writing, beginning in Nevada and California in 1863, and ending with his first novel, *The Gilded Age*, in 1873. While several arguments rely on the biographies of these women, their biographies serve to illustrate how Twain watched and judged women, often as a way to explore justice, sexuality, and the transgression of conventional femininity. Adah Isaacs Menken, a sexually provocative actress whose stage career at once captivated and repulsed Twain, received Twain's disdain when he masculinized her in writing. When Julia Bulette, the Virginia City, Nevada, prostitute, died, Twain was outraged. Twain victimized Bulette in order to feminize and rebuke her male murderer, John Millian, while displaying disgust and fascination with the implementation and spectacle of execution. Laura Hawkins, a fictional character that Twain based on Laura Fair, an elite San Francisco prostitute, murdered her lover and escaped state punishment, appeared in *The Gilded Age*. Though Mark Twain may or may not have been actually pondering Menken or Bulette, or their sexuality, when he wrote about other contemporary or fictional women like Laura Hawkins (or Becky Thatcher, or even men like Sherburn or Slade), Twain certainly reflected his fascination with masculinity and femininity that he produced and reproduced in his writing. Additionally, these three cases show that Twain's judgment of women was related to his responses to men who judged and violated women.

Admittedly, this case is built on circumstantial evidence, but one should not, as Brook Thomas suggests, "exclude a case merely because it cannot be established beyond a reasonable doubt as a 'source.'"[7] This kind of reasonable doubt could certainly exist in the case of Bulette. Because Twain did not write directly about Bulette and only mentioned her as the victim of a male murderer whom Twain eviscerated for violating his view of masculinity in the West, it is not clear if Twain admired her. Twain, however, used these women's performances, and the equally performative reactions of the men (including "Mark Twain") who judged them, to assess justice and to reveal his attraction to women who contested sexual mores, violated the law, and complicated his ideas about gender and justice. What appears in Twain's fiction, he also experiences in his life; so that, like Colonel Sherburn—backing down the mob of men, who lack "pluck enough to lynch a *man*!"—Twain experiences masculinity as a performance, staged in response to the treatment of women. Ultimately, in his writing, Twain finds pluck enough to "execute" his symbol for subversive femininity, "Laura."

"The Menken"

During his time as a reporter for Virginia City's *Territorial Enterprise* and San Francisco's *Daily Morning Call*, among other papers in the West, Samuel Clemens often wrote about violent men—murderers like J.A. Slade or John Millian, and victims of murder like Julia Bulette. But he also wrote about and interacted with women who subverted the gender roles that western males supported. Adah Isaacs Menken was a controversial stage performer, best known for playing the lead role in *The French Spy* and *Mazeppa* in 1863 and 1864. American born to a "Negro father" and French Creole mother, Menken was four-times married, and converted to Judaism for one of her husbands.[8] In anachronistic terms, Menken symbolized the nineteenth-century combination of Marilyn Monroe and Betty Page, one part admired sexualized actress, and one part fetishized pin-up girl. Menken became famous for playing Mazeppa, tied to the back of a live horse, and dressed in a flesh-colored body suit that made her appear to be nude. "The Menken," a dehumanizing, desexualizing title that Twain called her in print, also posed partially nude for a publicity photograph, which clearly showed Menken as a woman, rather than advertising her as an actress. Twain first saw Menken perform in San Francisco, September 1863, at McGuire's Opera House. In a November 1864 sketch, "A Full and Reliable Account of the Extraordinary Meteoric Shower of Last Saturday Night," Twain referred to a meteor shower as the "Great Menken." He satirically noted that his metaphor was a "more modest expression" for a beautiful, "flaming" night display than the Great Bear, the symbol for California. The following article, "The Menken—Written Especially for Gentlemen," is his review of her stage acting and appeared on September 17, 1863, in Virginia City's *Territorial Enterprise*. From the opening sentence Twain plays with images of femininity, masculinity, and sexuality. He first calls Menken a "body," a sexualized object with the title "the." Twain then marks Menken as a "manly young female," dressed in what appeared to be nothing more than a diaper. Here, he draws attention to Menken's infantile defiance of modest, feminine behavior in public, even on stage:

> When I arrived in San Francisco, I found there was no one in town—at least there was no body in town but "the Menken"—or rather, that no one was being talked about except that manly young female. I went to see her play "Mazeppa," of course. They said she was dressed from head to foot in flesh-colored "tights," but I had no opera-glass, and I couldn't see it, to use the language of the inelegant rabble. She appeared to me to have but one garment on—a thin tight white linen one, of unimportant dimensions; I forget the name of the article, but it is indispensable to infants of tender age—I suppose any young mother can tell you what it is, if you have the moral courage to ask the question ... some of her postures are not so modest as the suggestive attitude of the latter. She is a finely formed woman down to her knees.[9]

Twain's discourse here illustrates his conservative opinion—a review based on a stage performance, but one also based on Menken's performed infantilized femininity. In this case, the gender-bending act as Mazeppa bears particular significance, for the character, Ivan Mazeppa, is male. The play was based on Lord Byron's 1819 narrative poem "Mazeppa," which tells the story of young Ivan Mazeppa's love affair with a countess. When her husband discovers the affair, he publicly punishes Mazeppa by strapping the young lover naked to the back of horse. The man journeys through the wilderness, tormented both physically and emotionally. In the western play that Twain saw and reviewed, such events were dramatized on stage, so that the spectacle of the physical torture took precedent over the more poetic exploration of Mazeppa's emotional torment in Byron's poem.

In 1863 and 1864, Menken's portrayal of a man was sensational, but not uncommon. She also played the male lead in *Jack Sheppard*, and Dick Turbin, the highwayman who was hanged for his crimes, in the dramatic rendition of William Harrison Ainsworth's gothic romance *Rookwood* (1834). Though Mazeppa was a man, the role called for nudity, which is why Menken wore a body suit and a "white linen" cloth. Twain's review, then, worked on multiple levels: he summarized the plot, he literally accounted for a woman playing a male character, and he offered an opinion of the play and of Menken's dramatization. Of course, Twain's writing was also a masculine production that judged the woman behind that titillating performance. Twain subtitled the review "Especially for Gentlemen," which evoked an insider's sexualized view of a female performer with a male audience in mind. Indeed, "the Menken" performed with a "suggestive attitude," and she was a "finely formed woman." These descriptions were meant to attract male attention, just as Adah Isaacs Menken's stage performance was meant to attract male attention. Appealing to men, and to male readers, meant that the reporter needed to inscribe the female body with sexuality. Twain intended to put Menken on display so his "gentlemen" readers could wag tongues and admire her cavorting but also to judge her. While Twain certainly positions himself as one of his "gentlemen" readers who inhabit a higher social position than a female stage performer, Twain's masculine production as a writer judging a woman's performance on stage creates a curious portrait of the event. The male character Mazeppa required that Menken "play" maleness with a certain amount of ambiguity. She played a male lover, but her womanly "nakedness" attracted male attention. Twain's review, then, diminished the "maleness" of the character so that "gentlemen" readers would understand the "womanliness" of the performer.

And yet, Twain's discourse also diminished Menken's "womanhood." By describing her one article of clothing as a diaper (though he suppressed the word diaper) and not as a loincloth or even as undergarments, Twain shied away from the sexuality of an adult woman. An infant had the freedom to be nude. Perhaps for Twain, a woman did not. According to Ron Powers, Twain was "invested in his own countercultural spree" in Nevada, but like most men in the second half of the nineteenth century, he struggled with offering the same freedoms, agency, and "countercultural" behavior to women.[10] Clemens had grown up the Missouri's traditional Upper South in a small slave-holding family. He was the youngest child of three surviving children, and he treated his older sister Pamela with much respect, affection, and protection, much as he did his mother. When Clemens was a young boy, his father, Judge John Marshall Clemens, died of pneumonia. Though the Judge had practiced law and served as the justice of the peace and head of the family, after he died, Clemens's mother and sister took on many of the male familial responsibilities. These views of women Twain transported to the West.

Menken, however, flaunted her disinterest in social conventions for women, even in the bohemian mining towns of San Francisco and Virginia City. According to the popular myth about western women, many unmarried women were prostitutes. While prostitution satisfied one means for women to survive in the West, single women often worked as servants.[11] Some single women, not engaged in domestic servitude, even performed on stage and danced with men for a fee, but these women, or "hurdy-gurdy" girls, were not necessarily prostitutes.[12] Most women in the mining towns of Nevada were married.[13] These wives who performed the bulk of familial and domestic duties also volunteered at church and in organizations affiliated with churches, such as groups serving the community for disaster relief, social reform, and charity. And though most married women occupied the domestic space, volunteering allowed "respectable" women to perform in the public sphere. Some of these wives danced and performed on stage as a way raise charity funds through ticket sales.[14] Menken's sexualized performance, however, excited not female charity but male interest and attraction. But, as Twain viewed her, Adah Isaacs Menken was something other than a "woman" on stage. She became a "body," not a person. He quickly shifts from referring to the actress as the only "one" people were talking about to the only "body" that excited San Franciscans, especially the writer of the review. On stage, Menken's "body" could be sexualized, but a woman—a man's wife, sister, mother, or daughter—had to be respected. Even though most women needed men to survive and thrive in the mining towns of Nevada, the rarity of women in the region also allowed the right kind of women, the pure in behavior and speech, to experience a level of power in courtship. These women, not unlike their eastern counterparts, usually satisfied the traditional, religious gender norms of the mid–nineteenth century.[15] Indeed, many of these women, and the men, had emigrated from the East. These male emigrants and westerners, both married and single, comprised the audience to which Twain wrote in his review of *Mazeppa*.

Twain positioned himself as a member of the audience that viewed Menken's acting on stage to devise a persona that created and shared male readers' view of an unconventional woman. Though Twain initially portrayed Menken as a sexualized "body," then as a "manly young female," and then as an infant, he finally moves toward an ironic view of the actress as a graceless, masculine performer by writing active, masculine verbs associated with work and action, an appropriate technique to discuss a male Mazeppa:

> Every tongue sings the praises of her matchless grace, her supple gestures, her charming attitudes. Well, possibly, these tongues are right. In the first act, she rushes on the stage, and goes cavorting around after "Olinska"; she bends herself back like a bow; she pitches headforemost at the atmosphere like a battering ram; she works her arms, and her legs, and her whole body like a dancing-jack: her every movement is as quick as thought; in a word, without any apparent reason for it, she carries on like a lunatic from the beginning of the act to the end of it. At other times she "whallops" herself down on the stage, and rolls over as does the sportive pack-mule after his burden is removed. If this be grace then the Menken is eminently graceful.[16]

Twain uses the sexualized trope "tongue" twice in the opening descriptions of how men discuss and "praise" Menken. These tongues might be singing praises, but they are also in view, as if hanging out of men's mouths in sexual pleasure and delight. He did not intend to evoke the "grace" of Menken's movements, for tongue-wagging men wanted not grace but sex. He describes Menken's "cavorting," and how she "rushes," "bends," "pitches," "works," and "'whallops'" in order to show her as a male "battering ram." Though Menken's movements were graceless, Twain's words describing her actions objectified her, so that the woman revealed her body and then became a "battering ram," a phallus. Such a marker removed her grace and femininity. He also seemed to dislike her performance and perhaps even Menken herself as a performer, for she was sexual but also masculine. Because the review was over a thousand words in length, however, little argument can be made that he merely dismissed her. Rather, her "lunatic" performance and masculine yet sexualized appearance troubled Twain's conservative sensibilities but excited his fascination. He even withheld the information that the character was actually male. His only linguistic marker for this detail comes at the end of the review when he shifts from referring to Menken with feminine pronouns, such as "digging her heals" or "her sufferings,"[17] to discussing Mazeppa with masculine pronouns. For example, in the closing of the review, Twain describes Mazeppa as "insensible—"ginned out" by "his trip" of torture, strapped to the back of the living, panting horse.[18] Twain continues to use "he" and "his" to explain Mazeppa's actions on stage, but Twain never explains that Menken was portraying a male lover.

So, why offer up Adah Isaacs Menken on a platter meant for male consumption, then describe her as graceless and masculine, yet never explain the obvious and literal gender reversal? Twain certainly knew Byron's poem, for in the review Twain borrowed Byron's phrase "noble steed." Probably, too, spectators knew enough of the poem, or the gossip about the play, to expect a spectacle. In addition, even in the West, when Clemens was young, he understood how to write a sensational story or article that enticed male and female readers. And "The Menken," a nude woman cavorting on stage, subverting the expectations of viewers (and later readers of the review) who purchased a ticket to watch a famous actress play a male character, certainly delivered on those expectations. Twain continued to exploit this expectation in his review. He participated in this sensational performance that in writing could live beyond the transient stage performance and continue to influence his own thinking and writing, as well as the thinking of consumers and spectators. Perhaps, then, Twain had not intended to review accurately a play or Menken's portrayal of a man. Menken had gained popularity in the West, not just *for being* a beautiful and talented performer. She was also known *for playing* men. On the front page of the San Francisco *Daily Morning Call*, dated January 3, 1864, for example, the writer of "Theatrical Record" does specify that Menken was playing a "hero." The parenthetical phrase "(or heroine)" follows "hero" as a means to clarify the difference between male character and female performer. But Twain did not write this review, and the point of the "Record" is to deliver information without judgment. The "Record" also notes that Menken had already gained "success" playing Dick Turbin in *Rookwood*.[19] For this reason, Twain's review did not state the obvious or need to include information that readers already possessed. The review advanced what Twain thought would obviously attract male attention to the play and its player but also this attention to his article.

Menken's interpretation of Mazeppa captivated Twain, and ultimately Twain's "gentlemen" readers, and her final sensational act—wearing a flesh-colored body suit that made her appear nude on stage while strapped like a captive to the back of a living horse—stirred up a "tempest of applause":

After a while they proceed to strip her, and the high chief Pole calls for the "fiery untamed steed" ... They strap Mazeppa on his back, fore and aft, and face upper most, and the horse goes cantering up-stairs over the painted mountains, through tinted clouds of theatrical mist, in a brisk exciting way, with the wretched victim he bears unconsciously digging her heels into his hams, in the agony of her sufferings, to make him go faster. Then a tempest of applause bursts forth, and the curtain falls.[20]

Though Twain continues to pursue the sexuality of Menken by noting for his "gentlemen" readers that the actress was stripped on stage and strapped to a horse, the writer also becomes concerned with the final message of the play. An additional theme appears at the end of this review—justice. The spurned husband publicly punishes Mazeppa. The act illustrates a visual method to represent sexuality, retribution, and satisfaction, thus allowing the audience to participate in the spectacle. Twain imagined an abused and naked man receiving punishment. But a woman played the man in the same condition, which attracted a greater sense of astonishment and wonder in the audience, whose applause was like a "tempest." *Her* sexuality, then, is exposed through an act of justice that also visually punishes Mazeppa for *his* sexuality.

In this case, however, the audience witnessed the writhing punishment of a "nude" woman acting like a man. Because of the actress's thrilling stage appearances, perhaps aided by Twain's sensational review, Adah Isaacs Menken, her performance, and *Mazeppa* were popular in San Francisco and soon became popular elsewhere, especially in Virginia City, Nevada Territory. According to Twain, "'Mazeppa' proved a great card for Maguire here; he put it on the boards in first-class style, and crowded houses went crazy over it every night it was played. But Virginians will soon have an opportunity of seeing it themselves, as 'the Menken' will go direct from our town there without stopping on the way."[21] In 1864, Menken arrived in Virginia City, a bohemian mining town squatting near the Sierra Nevada range. Here, she performed *Mazeppa* with John Wilkes Booth's brother, J.B. Booth, at the other famous Maguire's Opera House.[22] In this town, Clemens finally met and socialized with Menken and began to view her in more complicated ways than merely as a sexualized stage performer. The word friendship is probably too strong to describe their relationship, but Clemens began to admire certain aspects of her personality that he exploited in later literary depictions of both men and women, both actual and imagined. Menken was charming, social, subversive, bold, and found a place within Clemens's male social circle. Because Menken's performed sexuality had tested the bounds of Clemens's acceptance of a woman in the West, he, and his friends, did not accept her into their social circle without first watching her and hoping to abuse her in writing. After all, Twain himself had been "tested" when he began contributing letters to the *Territorial Enterprise* under the penname "Josh." William H. Barstow, on staff in the paper's business office, liked the letters and helped Twain secure a permanent spot on the staff. Twain's talent, with the help of Barstow, won the attention of the paper's editors and owners.[23]

Twain initially considered Menken to be "overrated" and looked forward to having "an opportunity of doing some vast vivisecting"[24] of Menken's acting in a review for the *Territorial Enterprise*.[25] He took that opportunity with the writing of "The Menken—Written Especially for Gentlemen" in 1863. The following year, in March, a number of small reviews were published in local columns in Nevada Territory and California that responded to Twain's review in the *Enterprise*. While none of these reviews offered the extended sass that *Enterprise* readers discovered in "The Menken—Written Especially for Gentlemen," many of them contain judgments of Menken, as well as a review of the play. One review published in the *Virginia Daily Union* ranked the play among one "of the scandalous obscene exhibitions now nightly on display at the Maguire" and called it an "exhibition" of "the most lascivious nature."[26] Two of the final items illustrate a shift away from a harsh critique of Menken's acting toward a softer view of the actress, though in the first, the writer appropriates Twain's use of "The Menken." On March 14, "Splendid Acting" appeared in Stockton, California: "The Menken has been acting the nude Mazeppa to audiences in Virginia City for a few days past with wonderful effect. Both the editors of the *Enterprise* have gone crazy—but they didn't have far to go. The *Union* still preserves its gravity."[27] Though the review is positive, and humorous, the reporter has yet to relinquish the use of the dehumanizing definite article "The" posted prior to her last name. He also notes the "nude" performance, which insignificant to the plot or acting, was the most sensational aspect of the play. Finally, the reporter plays with the idea that "editors of the *Enterprise*," Twain and probably Dan De Quille, are part of this story. They, too, are performers, whose "crazy" behavior complements the "lunatic" performance of Menken. The editors' behaviors contrasted with their counterparts' "gravity" on the staff of the *Union*, which was the rival paper in Virginia City.

The second short review, published five days later in Humboldt, Nevada Territory, withholds the judgment that the previous reviews contained and even makes a kind of apology for the editors of the *Enterprise* for being critical of Menken's "nude" performance: "Miss Menken, the great unadorned, still performs nightly in Virginia. The local of the Enterprise doesn't pile it up quite so steep onto her this week. Guess Dan has discovered that she wears drawers."[28] Finally, the reporter has dropped the definite article before Menken and has instead used a more respectful tone with "Miss Menken." He still plays with the idea that she is "unadorned," but then he introduces the idea that Twain and Dan De Quille have abused Menken in their writing but not this week. Dan De Quille, the reporter humorously asserts, has discovered that Menken wears "drawers" to hide her nude femininity.[29] This seems to have been a turning point for the reception of Adah Isaacs Menken in Virginia City, one that would allow the actress to be accepted into Twain's masculine social circle because he and other editors had stopped abusing her in writing.

Four decades later, reflecting on Menken's arrival in Virginia City, and of Mark Twain's reception of the actress, Joe Goodman, fellow *Territorial Enterprise* reporter and co-owner, noted that he, Twain, and Dan De Quille each wrote a review of Menken's acting, but that not one of them "vivisected" her. Though to vivisect Menken like an animal would be a dehumanizing act, Twain also uses vivisect to mean the act of criticizing mercilessly the performer and to objectify her through the male gaze. Instead the male reporters wrote positive reviews, among which Goodman's was published in the newspaper. Menken was pleased with the review and invited Goodman, De Quille, and Twain to join her "in a succession of Bohemian dinners."[30] Two of these gatherings yielded conflicting results for Twain. In one instance, Menken invited Twain and a few guests back to her hotel room, where she did not allow her husband, Orpheus Kerr, to attend. According to rumor, she had abandoned her husband to have sex with another man. But in the hotel room that night, Twain noticed the absence of Kerr and the overwhelming presence of Menken's nineteen dogs. Twain became annoyed with the dogs, and with Menken, attempted to kick away one of Menken's many dogs that filled the room, and "accidently" kicked Menken instead.[31]

This party scene illustrates the kind of relationship Mark Twain had with Adah Isaacs Menken, one troubled by a conflict between two performers. Menken and Twain clashed over the appropriateness of these performances on stage, in writing, and in social gathers, and both performers wanted the spotlight. Perhaps a room occupied by The Menken and her many dogs allowed too little space in which "The Mark Twain" could perform. Furthermore, Clemens was a product of a slave-holding, conservative Missouri family and could not divorce entirely the classically portrayed image of a woman, even if later, in 1868, he would fall in love with Olivia, a feminine, funny, and politically minded woman from a liberal family. Still, in 1864, Twain struggled with how to interact with Menken, a bold and boisterous woman.

Menken's feisty behavior made a better impression on Twain during a second of these dinners. Her inclusion, and the exclusion of the other actors, created a rift between the famous Menken and the rest of the theater company, which the theater manager, Mr. Graves, did nothing to stop. The other performers at Maguire's Opera House, jealous of Menken's new friendship with the already popular journalists, set up a series of "gags" against the *Enterprise*.[32] Apparently, Twain, De Quille, Goodman, and Menken, in a night of drunken carousal and bonding that would change Twain's perception of Menken, decided that Menken should refuse to take the stage until Mr. Graves stopped the theatre troupe's war against the newspaper. According to Goodman, Menken told Mr. Graves that because he had "paid no attention" to her requests or the requests of the journalists to end the feud of jealousy, she decided to take "the matter into [her] own hands," and she had "nothing further to say" to him. Goodman noted that after she snubbed Mr. Graves, Menken "began talking to Mark Twain."[33] The "little Graves" and Adah Isaacs Menken ended the feud the next day, and Menken returned to perform in the sold-out opera house.[34]

Menken had single-handedly suppressed the cowardice of one "little" man and a theater troupe acting like a mob. Acts of personal justice excited Twain throughout his writing career, and mobs he always detested. More than it illustrates an act of personal justice, however, this case reflects Menken's agency as a woman, and as a famous woman, which allowed her to effect a situation within the control of a man, Graves. For this reason, such an experience calls for special attention not because it illustrates Twain's disdain for mob violence, corrupt or ignorant juries, or state justice, but because it shows a turning point in how Twain viewed Menken as a subversive woman, and especially as a person willing to stand against a man. When Menken performed this kind of masculine boldness, Twain noticed. Twain reproduced this ethic in characters such as *Huck Finn's* Sherburn, Slade from *Roughing It*, and Laura Hawkins in *The Gilded Age*. Twain admired acts of justice and boldness and found acts of cowardice unbecoming, even though he did not always choose the expected masculine or courageous path in his personal life. And, of course, he performed his masculinity in his writing, often a subversive act. If he could not respect

Menken for the way she performed her gender on stage, perhaps the writer could admire Menken for her performative act of writing.

On March 18, 1864, Samuel Clemens wrote a letter to his sister, Pamela A. Moffett, describing one of his experiences with Menken in Virginia City. As acting editor of the *Enterprise*, he had read a literary sketch that Menken hoped the newspaper would publish. It is apparent in the following letter that Clemens claimed not to "know" her when he received her submission, but we also know that he had already thrashed her in his "Written Especially for Gentlemen" review. But by the time he wrote the letter, after the feud with Graves,[35] he had come to respect Menken:

> Miss Menken, the actress—Orpheus C. Kerr's wife—she is a literary cuss herself. Although I was acquainted with Orpheus, I didn't know *her* from the devil, & the other day (I am acting in place of *both* the chief editors, now, & Dan has the local all to himself,) she sent a ~~note~~ brief note, couched in stately terms & full of frozen dignity, addressed to "Mr Mark Twain," asking if we would publish a sketch from her pen.... It was extravagantly sociable & familiar, but I swear it had humor in it, because I laughed at it myself. It was bad enough as it was when first finished.[36]

Twain thought Menken was humorous. Menken went on to contribute "a number of remarkable poems and articles to the paper,"[37] illustrating that Twain, Goodman, and De Quille—editors and writers for the most popular newspaper in Nevada—respected Menken, and her writing, enough to publish multiple pieces. This was no small compliment. These male journalists competed among themselves to write the most sensational, the most humorous pieces, in the newspaper. Because Goodman, De Quille, and especially Twain reconsidered and repositioned Menken as a comedic writer and performer of humor and grace, rather than as a graceless, masculine, grotesque "Roman slave," it becomes clear that Menken offered something both feminine and masculine, something bohemian and trickster, that simultaneously repulsed and excited Twain. In this letter to his sister, however, he could not compliment Menken without then knocking her down a notch by criticizing her penmanship. He stated that he removed the manuscript from

> the envelop & added an extra atrocity. She has a beautiful white hand but her handwriting is infamous; she writes very fast, but and her letters chirography is of the doorplate order—her letters are immense. I gave her a conundrum—thus: "My Dear Madam—Why ought your hand to retain its present grace & beauty always? Because you fool away devilish little of it on your manuscript." I think I can safely say that woman was furious for a few days. But that wasn't a matter of much consequence to me, & finally she got over it of her own accord, & wrote another note. She is friendly, now.[38]

Though Twain did not mock her acting in this letter, he derided her handwriting—her letters were large and quickly scribbled, perhaps, like a child's or one who was untrained. Still, she appeared to be feminine, for her hand was "white," and she was beautiful, but she lacked femininity on the stage with her graceless, abrasive actions, and now, in her penmanship, she also lacked elegance. As if Twain had not considered the obvious flaw with this judgment, Menken's penmanship would not matter once the piece was published, a point that makes Twain's comment seem viscous and influenced by his disdain for her progressive femininity more than for her amount of talent. Eventually, however, they became "friendly," because she had first reached him through her act of justice and then through the act of writing. Her use of humor and courage, in addition to her sensational and sexual stage performances, left a lasting impression on Twain, one that writhes underneath the prose of Twain's future writing concerned with gender and justice.

Julia Bulette and John "Melanie"

The Chinese servant who found the corpse of Julia Bulette, "lying on her left side, with a pillow over her head and face, the bed clothes beneath her head saturated with blood," on the morning of January 20, 1867, did not find the prostitute's murderer.[39] Frenchman Jean Marie A. Villain, better known as John Millian, had escaped the murder scene in the night and "secreted himself under the bed of another woman of the town, and in the middle of the night was crawling out with a slung-shot in one hand and a butcher knife in the other, when the woman discovered him, alarmed the neighborhood with her screams, and he retreated from the house.... He was arrested and then his later intended victim recognized him."[40] For Twain, the murder of a woman who knew how to handle herself in the dangerous mining town marked Millian as a kind of animal worthy of execution.[41] Twain used the story of Bulette's murder to illustrate male cowardice and the nauseating attraction to the performance and spectacle of execution. Like Menken, Bulette operated on the fringes of acceptable notions of femininity and within occupations that excited male viewers and consumers.

Though no evidence suggests that Twain wrote any letters, stories, or journalism specifically about Julia Bulette before she died, he had certainly read the now-lost articles published in the *Territorial Enterprise*, where he had been a full-time staff reporter until 1864. In 1867, when Bulette was murdered, he was a friend with the paper's owner, Joseph Goodman, and its writers, including Rollin Mallory Daggett. Twain had also likely read the sensational series of articles about Bulette's murder and the capture of her murderer, Millian, published in the popular *National Police Gazette* in 1867 before he wrote his letter, "Novel Entertainment, Nevada Execution—Horrible Nonchalance of the Victim," on May 2, 1868, and published in the *Chicago Republican* on May 31. The *Police Gazette* series introduced three ideas that Mark Twain used as components of his letter that focused more on the execution of Millian, and the justice that the hanging satisfied, than on the life and murder of Bulette, whose name and occupation he omitted. These elements include, first, the portrayal of Bulette as "very kind-hearted, liberal, benevolent and charitable," belonging to a "class denominated 'fair but frail,' and having "more true friends" than most of "her class."[42] This article, "The Assassin in Nevada," does not name Bulette as a prostitute, but only as a woman belonging to a "fair but frail" class whose women generally have few friends. Moreover, Twain signaled Bulette's profession, and name, and marked her only as "a woman of the town who lived alone," a euphemism for a prostitute or a woman of contested social position.[43] The *Police Gazette* also noted that she was an "honorary member of Virginia City Engine Company No. 1," one of the local fire departments, and the one that buried her.[44] Apparently, the department honored her with membership "in return for numerous favors and munificent gifts bestowed by her upon the company."[45]

In Bulette's most famous photograph, she appears posed next to an Engine Company No. 1 helmet.[46] She is stoic. One arm hangs at her side; the other is bent with hand on the hip hidden underneath a flowing silk dress drawn in by a corset, of which she owned two.[47] We also know, though not by inspecting the photograph, that she owned four such silk dresses of different colors, worth a total of sixty dollars in 1867.[48] In early twenty first-century dollars, these dresses would be valued at nearly one thousand dollars. While this figure might seem large and suggest that Bulette was wealthy because of her profession, the value of these dresses actually tells a contradictory story. Except for two pieces of jewelry, a "diamond ring & purse," valued at fifty dollars, and one "pair of gold bracelets" worth thirty, these four silk dresses were the most valuable items Julia Bulette owned.[49] They represented 6 percent of her total assets. Adding just two pieces of jewelry to the value of the dresses, these six items totaled 13 percent of

"Julia Bulette." Bulette was a well-known prostitute in Virginia City, Nevada Territory. Firefighters of Virginia Engine Number 1 named Bulette an honorary member (courtesy the Nevada Historical Society).

her wealth. Most of her property, found in her rented crib in Virginia City's "entertainment district," was clothes or jewelry. Perhaps this is not surprising, considering that her job required a certain amount of allure. But the probate records illustrate that when Bulette died, she was in poor health, in debt, and owned precious little, other than dresses and jewelry.[50] She needed to spend what few profits could be made on purely visual items that would attract potential clients. Such circumstances were the reality for a working-class prostitute in the West.

Western prostitutes rarely became financially secure. Most such women, in fact, lived in poverty in poorly constructed dwellings.[51] Despite the romantic view that Bulette was a beautiful, popular, wealthy prostitute with a heart of gold, Bulette was in fact a typical "working woman." Her clothes and jewelry comprised most of her assets, and she lived "in one of the hastily-constructed cribs which lined Virginia City's D Street."[52] Little space existed for the image of the romantic, glamorous madam that sometimes invades popular western narratives, or even the *Police Gazette's* portrayal of Bulette as a "very kind-hearted, liberal, benevolent and charitable" woman, whom all locals of Virginia City loved and admired. In reality, only the men of Engine Company No. 1, patrons of Bulette, and the male-dominated press admired her. The press advanced the idea that Bulette was a "generous citizen." Her contributions to No. 1 were her only recorded benevolence.[53]

The second element of the murder series, the narrative of the murderer's discoverer, found much more attention in the *Police Gazette*. Here again Twain offered only a few details in order to build toward his celebration of Millian's execution. The murderer eventually was caught because a second person, which Twain noted as "another woman," found Millian hiding underneath her bed. She alerted the police, and he was soon captured. She had purchased "articles" and dress goods from a shop in Virginia City where Millian had sold Bulette's dresses and patterns to the owners. The owner recognized the man as the merchant.[54] The *Police Gazette*, however, offered details about the heroics of this second woman, Martha Camp, and the storeowner, who became a kind of detective to help solve a mystery. When Twain wrote his letter, he, and his friends on the staff of the *Enterprise*, were probably less interested in the heroic stories of these women than were the *Police Gazette* and more interested in hanging Millian in the newspaper even before the noose found his neck. In the *Gazette's* second article in the series, "A Mysterious Murder Chased Up," the writer asserts that "the *Enterprise*, in a characteristic manner, threw discredit upon the woman's story."[55] Though Twain no longer worked for the paper, his friends Joseph Goodman and Rollin Mallory Daggett did. The *Police Gazette*, in fact, named Daggett as the reporter "not sworn in the case," and therefore unable to "impeach any person's character."[56] Years later, in November 1908, Joseph Goodman recalled in the "By-the-Bye" column of the *Nevada Mining News* this story and what he called "the shrewdness of women," which had caused the capture, trial, and execution of the murderer, Millian.[57] Even if forty years prior he and Daggett had "impeached" the character of Martha Camp, meaning that they insinuated that she, like Bulette, was a prostitute, Goodman now praised Camp, "a sensible and determined woman," for having "sharp eyes" that were "the means of unraveling a great mystery."[58] Though Goodman might have tried to redeem the aspersions he and Daggett had cast against Camp at the turn of the twentieth century, Twain never impugned the character of Martha Camp. He simply did not offer compliments for her courage. Instead, he focused on the cowardice of Millian, for the murderer had twice "secreted himself" so as to harm women. And though Twain might have struggled to accept unconventional women in the 1860s, he certainly did not think that Bulette, or Camp, deserved to be harmed by men preying upon women who lived alone.

The portrayal of Millian as a "cold-blooded murderer," marks the third and final component of the Bulette series that influenced Twain when writing his letter. Most of "Novel Entertainment" is devoted to indicting Millian as a feminized man worthy of the gallows. The writer of "The Assassin in Nevada," like Twain, wanted to see Millian hung: "It certainly is to be hoped the murdering villain may be captured and eventually adorn the end of a rope."[59] Twain's comment is similar: "This is the man I wanted to see hung."[60] Though the first Bulette article in the *Police Gazette* includes very little information about Frenchman Millian, the second article closes with an entire paragraph about the murderer. In addition to being a "cold-blooded murderer," Millian apparently was disliked, even among the French in Virginia City. Moreover, he was "a great braggart, and what is commonly called a 'blowhard'; frequently boasting that he wasn't afraid of anybody."[61] In the letter to the *Chicago Republican*, Twain played with this image of Millian. Twain turns Millian into a pusillanimous "happy girl" at the base of the gallows, and yet a "heartless assassin," whose victim was a kind, charitable woman surviving in a town known for mining and murder.

Like the life of Adah Isaacs Menken and her performance of femininity, Bulette's subversive social presentation provided Twain a story to create a narrative. Menken's allowed Twain to write a sensational review that invited men to view a sexualized performance. Yet, unlike Menken's story, he did not use Bulette's murder to draw attention to her sexuality. Instead, Twain used the murder to judge a male murderer as a coward within the sensational spectacle of execution. Though both women subverted the traditional gender norms for women in the West, a startling difference exists between the two women. Menken's fame brought her glamour and opportunities outside of a mining town, whereas Bulette's fame within Virginia City offered a meager wage for dangerous, eventually fatal, work. But four years before he wrote about Bulette's murderer and execution, Twain had learned from Menken that he (and other men) viewed, abused, and admired subversive women in ways that influenced his own writing.

Though Menken and Bulette's experiences in the West shared some common ground in the way they performed subversive femininity, Twain's inspection of these women illustrates a greater importance than a mere overlap in their experiences. Understanding Twain's conflicted view of Menken allows for a new interpretation of Twain's desire to see justice satisfied, especially within a framework of gender, and probably because of this framework. In the case of Bulette, Twain's use of vehement discourse about her alleged murderer John Millian complicated Twain's beliefs about execution when he often supported the rights of the individual over the rights of the group—mob, jury, or state.

Twain, at the time and later in life, wrestled with the justice of legal and extra-legal execution, but in a letter titled "Novel Entertainment, Nevada Execution—Horrible Nonchalance of the Victim," published in the *Chicago Republican* on May 31, 1868, Twain did not seem conflicted about the hanging of Millian. Rather, the journalist found justice in the execution:

> I saw a man hanged the other day. John Melanie, of France.... I never had witnessed an execution before, and did not believe I could be present at this one without turning away my head at the last moment. But I did not know what fascination there was about the thing, then. I only went because I thought I ought to have a lesson, and because I believed that if ever it would be possible to see a man hanged, and derive satisfaction from the spectacle, this was the time. For John Melanie was no common murderer—else he would have gone free. He was a heartless assassin. A year ago, he secreted himself under the house of a woman of the town who lived alone, and in the dead watches of the night, he entered her room, knocked her senseless with a billet of wood as she slept, and then strangled her with his fingers.[62]

Twain's prominent argument for the execution of "Melanie," a feminized form of Millian's name to further emasculate the criminal, is the lack of masculinity the murderer displayed by sneaking into Bulette's house in the night to prey upon a woman "who lived alone." Suppressing the fact that Bulette was a prostitute, Twain also omits Bulette's name. A nameless woman, a victim, Bulette could have been any woman—even a single, capable one, surviving within a dangerous mining town. Twain, of course, later created famous fictional women who lacked, but did not need, male protectors: Widow Douglas, Aunt Polly, and Miss Watson. But in articles, letters, and fiction influenced by the West, Twain often wrote about murderers, like the desperado Jack Slade, with a sense of respect and admiration, for they did not abuse women.

Twain, however, gives "Melanie" no respect. John Millian was "a heartless assassin," not a "common murderer." For Twain, Melanie was a coward, and not a man, for committing such a crime against a woman, especially a workingwoman and a survivor in the mining town. Twain understood that men settled disputes with other men face to face, and that murder was justified through personal acts of retribution, and not against women. "Melanie," according to Twain's view of justice, performed no such gender expectation and therefore deserved to be hanged:

> This is the man I wanted to see hung. I joined the appointed physicians, so that I might be admitted within the charmed circle and be close to Melanie. Now I never more shall be surprised at anything. That assassin got out of the closed carriage, and the first thing his eye fell upon was that awful gallows towering above a great sea of human heads, out yonder on the hill side and his cheek never blanched, and never a muscle quivered! He strode firmly away, and skipped gaily up the steps of the gallows like a happy girl.[63]

Here, Twain calls "Melanie" a "happy girl," for he did not perform in the ways a masculine murderer should. He "skipped gaily," and mocked the gravity of the gallows by performing as a girl. The reporter turns Millian into a girl not because a gender reversal allowed Twain to celebrate a hanging but because the reversal enabled Twain to mock a male, not a man, and to abuse him as a frightened female child.

A few years later, when the writer turned Slade into a legend in *Roughing It*, Twain applauded Slade's fear before the makeshift gallows as true masculine courage: "Slade showed that he was a man of peerless bravery. No coward would dare that."[64] "That" refers to Slade's tears and lamentations to his wife before his accusers summarily hanged the man. As for Millian, Twain admits that Millian's muscles did not quiver—perhaps an act of courage, but also perhaps an act of defiance. This detail marked Millian as a conflicted masculine character, like Slade, for although "Melanie" appeared to perform acts of girlhood, "Millian" also rejected biological fear and showed no sign of trepidation. In *Roughing It*, Twain called this kind of masculine behavior "dying game" or "dying with his boots on," a pantomime of maleness that excited spectators during an entertaining execution. Twain glorified male masculinity in both of the cases of Slade and John Millian, while Twain mocked and feminized Millian and not Slade. "Melanie" becomes Twain's written marker for the feminized cowardice that both repulsed and excited Twain. In this way, Twain's discourse actually shows signs of conflict about the execution of Millian. Such tension existed in Twain's anti-gallows discourse that supported the salvation of Edward Howard Rulloff and Slade—men Twain deemed useful. Melanie, however, is not useful, even if he is pitiful. He is barely even a man.

In the subtitle of the article, Twain calls Millian "the victim." To portray Millian as a victim, Twain first transforms the assassin into "Melanie," a feminized yet nonchalant victim. Yet, at the beginning of the section of the letter that detailed the execution, Twain calls the hanging "Novel Entertainment." But this kind of entertainment was not infectious, at least not for Twain: "I saw it all. I took exact note of every detail ... and I never wish to see it again. I can see that stiff, straight corpse hanging there yet, with its black pillow-cased head turned rigidly to one side, and the purple streaks creeping through the hands and driving the fleshy hue of life before them. Ugh!"[65] While the execution provided entertainment for some spectators, a deterrence for potential criminals, retribution for the State, and torture for the hanging murderer (victim), the torture represented a final image of Twain's conflicted view of justice, especially concerning codes of femininity and masculinity. Twain thought that Millian deserved to die, but perhaps not to be tortured at the gallows. Twain's analysis of this hanging depends on the viewing of a spectacular, excessive event. Millian jerked at the end of rope, his body painted new colors with the blood rushing then stopping in his veins. The culmination of the spectacle ends in death, but the display of the "victim" must elicit a response from the viewer. That response, on some level, must be satisfaction.[66] Twain, in fact, did agree that justice was satisfied on that day of Millian's execution, April 24, 1868, but this justice still sickened him. Perhaps Twain was disgusted with his own satisfaction, even though he wanted to see this man hanging before a crowd of four thousand spectators eating picnic lunches.[67] Still, Twain wanted to see justice performed truthfully. In the case of Millian's execution, the "truth" of the crime was the murder of a woman and what that might symbolize for Twain—the masculine view of women that often included their use and ended with their abuse. In Twain's letter, this kind of "truth" overshadows Millian's repeated claim that he was innocent.

In his confession recorded by his attorney, Charles E. DeLong, Millian claimed that two men had framed him for the murder of Bulette. Millian assured his attorney numerous times that Martha Camp's testimony that led to Millian's arrest was incorrect.[68] Twain does not mention this aspect of the legal case in "Novel Entertainment." He does, however, allude to an "abusive manuscript," a "thin sheet of paper," from which Millian read just before he was hanged.[69] This paper was probably Millian's final statement of gratitude for the women of the "Sisters of Charity" who had come to "minister kindly to his wants" in prison.[70] But in this statement, Millian also claimed his innocence.[71] And yet Twain does not mention the possibility of Millian's innocence or the man's confession in "Novel Entertainment." Perhaps Twain's use of the word "victim" to refer to Millian marks not only Twain's conflicted views about execution, but also his possible uncertainly about the guilt of Millian. Millian's printed claim of innocence may have influenced Twain to recognize Millian as a victim if he had not murdered Bulette. More importantly, Twain's literary vehemence toward Millian clearly supports the writer's view that Bulette was the real victim. Her social status allowed Twain to sympathize with her and to view her, not "Melanie," as the abused and murdered victim. Though Bulette died in the sexual service of men, and Adah Isaacs Menken survived, both women gained notoriety and income from their subversive behaviors. Moreover, aspects of each of these women, and also "Melanie," became the defining traits and behaviors of Twain's abused, provocative performer and murderer Laura Hawkins.

Laura Hawkins and Laura Fair

In 1873, Mark Twain published his first novel, *The Gilded Age*, which was also his only collaborative one. The plot depends on the murder trial of Laura Hawkins, a character based on Laura Fair, an elite prostitute in San Francisco. It is important to make clear the legal case of Fair in order to frame ways in which the real Laura influenced Twain's "Laura." Laura Fair shot her married lover on board a ferryboat in 1870 and was then tried for murder. According to Marion S. Goldman, Laura's "trial involved conflicting claims about the nature of chastity, feminine hysteria, culpability in adultery, and feminists' right to attend murder trials."[72] While the accused murderess waited in jail, Elizabeth Cady Stanton and Susan B. Anthony visited Fair. They then mentioned her in a suffrage speech as evidence for the argument that "a woman must be taught to protect herself" and not to rely on men.[73] Fair was found guilty and sentenced to die, but her conviction was eventually overturned after an appeal granted her a second trial. These sensational courtroom scenes led writers and artists to satirize the state justice, or injustice, which surrounded the case.

On May 11, 1871, in Boston, the *Zion's Herald* published a condemnation of Laura Fair, titled "A Foul Fair." The writer, like others, played with the "foul" nature or the less than "fair" trial of Fair. The article begins by insulting the woman:

> Mrs. Fair, another member of the Samaritan women so common to-day in America, has lately fed the prurient taste, in her trial for the murder of a lawyer in San Francisco, Mr. A. P. Crittenden.... He fell in love with her because she shot her fourth "husband" for daring to hoist the Stars and Stripes over her hotel in Virginia City, Nevada. Down came the flag, and the "husband" with it.[74]

Avoiding the word prostitute, the writer marks Fair's contested social status with Samaritan, one who "helps" men in need, and by using the word husband to denote her lovers. Crittenden was a client of the *prostitute* Fair and then became the victim of the *murderer* Fair. In the first trial, the "jury found her guilty of murder in the first degree, and served her right, as will the sheriff that hangs her,"[75] but a Supreme Court appeal gained her a second trial and then an acquittal in September 1872. During the first trial, however, the journalist of "A Foul Fair" notes that she "used every art, money, accomplishments of dress and person, feigned insanity and sickness, pleas of free-love and its obligations" to influence the jury. Though she was found guilty, and she was guilty, her case eventually did affect a new judgment. Another article, published after the acquittal in 1872, announced that "people conclude that it is her womanhood which shielded Mrs. Fair from the punishment of her crime, and jump to the conclusion that American men will not hang a woman; but it would be nearer the truth to say that they will not hang a charming woman."[76]

Laura Fair was beautiful by contemporary standards, which many people thought helped her case. Even without beauty, "every woman," according to this journalist, "who has committed a capital crime" has "escaped the penalty, though the sympathies of American jurors. Women who are charming may do what seemeth good unto them, so far as the extreme rigor of the law is concerned."[77] These were the sentiments of Jane Grey Cannon Swisshelm, journalist and advocate for rights of women. Ironically, Twain had met Swisshelm, before he began writing *The Gilded Age* and before Laura Fair had committed her crimes, in the fall of 1869. Twain was lecturing in Pittsburg where Swisshelm lived, and the two met and drank at the saloon for the opening banquet.[78] The two became friends and corresponded in writing until she died in 1884. Twain agreed with Swisshelm's condemnation of Laura Fair, which became the dominant opinion in the press. Fair's charm, beauty, sexuality, and womanhood became the focus of her acquittal in order to illustrate the court's poor decision not to satisfy justice. These kinds of criticisms also entered into the popular reception of the case, including newspaper articles and published illustrations. One such image, a lithograph entitled "A wolf in the fold, or a fair trial of Laura" (ca. 1871), depicted Laura Fair's murder scene, imprisonment, and her trial as a mockery.[79]

Each jury member appears in a panel surrounding the central panel of a seductive Laura in her bedroom, wearing only undergarments. Most of the jurors are depicted as animals—a wolf, a rat, a fox, a horse, dogs—and each frame includes a "deprecatory limerick."[80] Below the Horse juror, a conductor, appears the poem "A Conductor that rides, behind a blind Mare/Favored the acquittal, of Laura D. Fair." The language suggests that justice was "blind" behind the female horse, perhaps Fair, and that the juror himself was blind, unable to render justice. Beneath the image of the Rat, a juror whose apparent profession was a wagon or cart driver, appear the lines "A Rat of a draymen, must have been very drunk/Or else he'd convicted, that old flea-e she skunk." Again, the language of the limerick exposes the juror as inept, a drunkard, and finally wrong. But perhaps he was unable to resist the wiles of Laura Fair, a skunk, a seductive and poisonous creature. Even the title of the lithograph plays with the idea of fair—Laura's surname Fair, but also the fairness of the trial. According to images in the lithograph, Laura had seduced the jury with her beauty and her femininity.

Mark Twain never wrote an article about Laura Fair. By the time Fair's case went to trial in San Francisco, Twain had moved to New York, married Livy, and was writing *Roughing It* (1872). But Twain's writing at the time continued to show his interest in and rebuke of state justice, just as it had in his journalism in Nevada. He wove his anti-gallows and anti-jury sentiment throughout *Roughing It*, and he was critical in writing of the New York Supreme Court and the jury system, which appeared in his April

"A wolf in the fold, or a fair trial of Laura" (ca. 1871). Robert B. Honeyman, Jr., collection of early Californian and Western pictorial material, BANC PIC 1963.002:0874-B (courtesy the Bancroft Library, University of California, Berkeley). Laura Fair, an elite prostitute in San Francisco, shot her married lover on board a ferryboat in 1870 and was then tried for murder. Fair was found guilty, sentenced to die, but her conviction was eventually overturned after an appeal granted her a second trial.

29, 1871, letter Whitelaw Reid, editor of the *New-York Tribune*. In *The Gilded Age* Twain played with this idea of Laura—her performance in the courtroom and on a lecture stage, her beauty, her danger—and used the "Fair trial" as inspiration for his character Laura Hawkins to deride the corruption in the courts and the jury system by giving agency to a sexual, influential woman. Twain had watched and judged subversive women for the past ten years, and now he perched one on the seat of justice.

Within this context, the most important plot strand of the sprawling novel involves Laura Hawkins, a Washington, D.C., lobbyist who murders her married lover. Though she is actually guilty, the jury finds her not guilty. Hawkins, because of her newfound fame, tries to become a public lecturer, fails, and dies of "heart disease." A year after Twain and Warner published the novel, the novelists discovered that a journalist in San Francisco named Gilbert B. Desmore had dramatized the novel and created a stage production without obtaining the permission of Twain or Warner. Peeved at the injustice of the theft of his literature and the potential for additional profits to be made from the play, Twain purchased Densmore's script and dramatic rights, and revised the play to his own standards for a New York production. He renamed the play *Colonel Sellers* after one of the major characters.[81] Laura Hawkins also appeared as a prominent character in the stage version, but with one major difference between the dramatic and fictional Lauras. In the novel, Laura is found not guilty in court, but the dramatic script allowed the director and performers to make a choice on the night of the play's staging. Depending on which night the play was staged, Laura was sometimes convicted of murder, and during other performances the character was acquitted for being insane. The editors of the Mark Twain Papers have noted that "according to the few reviews that mentioned the climax of the play, it was in fact performed in two versions. Laura was convicted in performances on 31 August 1874 in Rochester, on 7 September 1874 in Buffalo, and on 16 September 1874 in New York (the present occasion). She was acquitted by reason of insanity on 17 September 1874 in New York, and on 19 April 1875 and 1 May 1875, both in Boston." The editors also note that Laura "is acquitted in two of the three surviving amanuensis copies of the play."[82]

Critic Andrew Carpenter Wheeler saw the play just after it opened in New York in September 1874. He praised the play, the acting and especially actor Mr. John T. Raymond, who played the title character, and Mark Twain for writing his excellent debut drama. Wheeler noted that Twain was present, and after Raymond, the star of the play, came forward for a call, so too did the playwright. Wheeler described this call, which includes Twain's explanation for allowing Laura's guilt to be decided in the courtroom of the theatre each night:

> I thank you for the compliment of this call, and I will take advantage of it to say that I have written this piece in such a way that the jury can bring in a verdict of guilty or not guilty, just as they happen to feel about it. I have done this for this reason. If a play carries its best lesson by teaching what ought to be done in such a case, but is *not* done in real life, then the righteous verdict of guilty should appear; but if the best lesson may be conveyed by holding up the mirror and showing what *is* done every day in such a case but ought *not* to be done, then the satirical verdict of not guilty should appear. I don't know which is best, strict truth and satire, or a nice moral lesson void of both. So I leave my jury free to decide.[83]

Twain's explanation was helpful for his audience's understanding, but this defense carries a larger meaning. He wrote this possible contradiction into the play for a "reason," which is to teach a lesson about what should be done in the courts. The point—Laura should be found guilty, for she was guilty. Twain understood, however, that his novel, and the play on certain nights, reflected reality, not a "righteous" verdict. Laura Fair was acquitted of her crimes in San Francisco, which is why Twain wrote Laura Hawkins to reflect the actual corruption that existed within the courts. Guilty criminals, according to Twain, were found not guilty "every day," even though this practice "ought *not* be done." Though the guilty were released without punishment each day, Twain called such an act "strict truth and satire." Laura's verdict of not guilty is rendered satirical by its reflection of reality. Twain's subversion of reality only occurred on the nights the "jury" found Laura guilty. But this verdict did not reflect the actual legal practices Twain critiques in the novel and in the play. This verdict offered "a nice moral lesson void" of truth and satire.

In other published instances, Twain did not always view execution as a just act. In the case of Laura, however, Twain seeks a divergent verdict. The fictionalized Laura's acquittal illustrates another side of the law and its protectors and executors of justice. The courts cannot be trusted to enact justice when a person should not be executed or when a person should be punished. In *The Gilded Age* Twain is concerned less with showing the brutality of legal or extra-legal execution and more interested in incriminating a corrupt political and legal system.[84] In both cases, Twain argues that justice has not been served; but with Laura's verdict of not guilty, Twain allowed his viewers to witness the truth and satire built into the court's interpretation of justice. The satire also depends on Twain's view of femininity. He, and others in the press, did believe that Laura Fair received special treatment in the courts because she was a woman. Such ambiguity in the decision of guilt reflects Twain's ongoing verdict of the justice system, specifically trial by jury. Twain judged the New York justice system that had judged Edward Howard Rulloff, and with *The Gilded Age* Twain continued to rail against the corruption and ignorance built in to the legal system of justice. For this reason, when the "jury" returned a guilty verdict, Twain permitted his audience to see justice but without the application of truth, which is a more complicated way to view justice.

Wai Chee Dimock, relying on a reading of John Rawls's *A Theory of Justice* (1971), views justice as "analogous to truth not only because it presides as an absolute ideal but also because it exists as an ontological given."[85] Although justice may exist with or without an application of law actually achieving an application of justice, the law sees justice "as having an objective reality," one that is "discoverable through a rational process of deliberation."[86] In the legal case of "Laura," Twain's reimagining of Laura Fair being found guilty, and subject to both justice and to truth, subverted his understanding, his witnessing, of a verdict. Justice in Twain's view, in reality, rarely occurred, even if he allowed justice to be performed on occasion, for his jury "to decide."[87] On those nights, Twain might have been pleased to see the "correct" verdict returned, for it probably satisfied his personal sense of justice. But, on those same nights, Twain's growing insistence on writing "realism" must have left him disappointed. Finding guilt in the guilty did not seem to be realistic.

With the novelistic and dramatic forms of *The Gilded Age*, Twain derided the corruption of the courts and the jury system, but he also illustrated the sexuality, agency, and influence a woman like "Laura" could have over corrupt and ignorant men. Even though Laura is not a positive or respectable character, she is a powerful one, at least for a time. She finally fails as a mild celebrity and speaker and dies alone. Ann M. Ryan has argued that Twain wrote Hawkins as a woman abused and mocked by men, an object of laughter and ridicule and not a symbol of female agency and power. Bryant Morey French has argued a similar point, claiming Twain's "handling of Laura's motivation" to be "negative and unconsciously cynical." French explains this handling of a subversive female character to be typical of the author's "life-long tendency to idealize and romanticize women."[88] Susan K. Harris has argued against French's claims about how Twain handled "Laura," but Harris also suggests that because Twain moved "Laura into the male sphere, Twain found that he could identify with her."[89]

Ultimately, Harris believes that Twain wrote Laura to be a "regressive" female character, for she fails in the public space because Twain pursued Laura as a failure of innocence and as an object of male objectification.[90] In this view, Twain created a subversive, sexual woman in Laura Hawkins and killed her at the end of the novel because he was affirming conservative views of women. In other words, by killing the one female character that represented subversive femininity, Twain was actually portraying women as victims of men. Judith Butler views such a judgment as being from a culture in which "the female body is marked within masculinist discourse, whereby the masculine body, in its conflation with the universal, remains unmarked."[91] Linda A. Morris has applied Butler's ideas when discussing how Mark Twain handled gender when writing *Huckleberry Finn* and *Pudd'nhead Wilson*, which also helps untangle Twain's portrayal of Laura: "I do not mean to suggest that he consciously doubted 'the reality of gender' but as his works make clear, he understood that gender norms could be called into question, and that they are to some extent an artifice."[92]

The positions of Ryan and Harris establish Laura as a regressive female character, especially when viewing the novel as a beginning of Twain's new metropolitan sentiment after he permanently left the West. Their arguments are strong, but perhaps the evidence could also support an alternate use of "Laura," who is a female character developed as a culmination for Twain's western ideology that offers a transition to his metropolitan sentiment. Twain's fictionalized view of an actual western, elite prostitute Laura Fair, who, like Laura Hawkins, escaped capital punishment, illustrates Twain's simultaneous fascination and dismissal of Hawkins, his "lifelong tendency to idealize and romanticize women," while also rebuking the legal system. The woman Twain wrote is alluring, though she is a criminal. She is frail yet courageous, and she performs on stage amidst verbal and physical abuses. And, perhaps most importantly, she is so alluring and powerful that she becomes an agent in the corrupt political society. In reality, men mostly occupied this space, and yet Laura Hawkins uses her beauty, charm, and intelligence to beguile politicians, jurors, and judges. According to Ron Powers, one of the strengths of the Laura Hawkins character is that "she leads the reader into a demimonde of crooked senators, money-grafting lobbyists, toadying journalists, sinister bosses, and lecherous committee chairmen."[93] In other words, she is able to lead the reader through Twain's literary judgment of political and legal corruption precisely because she is a woman. Twain constructed such a powerful woman from the bits and pieces of Fair, Menken, and Bulette—all women he viewed with a certain amount of respect, even if his conservative sensibilities did not allow him to create a strong woman in Laura who could succeed and live.

Hawkins's failure as a public speaker could be used as evidence for Twain's *disrespect* for his female character, especially if only men view and abuse Laura. But the crowd of spectators who mock Hawkins is comprised of "a handful of coarse men and ten or twelve still coarser women."[94] If this scene depicts men as the Laura's abusers, then it also illustrates women spectators contributing to Laura's failed lecture. In fact, this accumulation of "ten or twelve coarser women" comprises an extra-legal jury of Laura's peers. Their judgment, unlike the one rendered in court, is not based on evidence but on sentiment. The women "jurors," and the "course men," have decided that the legal jury failed to render justice. Analyzing this same scene, Ryan has also argued that Twain "exposes" Laura to laughter and ridicule, but that he also "sympathizes" with her.[95] This complicated or conflicting method to expose Laura Hawkins to shame and sympathy is, perhaps, Twain's way of depicting a female character that is both alluring and despicable but ultimately unredeemable. Though Twain wrote none of the trial scenes that eventually led to a verdict of not guilty, and Charles Dudley Warren wrote these scenes of vindication, Twain created the Laura character and designed the plot. Twain also wrote the scenes that depict the failure of Laura on the lecture circuit. This novel allows the reader to render a new decision each time the narrative is consumed.

Fiction need not "decide." But Twain has certainly judged Laura, because of her subversive gender performance and because legal justice is not satisfied. After the extra-legal judgment of Laura, Twain finally builds a case for the justice of Laura's death by providing evidence that she is a "heartless seducer of the affections of weak and misguided men."[96] Such language suggests that Twain did not need to find morality in Laura, but he did need to find in her strength. After all, the men she seduces are not admirable or strong—at least not to Twain. Even though men "always spoke of her in terms of mocking eulogy and ironical admiration,"[97] a mixture of contradictory emotions, Twain places his "determined" Laura on public display, to be mocked, but also to "show these people what a hunted and persecuted woman could do."[98] Before taking the stage, Laura tells the lecture agent not to "fear" for her—she is bold and has been a successful lobbyist and seducer of men. "These people" are men and women, which creates a possibility of non-gendered judgment, unlike the legal judgment in court. The legal jurors are all men. In court, Laura seduced men and influenced justice, and yet this quarrel between men and women is not the determining factor that brings Laura to her final public judgment. This ideological space between men's and women's views, what Dimock calls "a zone of problematic residuum,"[99] exists in justice, perhaps in court, but in the crowd both men and women "jurists" judge Laura. In spite of Laura's confidence and ability, her "determination," however, she does not succeed as a lecturer. Spectators mock and batter her, and she admits that her "pride was humbled, her spirit was broken."[100] Twain, exerting his authorial authority as judge and executioner, finally kills Laura with heart disease. This failure and subsequent death could be Twain's final abuse of Laura Hawkins. Or, Twain might have ended her life because, in his experience, female performers and criminals must pay for their subversive acts with their lives, even ones based on women, and girls, who had attracted Clemens's gaze for the first half of his life.

Samuel Clemens's actual childhood sweetheart was named Laura Hawkins. He based the character of Becky Thatcher on Laura, and we know that Tom is immediately attracted to Becky when first they meet. Mark Twain did not give the fictional Laura Hawkins the name of Samuel Clemens's sweetheart as a simple way to demonstrate his affection for a political and sexual seducer of men, but he did intentionally choose the name of a girl of personal import for his complicated female character. The allure of Clemens's Laura, and later of other "Lauras," inspired his creation of Twain's fictional Laura.[101] Laura's charisma reflects a mosaic of many women's identities, experiences, and deaths. The fictional Laura Hawkins dies at 28 of heart disease, a physical manifestation of her emotional wound.[102] Twain undoubtedly knew that Adah Isaacs Menken had also died young, at the age of thirty-three. She died in poor physical health in 1868, four months after Mark Twain published his article about the execution of John "Melanie," one year after Millian had murdered Julia Bulette, and a handful of years before Twain began collaborating with Charles Dudley Warren to write *The Gilded Age*. And finally, the actual "Lauras": Laura Hawkins (married name, Frazer) lived past 90 and became "the matron of a Hannibal home for orphans and the indigent."[103] Laura Fair got away with murder. She continued to live a sexually promiscuous life that ended in old age. It may seem obvious that to illustrate a view of gendered judgment Twain selected the life, and trial, of Laura Fair, rather than Adah Isaacs Menken, Julia Bulette, or John "Melanie," as the subject of a novel and a play. But Twain had already abused Menken in print and then befriended her before she died young. Bulette was murdered, and

Millian was hanged. Twain celebrated the legal decision to hang Bulette's murderer. Laura Fair's legal case, however, allowed Twain to reassess justice and to "re-decide" an unjust decision.

So, did Twain retry Laura Fair in the literary courts of *The Gilded Age*? Literature, unlike law, seeks multiple possibilities. Law judges guilt or not guilt, but literature explores complex ways to view justice. According to Dimock, "literary justice" differs from legal and philosophical justice. Literary justice holds the residues of "a different tradition and carrying with it a different vocabulary, a different language with which to describe the world and what matters in the world." This treatment of justice stands "as a supplement and as a corrective to any legal or philosophical propositions."[104] And, in the cases of the "Lauras," Twain gave a personality to the "problem of justice" largely because he had watched and judged these women.[105] He also viewed gender performance in compound ways that surpassed the conservative binary of male and female. Twain marked Menken as both "manly" and as a "finely formed woman," but he also infantilized her. Menken flaunted gender norms, which complicated Twain's need to marvel at Adah Isaacs Menken and his desire to judge "The Menken." But this experience solidified into a concrete ideology at the execution of John Millian: "This is the man I wanted to see hung." Perhaps this desire influenced Twain's decision to kill Laura at the end of the novel when the jury decided not to. Such a method might also be at play in the dramatizations that did find Laura guilty. Millian's execution, like Menken's performance, and later Laura's, still attracted Twain's marvel and judgment. A brave, "nonchalant" victim and yet a "happy girl," Millian represented for Twain the satisfaction of justice. The spectacle of justice, however, relied upon Twain's blurred binary of John Millian, a "man" and "Melanie," the skipping little girl. Twain reported these details about the man and his execution in "Novel Entertainment," and yet the journalist seemed more concerned with Millian's performance on the gallows and its resolution than with delivering the facts of the legal case. For nearly a year Millian had claimed to be innocent, and yet Twain marveled at the Frenchman whom Twain considered a "heartless assassin" who had invaded Bulette's crib. Twain also labeled Millian a calm, carefree girl performing the bravado of a "badman" skipping to the gallows like a "happy girl."

Twain' ability (or need) to admire and judge finally allowed him to conflate these women and men, including their performatives that often produced gender reversals, into the fictional Laura Hawkins. She is one of Mark Twain's most multifaceted inventions, who exists and dies because Samuel Clemens loved a girl in his youth, but especially because Mark Twain interpreted subversive women in the West as objects of marvel and disdain. This multi-vocal Laura displays the sexualized performer and controversial personality of Adah Isaacs Menken, and yet Menken did not commit murder. She performed in America and Europe and died in Paris at the age of thirty-three, perhaps due to complications from tuberculosis. She died poor and was buried as such in the "paupers' enclave of the Jewish section of Père Lachaise."[106] If Twain had found her subversive in 1864, perhaps he sympathized with a lonely and impoverished Menken in 1868, the same year Millian was hanged for murdering an impoverished and sympathetic Julia Bulette. Initially, though, Twain's fictional Laura Hawkins is more like Menken than Bulette in that Hawkins is publically influential and occupies a more elite social position than does Bulette. Laura Hawkins, like Bulette, becomes the victim of her own sexual subversion, though Hawkins is not the victim of murder. Laura Hawkins is, however, "Melanie," a murderer ridiculed by Twain, though Twain does not execute her. Instead, Twain torments Laura with a "mob" that hurls insults and stones that emotionally and physically wound her.[107] While she recovers, Twain gives her thoughts of her "girlhood," when she danced "in the budding grace" of her youth.[108] For the last moments of her life, she is a type of "happy girl," a girl whose heart is "full of music."[109] But then comes night, and sorrow, and Twain leaves Laura alone to die. Days pass, and "the keepers of house" become "uneasy."[110] They finally enter Laura's home, but they do not discover a fresh corpse in bed, with a smashed temple and bruises on her neck left by her male murderer, as the police found Julia Bulette. The housekeepers instead find a silent and still Laura seated at the table, "face upon the hands,"[111] where Twain withheld a violent death. A quiet death had come, and with it, Twain's final literary exploitation of Laura Hawkins.

Afterword: Mark Twain's Contradictory "Messiness": Murderer, Judge and Hangman

On the page, Mark Twain committed many acts of murder, judgment, and execution. *The Gilded Age*'s Laura Hawkins was neither his first nor his last quarry. Some, like Laura, expired gently, sadly. As if sleeping, head resting on her folded hands on the table, she died "from heart disease, and was instant and painless. That was all. Merely heart disease."[1] Laura's soft death that visits her in the lonely night represents Twain's final verdict of Laura, a murderess, a subversive, sexualized woman who escaped legal justice. In this case, Twain's literary murder is an act of extra-legal literary execution.

The verdict: Twain's western journalism and hoaxes, letters, *Roughing It* (1872) and *The Gilded Age* (1873) report on or expose violent acts, often by celebrating such violence, which signaled his anxieties about gender and justice. In addition, the reports on or creations of violence were literary productions intended to sell periodicals and papers, books, and eventually "Mark Twain." Finally, his western writing and the two books influenced by his time in West followed in a lineage of sensational literature produced in periodicals and novels spanning antebellum America to post-war America. Between 1862 and 1873, Twain judged the acts of men and women and offered verdicts beyond the scope of the law. Whereas a judge "pronounces" a sentence that reflects his legal legitimacy and authority, Twain pronounced judgments that do not illustrate his "uncontested power,"[2] but instead show *how* he contested power. Twain performs, or reclaims, power in his factual reporting that contains facts but, more importantly, facts told in exaggerated ways that depend on graphically described murders. Such journalism, and especially hoaxes, mixes enough factual details to make believable the fictional account of horror and murder. Twain's sensational journalism, hoaxes, and fiction were lies, often crafted from truths, meant not to harm but to offer information, or a way to assess information, about a factual or philosophical set of circumstances. In all cases, this kind of writing delivered subversions of facts, created warnings for readers, and promoted a kind of justice.

Literature, according to Wai Chee Dimock contains "residues" of justice that authors explore in complicated ways unavailable to law or philosophy. She argues that literary texts reject the formal logic of law and instead seek a justice "whose lineaments are traceable in the fate of some specific characters, generating not only an ever-widening horizon of meaning but also an ever-widening spectrum of queries."[3] Dimock eventually applies this idea to Kate Chopin's *The Awakening* (1899), especially to the ending in which Edna gives herself to the water and dies noticing "the hum of bees, and the musky odor of pinks."[4] Laura's ending is not unlike Edna's in that they both generate a vast "horizon" of meaning. Specifically, both female protagonists fail to find total freedom, though Edna chooses here death and thereby selects an outcome unavailable to Laura. Laura expires a defeated woman, not a woman freed from the bounds of male control or familial dissatisfaction. Perhaps, then, this horizon of meaning is so large *because* it opens "an ever-widening spectrum of queries." By this I mean that queries depend on multiple meanings, that meanings suggest questions rather than satisfy questions. For Dimock, endings fulfill these questions because a final verdict, such as Chopin's or Twain's, "dissolves all conflict, clearing away all lingering doubt, all lingering messiness."[5]

Twain was not always consistent on views of justice or gender, perhaps, in part, because he wrote sensational views. Therefore, no verdict can possibly clear away all "lingering messiness." For example, he did not always support the agency of women in his literature. Nor did he always write them as victims. Laura is both powerful and a victim. Such a contradictory character grew from Twain's views on women as rape victims, prostitutes, murderers, wives, sisters, mothers, and as fellow writers. These residues exist in the character of Laura and in *The Gilded Age*. But this tension also appears in his San Francisco reports on rapists and "demoralizers." If Twain believed that the "beasts in the semblance of men" that raped women deserved punishment, he also believed that some women like Roberts or McQuinn, victims of men, had welcomed the violence the "beasts" enacted.

Furthermore, Twain did not always support the retribution of male murderers. He romanticized J.A. Slade in *Roughing It*, who in reality killed many men. Yet Twain found him to be the most "useful" man in the region and lamented Slade's extra-legal hanging. Twain later wrote that in drafting the chapters about Slade, he had a goal: "I thought I would just rescue my late friend Slade from oblivion & set a sympathetic public to weeping for him."[6] After all, though he was a murderer, he was also a useful "desperado" whom women travelers, powerful men and owners of companies, and criminals all feared. To a certain extent, as a journalist reporting on murder and murderers, Twain used Slade as a model for manliness and boldness. Such a man attracted attention, fear, respect, and Twain wanted such notice. He learned that writing about murder and other violence gained him success. A story about a murdered man got published. In *Roughing It*, Twain's narrator remembers discovering this truth and "wrote up the murder with a hungry attention to details."[7] Joseph Goodman, his boss at the *Enterprise*, encouraged him to do this always, which caused Twain great pride. He notes, "I felt that I could take my pen and murder all the immigrants on the plains if need be and the interests of the paper demanded it."[8] In this reflection, we see that Twain did not commit these literary murders to reinforce codes of justice or to expose a murderer. He wrote about them because murder benefited him as a writer.

In 1871, Twain also thought Edward Howard Rulloff, the scholar-murderer, represented a social benefit too great to execute. When Twain wrote to the *New-York Tribune* for the commutation of Rulloff's death sentence, Twain hoped that his readers would notice, would care, would act. He wanted readers to "discover that regret is growing up in their souls that the man is going to be hung. If the *talk* gets started once, that is sufficient—they'll *all* talk, pretty soon, & then the *acting* will come easily & naturally."[9] In this case, Twain's response to punishment was not meant to bring attention to him, the man and the writer, though this might have been a side effect. Rather, Twain intended for people to consider the man Rulloff. And yet, these literary responses to Rulloff and to Slade, whose lives both ended on the gallows, do not clear "away all lingering doubt" that Twain opposed violence, murder, or legal and extra-legal hanging.

In yet another example, Twain portrays the usefulness of one man. When Colonel Sherburn backs down a lynch mob in *The Adventures of*

Huckleberry Finn (1884), justice is not the cause. Sherburn's show of manliness stops the mob. He calls the men in the mob cowards, less than men, without "pluck enough to lynch a *man*." They might be "brave enough to tar and feather poor friendless cast-out women," but they have not "grit enough" to touch a man.[10] Here, Twain celebrates singular manliness in the face of a crowd filled with lesser aims in opposition to the lone heroic man. Twain admired Slade for similar reasons. And, Sherburn, like Slade, is a murderer, but, according to Twain, neither man deserves to die.

Though Twain chose to save, or attempted to save, the lives of murderers such as Slade, Sherburn, and Rulloff, Twain also chose to execute a woman, Laura, who had done no worse. Such contradictions have led some literary critics such as Susan K. Harris and Myra Jehlen to argue that Twain used his novels, especially *Huckleberry Finn* and *The Gilded Age*, to mock women and femininity. For such critics, these abuses tell a different story than the one this book has narrated. Harris and Jehlen argue that all of the "lingering doubt" and "lingering messiness" in Twain's writing of justice culminates with his criticisms of women rather than with explorations of their subversive performances. My argument differs because of its link to sensational journalism and fiction—a starting point for Twain's literary career—for it illustrates that Twain's writing about these women reflected his appreciation for or the usefulness of subversive women. Twain had accomplished something similar with the writing of Slade, Rulloff, and Sherburn. From Harris's and Jehlen's readings of Twain, which are necessary for my reading to exist, perhaps we do not see "an ever-widening horizon of meaning" for Twain's judgments of women. Instead, that horizon becomes narrowed so that we see less "messiness" and a clearer answer: subversive women deserve mockery and death; subversive men deserve applause and salvation.

Twain's writing in the West participated in a periodical marketplace and used a style developed by writers such as George Lippard, George Thompson, and Ned Buntline. Such an argument functions as an additive, rather than as a corrective, to scholarship about Twain's gender anxieties and his writing from the West and about it. Ann M. Ryan, Susan K. Harris, Linda A. Morris, and Laura Skandera Trombley have contributed foundational gender analyses to which I owe credit. Several scholars' work about Twain's western experience also deserve notice. Roy Morris, Jr.'s *Lighting Out for the Territory: How Samuel Clemens Headed West and Became Mark Twain* (New York: Simon & Schuster, 2010) offers a literary biography, and Joe B. Fulton's *The Reconstruction of Mark Twain: How a Confederate*

Bushwhacker Became the Lincoln of Our Literature (Baton Rouge: Louisiana State University Press, 2010) discusses Twain's western years as a time of "transformation" into the literary figure that Twain would become. Lawrence I. Berkove's *The Sagebrush Anthology* (Columbia: University of Missouri Press, 2006), Joseph L. Coulombe's *Mark Twain and the American West* (Columbia: University of Missouri Press, 2003), and James E. Caron's *Mark Twain: Unsanctified Newspaper Reporter* (Columbia: University of Missouri Press, 2008) have been especially influential. Berkove suggests that the literature produced by Twain's western contemporary writers is worthy to read and analyze, as is Twain's lesser-read western writing. Coulombe discusses Twain's masculine performance as a writer responding to western violence, and Caron analyzes and contextualizes Twain's performative voice and periodical writing.

I have built on this scholarly foundation to illustrate Twain's view of gender and justice within a sensational framework that relies on a writer's discourse of violence. Caron's book explores in detail "Mark Twain" as a "vehicle by which Sam Clemens expressed his comic genius."[11] I add to this claim that "Mark Twain" also advanced a sensational violent critique of violence, sometimes humorous, often times satirical, judgmental, and serious. Caron makes a nod to sensational literature, noting that Twain's description of his arrival into Honolulu harbor "exhibits stylistic flourishes typical of a blood-and-thunder tale, the sort found in the New York *Ledger* and other story papers that dominated American popular culture since midcentury."[12] Caron compares Twain's sensational style to two specific writers, claiming that Twain's "exotic narrative elements" are able "to hold their own with anything George Lippard or 'Ned Buntline' could conjure."[13] Though this statement connects Twain's writing to sensational, antebellum periodical writing, most of Caron's discussion of periodicals focuses on humor writing. Certainly, Twain showed his periodical readers a good time, but he also showed them what was wrong in the culture buy employing sensational techniques that expose these ills: he applied violent discourse to critique violence; he wrote responses to analyze how men and women performed gender. And like his sensational journalist and novelist predecessors and his western contemporaries, Twain helped to sell newspapers and eventually to sell "Twain" to a nation.

Twain was critical of legal justice and sometimes supported extralegal justice. Though these criticisms appeared in his early western writing, *Roughing It*, and in *The Gilded Age*, such judgments about justice continued to gain literary treatment even beyond *Huckleberry Finn*. For example, the resolution of *Pudd'nhead Wilson* (1894) depends on contradictory legal decisions. "Tom," a slave reared as a white man whose life has been switched with the actual Tom, is a man of poor character. Toward the end of the tale, he murders Judge Driscoll. In the conclusion, "Tom" confesses to murder and is sentenced to life in prison. Twain, however, is dissatisfied with a legal decision that has imprisoned a cruel imposter, while the "real" Tom has toiled as a slave his entire life. So Twain brings forth creditors who petition the court to recognize "Tom" as their property, for he is a rightful slave. They claim that had he *been* a slave, rather than *performing* as a free man, "Tom" could never have murdered the judge. They would have sold him to offset their losses long before he would have had the chance to murder anyone. And so the "Governor" decides to pardon "Tom" and return him to the creditors. Twain's final words deliver a complication with legal justice: "the creditors sold him down the river."[14] Though the court "decides" two legal judgments, the real justice occurs when "Tom" must now perform the social retribution of slavery. Being "sold down the river" is a harsher punishment that serving life in prison. Certainly, a pardon is a legal act, and yet it preserves the ironic application of extra-legal justice that being delivered into a new state of slavery must display. "Tom," then, signifies the deposit of Twain's contradictory judgment: the legal punishment is insufficient to satisfy the justice that "Tom" deserves.

For a final view of Twain's contradiction personified in one character, I offer Hank Morgan, Twain's hero in *A Connecticut Yankee in King Arthur's Court* (1889). According to Roy Blount, Jr., Morgan's narrative "voice is a flatter version of Twain's." The novel itself is less a novel and more "a performance by Mark Twain, preformed over the course of the period, 1886–89."[15] And the performance is a spectacular one, comprising a sensational act of extra-legal execution, in this case, electric execution. In one scene, Hank Morgan prepares an elaborate system of electric fences to annihilate an invading army in Medieval England. The troops are attempting to overthrow the just political system and eliminate the "improved" laws that Hank Morgan has helped to establish in a barbaric land. As the troops advance, he activates the fences, burning and killing "eleven thousand men." His victims' bodies explode with electricity, and he celebrates his success and the sensational sight:

> Land, what a sight! We were enclosed in three walls of dead men! All the other fences were pretty nearly filled with the living, which were stealthily working their way forward through the wires. The sudden glare paralyzed this host, petrified them, you may say, with astonishment; there was just one instant for me

> to utilize their immobility in, and I didn't lose the chance. You see, in another instant they would have burst into a cheer and made a rush, and my wires would have gone down before it; but that lost instant lost them their opportunity forever; while even that slight fragment of time was still unspent, I shot the current through all the struck the whole host dead in their track! *There* was a groan you could hear! It voiced the death-pang of eleven thousand men. It swelled out on the night with awful pathos.[16]

Hank's description, with all its exclamation points, provides gory details about a mass execution. So many bodies litter the earth that their corpses form "three walls of dead men." The invisible fourth "wall," established by Hank and his fences, contains this scene within a metaphorical institutional space, indeed, within the walls of a chamber of execution. Hank concludes the scene with an appeal, a "pathos," which occurs under the weight of eleven thousand groans, of death-pangs. A "terrible thing" precedes these groans: the silence of the men approaching the wall, "the absence of human voices," the cheerless night that knew "no war cries."[17] As haunting and terrible as men's silence might have been just before they died, the groans of death are not terrible. Though Hank Morgan and Mark Twain appeal to our emotions at the end of this death scene, they have petitioned for the celebration of violence at its beginning.

And herein lies Twain's literary contradiction, not to be resolved, but to be examined and appreciated. Samuel Clemens's and Mark Twain's western journalism from the 1860s and Mark Twain's novels through the 1870s, 1880s, and 1890s depended on contradictions. Twain, and the sensational writers within this book, ask their readers to look at "what a sight!"; they then advance a pathos so that readers can consider the horror of the violence, understand its cause, and seek justice, even if mobs and courts do not. Finally, then, this book does not avoid these contradictions or seek "a verdict that resolves all conflict." Twain's western writing relied on contradiction: sensational literary responses to violent crime and punishment (whether journalistic or fictional) always involve the use and celebration of violence.

Twain wrote about violence with a discourse of violence. Fellow journalists Dan De Quille, Joseph T. Goodman, and Samuel Post Davis also responded to violence by portraying such acts as necessary or useful or simply existent. For twenty years before Twain used this technique, American writers George Lippard, George Thompson, Ned Buntline, Emerson Bennett, and John Rollin Ridge had glorified excessive violence in periodicals and novels as a means to expose the horrors of crime in the city and in the expanding West. In light of the cases presented in this book,

Twain's murders represent a kind of justice. Twain kills Laura Hawkins because the actual San Francisco jury could not sentence a beautiful murderess Laura Fair to die. Conversely, he saves Hank Morgan from being burned at the stake, so Morgan could later satisfy justice by murdering thousands of men. Twenty-five years before he rescued Morgan, however, Twain openly judged and condemned men and women. In a literary sense, he saved Slade, Rulloff, and Sherburn. Some characters, like Laura, were less fortunate. Still, in his journalism, Twain did clear "away all lingering doubt" for the punishment of many others—even if found not guilty in reality, or whose guilt did not warrant punishments equal to the ones he would have gladly given. He did not mind the killing. Twain depended on death, even if he had to create it. This method echoed the technique used by George Lippard and Dan De Quille, Ned Buntline and Bret Harte. And such "creation" reflected many emigrants' desires to recreate themselves by finding in the West rejuvenation. Though, as Twain learned, a western Eden did not exist. Instead he found murderers, rapists, and lynch mobs, overburdened police forces, female victims, and corrupt courts. In the West, Mark Twain found his literary voice of judgment, birthed from violence, written in blood.

Chapter Notes

Introduction

1. "Sam Clemens," 1863, Age 27, Carson City, Nevada, courtesy of the Mark Twain Papers, Bancroft Library.
2. SLC to Jane Lampton Clemens, 4 Nov 1868, New York, N.Y. (*UCCL 02762*).
3. James E. Caron, *Mark Twain: Unsanctified Newspaper Reporter* (Columbia: University of Missouri Press, 2008), 3.
4. For more about Twain and the West and his influences, see these works: Three works by Lawrence I. Berkove, *Insider Stories of the Comstock Lode and Nevada's Mining Frontier 1859–1909: Primary Sources in American Social History* (Lewiston, New York: The Edwin Mellen Press, 2007); "Nevada Influences on Mark Twain." *A Companion to Mark Twain*. eds. Messent and Budd. (Malden, MA: Blackwell, 2005); and *The Sagebrush Anthology* (Columbia: University of Missouri Press, 2006). Also, Tom Quirk, "Mark Twain and Human Nature." *A Companion to Mark Twain* eds. Peter Messent and Louis J. Budd. (Oxford: Blackwell, 2005), 21–37. In addition, Joseph L. Coulombe, *Mark Twain and the American West* (Columbia: University of Missouri Press, 2003). James E. Caron, *Mark Twain: Unsanctified Newspaper Reporter* (Columbia: University of Missouri Press, 2008). Gary Scharnhorst, "Twain and the Literary Construction of the West." *A Companion to Mark Twain*, ed. Messent and Budd. (Malden, MA: Blackwell, 2005). Finally, Joe B. Fulton, *The Reconstruction of Mark Twain: How a Confederate Bushwhacker Became the Lincoln of Our Literature* (Baton Rouge: Louisiana State University Press, 2010).
5. For excellent discussions of Mark Twain's realistic style, see Bruce Michelson's *Mark Twain on the Loose: A Comic Writer and the American Self* (Amherst: University of Massachusetts Press, 1995), especially the chapters "Mark Twain and the Escape from Sense" and "The Quarrel with Romance." Joe B. Fulton's *Mark Twain's Ethical Realism: The Aesthetics of Race, Class, and Gender* (Columbia: The University of Missouri Press, 1997), and to a lesser extent, his more recent book, *The Reconstruction of Mark Twain: How a Confederate Bushwhacker Became the Lincoln of Our Literature* (Baton Rouge: Louisiana State University Press, 2010), explores the idea of realism in Twain's writing. Brook Thomas's *American Literary Realism and the Failed Promise of Contract* (Berkeley: University of California Press, 1999) contains numerous discussions of realism and explores the laws concerning race in America against a reading of Twain in the chapter "Twain, Tourgée, and the Logic of 'Separate but Equal.'" Michael Davitt Bell's *The Problem of American Realism: Studies in the Cultural History of a Literary Idea* (Chicago: University of Chicago Press, 1993) also complicates the realistic tradition of Howells, James, and Twain. See especially the chapter "Humor, Sentiment, Realism: Mark Twain."
6. David S. Reynolds, *Beneath the American Renaissance: The Subversive Imagination*

in the Age of Emerson and Melville (Cambridge: Harvard University Press, 1988), 3.

7. Shelley Streeby, "Sensational Fiction," A Companion to American Fiction, ed. Shirley Samuels (Oxford: Blackwell, 2002), 183.

8. David S. Reynolds, Beneath the American Renaissance: The Subversive Imagination in the Age of Emerson and Melville (Cambridge: Harvard University Press, 1988), 88.

9. Reynolds, "Introduction" to Venus in Boston and Other Tales of Nineteenth-Century City Life (Amherst: University of Massachusetts Press, 2002), xv.

10. Ibid., xxvi.

11. Streeby, 181.

12. J. Randolph Cox, The Dime Novel Companion: A Source Book (Westport, CT: Greenwood Press, 2000), 25.

13. Mark Twain, Roughing It (New York: Penguin, 1981), 168.

14. See publisher's advertisement, The Bride of the Wilderness (Philadelphia: T.B. Peterson, 1854).

15. James W. Parins, John Rollin Ridge: His Life and Works (Lincoln: University of Nebraska Press, 2004), 78, 121.

16. SLC to Jane Lampton Clemens and Pamela A. Moffett, 25 Sept 1864, San Francisco, Calif. (UCCL 00087).

17. Branch and Hirst, 30.

18. Reynolds, "Introduction" to Venus in Boston and Other Tales of Nineteenth-Century City Life (Amherst: University of Massachusetts Press, 2002), xv.

19. John Rollin Ridge, The Life and Adventures of Joaquin Murieta, the Celebrated California Bandit (Norman: University of Oklahoma Press, 1955), xxxiii.

20. Editors' Note 2, MTP, SLC to Jane Lampton Clemens and Family, 20 Nov 1867, New York, N.Y. (UCCL 00155). Also discussed by R. Kent Rasmussen, Mark Twain A–Z: The Essential Reference to His Life and Writings (New York: Oxford University Press, 1995), 336.

21. SLC to Jane Lampton Clemens and Pamela A. Moffett, 24 Jan 1868, Hartford, Conn. (UCCL 00182).

22. Isaac Clarke Pray, Memoirs of James Gordon Bennett and His Times: By a Journalist (New York: Stringer & Townsend, 1855), 194.

23. "Mark Twain's Letters from Washington. Number IX," Virginia City Territorial Enterprise, 7 March 1868. Quoted in Branch and Hirst, Early Tales and Sketches, Volume 1: 1851–1864 (Berkeley: University of California Press, 1979), 21.

24. Branch and Hirst, 245.

25. Twain wrote "Horrible Affair" in April 1863 in response to a criminal, named Campbell, murdering two of Twain's friends and the lynch mob that came after Campbell. Twain published "A Bloody Massacre Near Carson," on 28 October 1863, in response to the Spring Valley Water Company's greedy water-hoarding practices.

26. Gary Scharnhorst, "Introduction" to The Luck of Roaring Camp and Other Writings (New York: Penguin Books, 2001), xii.

Chapter 1

1. Note 6, SLC to Orion and Mary E. (Mollie) Clemens, 19 and 20 Oct 1865, San Francisco, Calif.

2. Ibid.

3. SLC to Orion and Mary E. (Mollie) Clemens, 19 and 20 Oct 1865, San Francisco, Calif.

4. Joe B. Fulton cites portions of this letter, but not the section about "Self-Murder." See The Reconstruction of Mark Twain: How a Confederate Bushwhacker Became the Lincoln of Our Literature (Baton Rouge: Louisiana State University Press, 2010). Roy Morris, Jr., in Lighting Out for the Territory: How Samuel Clemens Headed West and Became Mark Twain (New York: Simon & Schuster, 2012), does briefly discuss this suicidal moment as a turning point in Twain's career: "he put down the pistol and picked up the pen" (158).

5. Mark Twain, "A Strange Dream," The New-York Saturday Press, 2 June 1866, MTP.

6. SLC to Orion and Mary E. (Mollie) Clemens, 28 Sept 1864, San Francisco, Calif. (UCCL 00088). In a letter to his brother and sister-in-law in 1865, Twain noted that he wanted to write for a paper with "an exalted reputation in the east, & is liberally copied from by papers like the Home Journal."

7. Ibid., 20.

8. Branch and Hirst, Early Tales and Sketches, Volume 1: 1851–1864 (Berkeley: University of California Press, 1979), 21.

9. Joseph Coulombe, Mark Twain and the American West (Columbia: University of Missouri Press, 2003), 48.

10. SLC to Orion and Mary E. (Mollie) Clemens, 19 and 20 Oct 1865, San Francisco, Calif.
11. Ron Powers, *Mark Twain: A Life* (New York: Free Press, 2005), 153.
12. Branch and Hirst, 399.
13. *Ibid.*, 21.
14. SLC to Orion and Mary E. (Mollie) Clemens, 19 and 20 Oct 1865.
15. In "Discourse in the Novel" (1934–35), Mikhail Bakhtin notes that, "Certain features of language take on the specific flavor of a given genre: they knit together with specific points of view, specific approaches, forms of thinking..." (289). Though Bakhtin is discussing fiction, these terms and ideas are relevant for the analysis of Twain's early work that depends on the construction of a literary persona so that he can offer competing ideas within one piece of work. Twain appropriates language in dialogic formation, which allows him to be both philosophic and popular. This idea complicates Coulombe's argument, for Twain's early writing delivered by an invented masculine persona advances Twain's, and his readers', voice within a certain set of conditions in the West—violent, growing in population, and the birthplace of Twain's literary popularity. Furthermore, the dialogic style of these news items suggests Twain's concern with context over text, or, to use another of Bakhtin's terms, heteroglossia.
16. "Man Shot," published on July 5 in the *Enterprise* and reprinted in the *Daily Morning Call*, 9 July 1863, MTP.
17. "Man Shot," *Daily Morning Call*, 9 July 1863, MTP.
18. Ronald M. James, *The Roar and the Silence: A History of Virginia City and the Comstock Lode* (Reno: University of Nevada Press, 1998), 172.
19. Mark Twain, *Roughing It*, 413.
20. Ronald M. James, *The Roar and the Silence: A History of Virginia City and the Comstock Lode* (Reno: University of Nevada Press, 1998), 171–172.
21. *Ibid.*, 245.
22. *Roughing It*, 414.
23. Frederick Jackson Turner, "The Significance of the Frontier in American History," 1893, excerpted from *The American Studies Hypertexts Project* at the University of Virginia, 7.
24. *Roughing It*, 415.
25. "False Report," *Daily Morning Call*, 9 July 1863, MTP.
26. *Roughing It*, 304.
27. *Ibid.*, 305.
28. "The Compositor," Typothetae Dinner, Delmonico's, New York, January 18, 1886. *Mark Twain Speaking*, ed. Paul Fatout (Iowa City: University of Iowa Press, 1976), 200.
29. *Ibid.*
30. Judith Butler, *Gender Trouble: Feminism and the Subversion of Identity* (New York: Routledge, 1990), xv.
31. Judith Butler, *Excitable Speech: A Politics of the Performative* (New York: Routledge, 1997), 40.
32. *Ibid.*, 49.
33. Ronald M. James, *The Roar and the Silence: A History of Virginia City and the Comstock Lode* (Reno: University of Nevada Press, 1998), 173.
34. "Brutal Affrays in Washoe," 19 April 1864, *Territorial Enterprise*.
35. "Another Innocent Man Killed," 16 September 1862. Cited by Barbara Schmidt, text recovered by Michael Marleau. Reprinted in *Mark Twain Journal* (Fall 2004): 11–12.
36. Though humor is one of Twain's signature stylistic markers, withholding humor in cases of innocent people's physical abuses or murders is also a common feature in his journalism. I would not necessarily extend this ethic to all of Twain's more popular works of fiction, however. For example in *Huckleberry Finn*, Jim is innocent of any crime (other than escaping slavery), and yet the narrative offers numerous gags at Jim's expense. The snakebite birthed from his superstition and Tom's elaborate plan to "rescue" Jim at the end, even though he is already free, are two good examples. Of course, race and slavery exist at the heart of this narrative, rather than violent crime in the West.
37. *Roughing It*, 336.
38. SLC to Pamela A. Moffett, 15, August 1862, MTP. In a letter to Pamela, Twain notes that his friend and cabin mate Dan Twing attended the funeral of Dr. Chorpening. He "was shot by Wm. Pooler for being too attentive to Pooler's wife." ("Esmeralda Correspondence," 20 August 1862, Sacramento *Bee*, MTP. Signed Veni, Vidi). This story also had regional significance because Dr. Chorpening was the brother of George Chorpening, who recently, in 1860, had become the

mail contractor in the Territories of Utah and Nevada and in California.

39. For additional stories about "affrays," especially those influenced by alcohol, disputes over mining claims, often set inside or outside of saloons, see *Roughing It*, "Chapter XLIX." Twain's narrator begins the chapter with an introduction and then a selection of such stories, noted here by their titles: "An extract or two from the newspapers of the day will furnish a photograph that can need no embellishment: "Fatal Shooting Affray," "Robbery and Desperate Affray," and "More Cutting and Shooting." The narrator ends this chapter with a lament for the legal justice system: "...as far as I can learn, only two persons have suffered the death penalty there. However, four or five who had no money and no political influence have been punished by imprisonment."

40. "Offices," 19 November 1863, *Daily Morning Call*, MTP.

41. Lawrence I. Berkove, *The Sagebrush Anthology: Literature from the Silver Age of the Old West* (Columbia: University of Missouri Press, 2006), 5–6.

42. Quoted by James, 172.

43. "Death—Robbery," 2 December 1863, *Daily Morning Call*, reprinted in Ivan Benson, *Mark Twain's Western Years* (New York: Russell & Russell, 1966), 178.

44. "Dispatches by the State Line (SPECIALLY TO THE *DAILY MORNING CALL*)" 3 September 1863, MTP.

45. "Homicide—Coroner's Inquest," 7 July 1864, *Daily Morning Call*, MTP.

46. Twain makes this point in a letter to his sister: SLC to Pamela A. Moffett, 18 March 1864, Virginia City, Nev. (*UCCL 00076*).

47. "Dispatches by the State Line," 3 September 1863, *Daily Morning Call*. Cited by Edgar M. Branch, *Clemens of the "Call," Mark Twain in San Francisco* (Berkeley: University of California Press, 1969), 287.

48. "A Brisk Business in the Shooting and Slashing Way at Washoe," 10 March 1864, San Francisco *Evening Bulletin*, MTP.

49. SLC to Orion and Mary E. (Mollie) Clemens, 19 and 20 Oct 1865, San Francisco, Calif.

50. SLC to Pamela A. Moffett, 18 March 1864, Virginia City, Nev. (*UCCL 00076*).

51. SLC to Orion Clemens, 23 July 1862, Aurora, Nevada (*UCCL 00055*).

52. SLC to Jane Lampton Clemens, 19 Aug 1863, Steamboat Springs, Nev. (*UCCL 00071*).

53. "A Brisk Business in the Shooting and Slashing Way at Washoe," 10 March 1864, San Francisco *Evening Bulletin*, MTP.

54. *RI*, 354.

55. *Ibid.*, 353–358.

56. James, 172.

57. *Ibid.*

58. R. Kent Rasmussen, *Mark Twain A–Z: The Essential Reference to His Life and Writings* (New York: Oxford University Press, 1995), 303.

59. *RI*, 355.

60. *Ibid.*

61. "Assassination in Carson," 11 December 1863, MTP. Text from *Mark Twain's Western Years*, Ivan Benson (Russell & Russell, 1966), 178.

62. Bahktin called this kind of linguistic marker a "concrete heteroglot conception of the world," a use of language that has a "taste" of something particular "Discourse in the Novel," *Dialogic Imagination*, 293.

63. James E. Caron, 323.

64. Roy Morris, Jr., 116.

65. The following scholars have written about Twain's hoaxes as early forms of his developing style: Lawrence I. Berkove, especially in *The Sagebrush Anthology: Literature from the Silver Age of the Old West* (Columbia: University of Missouri Press, 2006) and "Nevada Influences on Mark Twain" from *A Companion to Mark Twain* (Malden, MA: Blackwell, 2005); Edgar M. Branch and Robert H. Hirst in *Early Tales and Sketches, Volume 1: 1851–1864* (Berkeley: University of California Press, 1979). Henry Nash Smith offered little context or analysis of hoaxes in *Mark Twain of the Enterprise: Newspaper Articles & Other Documents, 1862–1864* (Berkeley: University of California Press, 1957). James E. Caron, in *Mark Twain: Unsanctified Newspaper Reporter* (Columbia: University of Missouri Press, 2008) provides the best analysis of the hoax, but his method relies on "Lying to the Public for Laughs," as the section heading identifies (135). For Caron, the hoax "neatly highlights these opposing reactions to Sam Clemens's comic character" (143).

66. SLC to Jane Lampton Clemens, 19 Aug 1863, Steamboat Springs, Nev. (*UCCL 00071*).

67. "Horrible Affair," *Territorial Enterprise*, between 16 and 18 April 1863. Reprinted in

Early Tales & Sketches, Vol. 1 1851–1864, 246–47.

68. MTP Editor's Note 1, SLC to Jane Lampton Clemens and Pamela A. Moffett 11 and 12 April 1863, Virginia City, Nev. Terr. (MS: NPV and CU-MARK, *UCCL* 00063)

69. SLC to Jane Lampton Clemens and Pamela A. Moffett 11 and 12 April 1863, Virginia City, Nev. Terr. (MS: NPV and CU-MARK, *UCCL* 00063)

70. *Ibid.*

71. Scharnhorst, xii–xiii.

72. Branch and Hirst, 244.

73. The complete text from this paper does not exist. Three other papers reprinted the item, however, and all three have survived. I have taken my source material from the reprinted article in the San Francisco *Daily Evening Bulletin*, printed on the evening of Halloween. Two other versions also exist, from the afternoon edition of the Gold Hill *News* on 28 October, and the second from Sacramento *Union* on 30 October. Cited by Branch and Hirst, *Early Tales & Sketches, Vol. 1 1851–1864*, 320.

74. "A Bloody Massacre Near Carson," 28 October 1863, *Territorial Enterprise*, reprinted in the San Francisco *Daily Evening Bulletin*, 31 October 1863, MTP.

75. Twain's style here is reminiscent of Puritan "plain style," especially popular in captivity narratives. Such language links Twain to a larger tradition of sensational and violent American narratives.

76. "A Bloody Massacre Near Carson," 28 October 1863, *Territorial Enterprise*, reprinted in the San Francisco *Daily Evening Bulletin*, 31 October 1863, MTP.

77. "Character speech" and "authorial speech" are terms Bakhtin uses in "Discourse in the Novel" to explain what is invented, created for a character, "almost always influences authorial speech" (315). In the case of Twain's hoax, the author may have misjudged the power of his language, and its reception, for the author's speech or intention competed with the narrator's (reporter's) speech. The fictional language affected a real outcome not contained within the scope of the writer's original plan.

78. "A Bloody Massacre Near Carson," 28 October 1863, *Territorial Enterprise*, reprinted in the San Francisco *Daily Evening Bulletin*, 31 October 1863, MTP.

79. "I TAKE IT ALL BACK," 29 October 1863, *Territorial Enterprise*. Text reprinted in *The Sagebrush Anthology*, 20.

80. Richard G. Lillard, "Contemporary Reaction to 'The Empire City Massacre,'" *American Literature*, Vol. 16, No. 3 (Nov., 1944): 203.

81. *Ibid.*, 198.

82. Such criticisms represent an early form of "muckraking" journalism. Newspapers used the term "muckrake" as early as the late-1860s. Ida B. Wells published her famous muckraking journalism about lynching in America in the *New York Age* in 1892, which became the material for *Southern Horrors: Lynch Law in All Its Phases* (1892).

83. Branch and Hirst, 323.

84. Richard G. Lillard, 198. He cites William Wright, "Reporting with Mark Twain (1893).

85. Branch and Hirst, 321.

86. Lillard, 199.

87. For rich discussions of law and extralegal justice in the West, see Ronald M. James *The Roar and the Silence: A History of Virginia City and the Comstock Lode* (Reno: University of Nevada Press, 1998); Roger D. McGrath, *Gunfighters, Highwaymen, & Vigilantes: Violence on the Frontier* (Berkeley and Los Angeles: University of California Press, 1984); Wayne Gard, *Frontier Justice*. Norman: University of Oklahoma Press, 1949; Ken Gonzales-Day, *Lynching in the West, 1850–1935* (Durham: Duke University Press, 2006).

88. "THAT 'SELL,'" 29 or 30 October 1863, Gold Hill *Daily News*, MTP.

89. Lillard, 199.

90. *Ibid.*, 201.

91. Powers, 51. The biographer discusses Twain's view that "truth" is "an impediment to good literature." According to Powers, the presence of such competitive discourses makes difficult the job of a scholar to determine what happened and what did not.

92. Lillard, 201.

93. This discussion relies again on Bakhtin's view of dialogic discourse. Bakhtin argues that the dialogic tension between two ideas "permits authorial intentions to be realized in such a way that we can acutely sense their presence at point in the work" ("Discourse in the Novel" 314). In a dialogic sense, perhaps Twain's hoax was not a linguistic failure. The author's presence, his very existence,

is the reason some editor's found the hoax distasteful, a lie. But, because Twain is not neutral, his biased authorial (performative) act betrays the competing discourses and allows one to overpower the other. In either case, the hoax became popular and allowed Twain to gain notoriety and eventually fame.

94. "A correspondent from Belmont, Nevada, in the *Enterprise*, Jan. 22, 1867, and quoted in Lillard, 203.

95. Lillard, 202.

96. SLC to Orion and Mary E. (Mollie) Clemens, 28 Sept 1864, San Francisco, Calif. (*UCCL 00088*).

97. Ibid. The "Home Journal" is the New York *Home Journal*.

98. SLC to Jane Lampton Clemens and Pamela A. Moffett, 25 Sept 1864, San Francisco, Calif. (*UCCL 00087*).

99. Note 6, SLC to Orion and Mary E. (Mollie) Clemens, 19 and 20 Oct 1865, San Francisco, Calif. (*UCCL 00092*).

100. "Letter from San Francisco," Sacramento *Union*, 3 November 1865. Reprinted in Branch and Hirst, *Early Tales and Sketches, Volume 1: 1851–1864*, 33.

101. SLC to Orion and Mary E. (Mollie) Clemens, 19 and 20 Oct 1865, San Francisco, Calif.

102. From "American Humor and Humorists," *Round Table*, 9 September 1865, 2. Reprinted in Branch and Hirst, *Early Tales and Sketches, Volume 1: 1851–1864*, 32.

103. SLC to Charles Warren Stoddard, 23 Apr 1867, New York, N.Y. (*UCCL 00124*).

104. Between November 1865, and June 1866, Mark Twain published six stories in Clapp's *New York Saturday Press*. In addition to Whitman, Howells, Trollope, and Collins, many other writers of note published in the paper: Horatio Alger, Jr., Ada Clare, Fitz Hugh Ludlow, and Charles Desmarais Gardette, whose poem "The Fire-Fiend. A Nightmare" was attributed to Edgar Allan Poe.

105. Twain, "A Strange Dream," The New-York *Saturday Press*, 2 June 1866, MTP.

Chapter 2

1. Twain, Letter to Horace Greeley, 17 August 1871, Hartford, CT, MTP.

2. Henry Nash Smith, *Mark Twain of the Enterprise: Newspaper Articles & Other Documents 1862–1864* (Berkeley: University of California Press, 1957), 99. Reprinted from the *Territorial Enterprise*, "Letter from Mark Twain," 12 December 1863.

3. *Roughing It*, 142.

4. Explanatory Notes, Note 2, Letter to Horace Greeley, 17 August 1871, Hartford, CT, MTP.

5. For a rich discussion of this topic, see *Public Sentiments: Structures of Feeling in Nineteenth-Century American Literature* (Chapel Hill: University of North Carolina Press, 2001).

6. Branch and Hirst, *Early Tales and Sketches, Vol. 1: 1851–1864*, 12.

7. *Roughing It*, 53.

8. Sixty-one letters still exist in the Mark Twain Papers at the Bancroft Library in Berkeley, California, from this nearly three-year period. Exclamations using "devil" to emphasize disdain, pity, mischief, humor, negation, a spirited person, and others have been used for centuries by writers such as Chaucer, Shakespeare, Emerson, Thoreau, Dickens, Trollope, among others.

9. Ronald M. James, 81.

10. SLC to Orion and Mary E. (Mollie) Clemens, 16 and 17 January 1862, MTP.

11. Ibid.

12. Ibid.

13. See Dan Rottenberg, *Death of a Gunfighter: The Quest for Jack Slade, the West's Most Elusive Legend* (Yardley, Pennsylvania: Westholme Publishing, 2008), 303. Rottenberg argues that even a few robberies or murders incited fear among settlers and travelers in the West. Rumors and newspaper accounts spread across the region like warnings for those seeking profits in the West.

14. Julie Nicoletta, "Redefining Domesticity: Women in Lodging Houses on the Comstock," *Comstock Women: The Making of a Mining Community*, ed. Ronald M. James and C. Elizabeth Raymond. (Reno: University of Nevada Press, 1998). In 1860, only six women spread among Virginia City, Silver City, and Gold Hill worked as lodging-house keepers. This number grew steadily over the next decade to thirty-two women keepers.

15. SLC to Jane Lampton Clemens, 26 Oct 1861, Carson City, Nev. (*UCCL 00031*).

16. SLC to Pamela, 8 February 1862, MTP. Strikethroughs and spellings appear as Twain wrote them.

Notes. Chapter 2

17. SLC to Jane and Pamela, 25 October 1861, MTP.
18. SLC to Pamela, 8 February 1862, MTP.
19. SLC to Jane and Pamela, 8 February 1862, MTP.
20. Orion and SLC to Mary E. (Mollie) Clemens, 29, 30, and 31 Jan 1862, Carson City, Nev. (*UCCL 00035*).
21. SLC to Pamela, 8 February 1862, MTP.
22. *Ibid.*
23. "The Indian Troubles on the Overland Route," *Weekly Appeal*, 5 October 1862. Reprinted from the *Territorial Enterprise*, 1 October 1862, MTP.
24. SLC to Pamela, 8 February 1862, MTP.
25. J. Ross Browne, "A Peep at Washoe," [Third Paper], February 1861, *Harper's New Monthly Magazine*, Vol. 22, No. 129, 289–290.
26. "A Big Thing in Washoe City," *Placer Weekly Courier*, 17 January 1863, MTP.
27. "Snow Slide," February, 1861, "A Peep at Washoe," [Third Paper].
28. SLC to Jane Lampton Clemens and Pamela A. Moffett, 8 and 9 Feb 1862, Carson City, Nev. (*UCCL 00036*).
29. SLC to Jane Lampton Clemens and Pamela A. Moffett, 16 Feb 1863, Virginia City, Nev. (*UCCL 00061*).
30. SLC to Jane Lampton Clemens and Pamela A. Moffett, 8 and 9 Feb 1862, Carson City, Nev. (*UCCL 00036*).
31. *Roughing It*, 252.
32. SLC to Jane Lampton Clemens and Pamela A. Moffett, 8 and 9 Feb 1862, Carson City, Nev. (*UCCL 00036*).
33. "Outgoing and Incoming," February, 1861, "A Peep at Washoe," [Third Paper].
34. "We are Waiting for You," January, 1861, "A Peep at Washoe," [Second Paper].
35. "Holding on to It," February, 1861, "A Peep at Washoe," [Third Paper] and "A Question of Title," January, 1861, "A Peep at Washoe," [Second Paper].
36. "Late from Washoe," *Sacramento Daily Union*, 22 July 1862, MTP. Reprinted from the *Territorial Enterprise*, 20 July, and written anonymously on July 13 by the Esmeralda correspondent, Samuel Clemens.
37. In Dante's *Inferno*, in the lowest region of the Ninth Circle of Hell, Satan (and Judas) is captured in ice. In this case, the worst of hell is not heat of torture but the cold of "treachery." Though Clemens is not referring to *Inferno*, he is participating in alternate views of damnation. And, he did return to medieval ideology in the writing of *A Connecticut Yankee in King Arthur's Court* (1889).
38. "A Big Thing in Washoe City," *Placer Weekly Courier*, 17 January 1863, MTP.
39. *Ibid.*
40. "Advertisement," *Placer Weekly Courier*, Vol. 6, No. 30, January 17, 1863, MTP.
41. SLC to Jane Lampton Clemens and Pamela A. Moffett, 8 and 9 Feb 1862, Carson City, Nev. (*UCCL 00036*).
42. Branch and Hirst, *Early Tales & Sketches, Volume I*, 387–388. William Wright wrote sketches, articles, and hoaxes similar to Mark Twain's, and the two writers' styles are often difficult to distinguish between each other in very short newspaper articles.
43. "Time for Her to Come Home," *Amador Weekly Ledger*, 14 November 1863, MTP.
44. "Time for Her to Come Home," *Amador Weekly Ledger*, 14 November 1863, MTP.
45. Branch and Hirst, *Early Tales and Sketches, Volume 1*, 172.
46. Berkove, *The Sagebrush Anthology*, 9.
47. Sam P. Davis, *The History of Nevada* (Reno and Los Angeles: The Elms Publishing Co., Inc., 1913), 242.
48. Edgar M. Branch, *Clemens of the "Call": Mark Twain in San Francisco* (Berkeley: University of California Press, 1969), 261.
49. Reported by Branch in *Clemens of the "Call,"* 288, and also Branch and Hirst in *Early Tales and Sketches, Volume 1*, 27.
50. Branch and Hirst, *Early Tales and Sketches, Volume 1*, 27.
51. *Ibid.*, 26–27.
52. *Ibid.*, 29.
53. Branch, *Clemens of the "Call,"* 259.
54. Branch, "Preface," *Clemens of the "Call,"* viii.
55. *Roughing It*, 401. George M. Marshall mentions his business relationship with Sheba Hurst and A.H. Rose in "Our Traveler's Letters."
56. "Our Traveler's Letters," 7 July 1864, Virginia City *Union*, 1, MTP.
57. *Ibid.*
58. Branch, *Clemens of the "Call,"* 260.
59. *Ibid.*, 259.
60. *Ibid.*
61. SLC to Orion Clemens, 24 and 25 Apr 1862, Aurora, Nevada (*UCCL 00045*).
62. SLC to Jane Lampton Clemens and

Pamela A. Moffett, 17 May 1864, Virginia City, Nev. (*UCCL 00077*).
63. SLC to Jane Lampton Clemens and Pamela A. Moffett, 17 May 1864, Virginia City, Nev. (*UCCL 00077*), n. 13.
64. Branch, *Clemens of the "Call,"* 260. Quoted by Branch from Albert S. Evans, "Our San Francisco Correspondence," *News*, 22 July 1864, 2.
65. *Ibid.*, 261.
66. SLC to Orion Clemens, 24 and 25 Apr 1862, Aurora, Nevada (*UCCL 00045*), n. 8.
67. Henry Nash Smith, *Mark Twain of the Enterprise* (Berkeley: University of California Press, 1957), 17.
68. *Ibid.*, 16–17.
69. *Ibid.*, 19.
70. Roy Morris, Jr. *Lighting Out for the Territory: How Samuel Clemens Headed West and Became Mark Twain* (New York: Simon & Schuster, 2012), 112.
71. *Ibid.*, 259.
72. James M. McPherson, *Battle Cry of Freedom: The Civil War Era* (New York: Oxford University Press, 2003), 116.
73. *Ibid.*, 599.
74. According to the U.S. Bureau of the Census, "Population of the Largest Urban Places: 1860," San Francisco ranked fifteenth, with 56,802 inhabitants. St. Louis, the second most western city ranked eighth, with a population of 160,773. In 1870, San Francisco ranked number ten and became the first western city to rank in the top ten most populated cities in the U.S. San Francisco tripled in size between 1860 and 1870. St. Louis's population doubled.
75. Branch, *Clemens of the "Call,"* 261.
76. *Ibid.*, 262.
77. *Ibid.*
78. "Letter from Mark Twain," reprinted in Branch and Hirst, *Early Tales and Sketches*, Volume 1, 293–294.
79. Berkove, *The Sagebrush Anthology*, 4.
80. Branch, *Clemens of the "Call,"* 263.
81. Berkove, *The Sagebrush Anthology*, 5.
82. Branch, *Clemens of the "Call,"* 265.
83. "Arrest of Charles L. Weller for Treasonable Utterances," *Daily Morning Call*, 26 July 1864, MTP.
84. Branch, *Clemens of the "Call,"* 258.
85. Greeley, "The Movement in Favor of Peace," *Daily Morning Call*, 26 July 1864, MTP.
86. Ronald M. James, 245.
87. Branch and Hirst, *Early Tales and Sketches, Vol. 2 1864–1865* (Berkeley: University of California Press, 1995), 9.

Chapter 3

1. Anonymous Correspondent, "Girls," *Daily Morning Call*, 3 January 1864, MTP.
2. "Another Victim," *Daily Morning Call*, 26 July 1864, MTP.
3. In 1865–1866, Twain attacked police corruption in San Francisco. According to Gary Scharnhorst in "Twain and the Literary Construction of the West" Twain was "a self-appointed vigilante" (311.)
4. Michael Schudson, *Discovering the News: A Social History of American Newspapers* (New York: Basic Books, 1978), 89–90. Schudson discusses newspapers in the 1890s, but he makes a larger point that journalism is supposed to deliver information and also to entertain. Michael Denning includes a succinct note that describes these positions in *Mechanic Accents: Dime Novels and Working-Class Culture in America* (New York: Verso, 1987), 251, though Schudson's book advances numerous larger points about journalism in particular.
5. *Ibid.*, 89.
6. *Ibid.*, 90.
7. *Ibid.*, 89. Schudson's phrase.
8. David S. Reynolds, Introduction, *The Quaker City, Or, the Monks of Monk Hall: A Romance of Philadelphia Life, Mystery, and Crime* (Amherst: University of Massachusetts Press, 1995), xxv.
9. Harris, "Four Ways to Inscribe a Mackerel: Mark Twain and Laura Hawkins," *Studies in the Novel*. Vol. 21, No. 2 (Summer, 1989): 138–153.
10. SLC to Orion and Henry Clemens, 26–28 Oct 1853, Philadelphia, Pa. (*UCCL 00002*).
11. David S. Reynolds, Introduction, *The Quaker City* (Amherst: University of Massachusetts Press, 1995), xxx.
12. *Ibid.*
13. *Ibid.*
14. Michael Denning, *Mechanic Accents: Dime Novels and Working-Class Culture in America* (New York: Verso, 1987), 88.
15. Lippard, 562.

Notes. Chapter 3

16. Denning, 24.
17. SLC to Jane and Pamela, 8 February 1862, MTP.
18. Edgar M. Branch included three of these stories about hackmen in *Clemens of the "Call": Mark Twain in San Francisco* (Berkeley: University of California Press, 1969). I also refer to and analyze stories Twain wrote about hack drivers not published in Branch's text. In "Appendix C," Branch lists other stories that he attributes to Twain, 288. Many of these stories are contained in the Mark Twain Papers in the Bancroft Library. Though Branch excluded most of these stories about hack drivers in his book, I am including them here.
19. "Beasts in the Semblance of Men," 12 June 1864, *Daily Morning Call*, MTP.
20. According to the U.S. Bureau of the Census, San Francisco tripled in size in the 1860s.
21. "Beasts in the Semblance of Men," 12 June 1864, *Daily Morning Call*, MTP.
22. Ibid.
23. "Rape," 23 July 1864, *Daily Morning Call*, reprinted in Branch, *Clemens of the "Call,"* 185.
24. Ibid., 186.
25. "Beasts in the Semblance of Men," 12 June 1864, *Daily Morning Call*, MTP.
26. Branch, "Rape," 23 July 1864, *Daily Morning Call*, reprinted in Branch, *Clemens of the "Call,"* 185.
27. Ibid.
28. "End of the Rape Case," 30 July 1864, *Daily Morning Call*, reprinted in Branch, *Clemens of the "Call,"* 187.
29. "Concerning Hackmen," 26 July 1864, *Daily Morning Call*, reprinted in Branch, *Clemens of the "Call,"* 186.
30. Schudson, 89.
31. In Lippard's *Quaker City*, Luke Harvey performs this role—a masculine man bent on ridding the city of usurpers of justice. Harvey, though, is not an officer of the law, and he hunts not just men but also Dora Livingstone, the seductress.
32. Branch, *Clemens of the "Call,"* 313, quoting Twain's article "Twainiana," San Francisco *Examiner*, 8 November 1865.
33. Ibid., 184.
34. "Rape," 23 July 1864, *Daily Morning Call*, reprinted in Branch, *Clemens of the "Call,"* 186.
35. "Concerning Hackmen," 26 July 1864, *Daily Morning Call*, reprinted in Branch, *Clemens of the "Call,"* 186.
36. Ibid.
37. Branch, *Clemens of the "Call,"* 313, quoting Twain's article "Twainiana," San Francisco *Examiner*, 8 November 1865.
38. "Attention, Hackmen," *Daily Morning Call*, 6 August 1864, MTP.
39. "Judicial Strategy," *Daily Morning Call*, 6 August 1864, MTP.
40. "Arrested for Theft," *Daily Morning Call*, 6 August 1864, MTP.
41. "After the Hackmen," *Daily Morning Call*, 7 August 1864, MTP.
42. "Hackmen Arrested," *Daily Morning Call*, 28 June 1864, MTP.
43. Ibid.
44. On Wednesday, August 18, Union forces attacked the Weldon Railroad at the Globe Tavern in Virginia. The attack resulted in a Union victory on August 21.
45. "Insolent Hackmen," *Daily Morning Call*, 18 August 1864, 3, c. 1, MTP.
46. Branch, *Clemens of the "Call,"* 185.
47. "Insolent Hackmen," *Daily Morning Call*, 18 August 1864, 3, c. 1, MTP.
48. Branch, *Clemens of the "Call,"* 185.
49. Ibid.
50. Ibid.
51. "Trial of a Hackman," *Daily Morning Call*, 22 September 1864, 3, MTP.
52. Branch, *Clemens of the "Call,"* 185.
53. "Demoralizing Young Girls," San Francisco *Daily Morning Call*, 23 July 1864, MTP. On loan.
54. Ibid.
55. Michael Denning, *Mechanic Accents: Dime Novels and Working-Class Culture in America* (New York: Verso, 1987), 24.
56. "Demoralizing Young Girls," San Francisco *Daily Morning Call*, 23 July 1864, MTP. On loan.
57. "A Merited Penalty," San Francisco *Daily Morning Call*, 24 July 1864, MTP. On loan.
58. "Lewd Merchandise," San Francisco *Daily Morning Call*, 26 July 1864, MTP. On loan.
59. "Vending Obscene Pictures," San Francisco *Daily Morning Call*, 26 July 1864, MTP. On loan.
60. Ibid.
61. Ibid.

62. "For Sentence," San Francisco *Daily Morning Call*, 26 July 1864, MTP. On loan.
63. "Obscene-Picture Dealers," San Francisco *Daily Morning Call*, 24 July 1864, MTP. On loan.
64. "The Movement in Favor of Peace," a reporter summarizes an overland dispatch in which we discover that Horace Greeley, famous editor of the *New-York Tribune* and stagecoach traveler out West, has met with "commissioners of the Rebel Government" in order to negotiate a proposition between the North and South. At the time Greeley served on a peace commission appointed by President Lincoln. In Twain's journalism and in *Roughing It*, Greeley's journey west had provided Twain with a legend to initially support and then later debunk.
65. "A Rough Customer," *Daily Morning Call*, 8 October 1864, MTP.
66. "The Roderick Case," *Daily Morning Call*, 9 October 1864, MTP.
67. *Ibid.*
68. *Ibid.*
69. Henry Nash Smith, *Mark Twain of the Enterprise* (Berkeley: University of California Press, 1957), 17.
70. Quoted in Branch and Hirst, *Early Tales and Sketches, Volume 1*, 27.
71. Branch, *Clemens of the "Call,"* 12.
72. *Ibid.*
73. Richard Slotkin, *The Fatal Environment: the Myth of the Frontier in the Age of Industrialization, 1800–1890* (Norman: University of Oklahoma Press, 1985), 15.
74. "Obscene Information," San Francisco *Daily Morning Call*, 29 July 1864, MTP. On loan.
75. "Demoralizing Young Girls," San Francisco *Daily Morning Call*, 23 July 1864, MTP. On loan.
76. "Another Obscene Picture Knave Captured—He Solicits the Custom of School Girls," 6 August 1864, quoted in Branch, *Clemens of the "Call,"* 173.
77. Benedict Anderson, *Imagined Communities: Reflections on the Origin and Spread of Nationalism* (New York: Verso, 2006), 33.
78. *Ibid.*, 33–34.
79. I am working with Michael Denning's idea that journalism, as a form of literature, knows not unity of plot, but only unity of date and place. Lippard and Twain both worked within this model as journalists, and

both men later used these journalistic techniques in their fiction, which also requires a plot. Denning goes on to argue "that reading Lippard is like reading a newspaper with a plot" (91).
80. Anonymous Correspondent, "Girls," *Daily Morning Call*, 3 January 1864, MTP.
81. Untitled, from "Facts and Fancies," 26 July 1864, Daily Morning Call, MTP.
82. Schudson, 89.
83. *Ibid.*
84. *Ibid.*, 90.

Chapter 4

1. This comment comprises part two of Sumner's response to two newspaper correspondents being "taken into custody by order of the Senate, for refusing to disclose" sources and imprisoned without due process ("Power of the Senate to Imprison Recusant Witnesses," May 18, 1871, *Charles Sumner; His Complete Works* (Boston: Lee and Shepard, 1900), 145.
2. SLC to T. B. Pugh, 27 July 1873, Edinburgh, Scotland (*UCCL 00957*).
3. SLC to Whitelaw Reid, 29 Apr 1871, Elmira, N.Y. (*UCCL 00607*).
4. "Life, trial, and execution of Edward H. Ruloff: perpetrator of eight murders, numerous burglaries, and other crimes; who was recently hanged at Binghamton, N.Y...." Courtesy of Fenimore Art Museum, "Murder Pamphlet Collection," 1871.
5. For more on this topic, see John Cyril Barton's *Literary Executions: Capital Punishment and American Culture, 1820–1925* (Baltimore: Johns Hopkins University Press, 2014).
6. James Fenimore Cooper (Preface, *The Ways of the Hour*).
7. Walter Whitman, "Revenge and Requital. A Tale of a Murderer Escaped." *The United States Magazine, and Democratic Review* Vol. XVII, No. LXXXV (July and August, 1845): 111.
8. David S. Reynolds, *Introduction, The Quaker City, Or, the Monks of Monk Hall: A Romance of Philadelphia Life, Mystery, and Crime* (Amherst: University of Massachusetts Press, 1995), xxxi.
9. SLC to Whitelaw Reid, 29 Apr 1871, Elmira, N.Y. (*UCCL 00607*).

10. Captain Ned Blakely's actual name was Edgar "Ned" Wakeman, who was also Twain's inspiration for the title character of Twain's short story "Captain Stormfield's Visit to Heaven."
11. For discussions of crime and punishment in America, including the anti-gallows movement, which preceded Twain's discussions in his journalism and novels, see the following works: Stuart Banner's *The Death Penalty: An American History* (Cambridge: Harvard University Press, 2002), Louis P. Masur, *Rites of Execution: Capital Punishment and the Transformation of American Culture, 1776–1865* (New York and Oxford: Oxford University Press, 1989); Daniel A. Cohen, *Pillars of Salt, Monuments of Grace: New England Crime Literature and the Origins of American Popular Culture, 1674–1860* (Amherst: University of Massachusetts Press, 1993); two works by David Brion Davis, "The Movement to Abolish Capital Punishment in America, 1787–1861." *The American Historical Review* (Vol. 63, No. 1, 1957): 23–46 and *From Homicide to Slavery: Studies in American Culture* (New York: Oxford University Press, 1988); Karen Halttunen, *Murder Most Foul: The Killer and the American Gothic Imagination* (Cambridge: Harvard University Press, 1998); John Cyril Barton, "The Anti-Gallows Movement in Antebellum America." *REAL*, Vol. 23. *Civil Liberties, Ltd*, ed. Brook Thomas. (Verlag: 2006): 145–178; and John Cyril Barton, *Literary Executions: Capital Punishment and American Culture, 1820–1925* (Baltimore: Johns Hopkins University Press, 2014).
12. SLC to Whitelaw Reid, 29 Apr 1871, Elmira, N.Y. (*UCCL 00607*). All italics in this letter represent Twain's emphasis. The strikethroughs are also Twain's.
13. Perhaps also an alternate resolution to the *lex talionis* justice that Twain and his circle of journalists often supported in the West.
14. SLC to Whitelaw Reid, 29 Apr 1871, Elmira, N.Y. (*UCCL 00607*).
15. *Ibid.*
16. Henry Sweets, the curator of The Mark Twain Boyhood Home & Museum in Hannibal, Missouri, explained this history in the Hannibal *Courier-Post*, 1 May 2009. http://www.hannibal.net/article/20090501/NEWS/305019857.
17. R. Kent Rasmussen, *Mark Twain A–Z: The Essential Reference to His Life and Works* (New York: Oxford University Press, 1995), 79.
18. SLC to Elisha Bliss, Jr., 15 May 1871, Elmira, N.Y. (*UCCL 00612*) and Note 5.
19. SLC to Whitelaw Reid, MTP.
20. Gary Scharnhorst, "Twain and the Literary Construction of the West." *A Companion to Mark Twain*, ed. Messent and Budd. (Malden, MA: Blackwell, 2005), 315.
21. *Roughing It*, 103.
22. *Ibid.*
23. Richard Slotkin, *The Fatal Environment: The Myth of the Frontier in the Age of Industrialization, 1800–1890* (Norman: University of Oklahoma Press, 1985), 110–118.
24. *Roughing It*, 107.
25. *Ibid.*, 109.
26. Erin Turner. *Badasses of the Old West: True Stories of Outlaws on the Edge* (Guilford, CT: TwoDot, 2010), 113.
27. *Roughing It*, 103.
28. Berkove, *The Sagebrush Anthology*, 4–5.
29. See John Rollin Ridge, *The Life and Adventures of Joaquin Murieta, the Celebrated California Bandit* (Norman, University of Oklahoma Press, 1955). Published in 1854, the novel based on the life of Murieta presents a complicated case. Anglo-Americans viewed him as a monster and a bandit. Native Californians and Mexicans considered him to be a patriotic hero fighting the larger force of Anglo-Americans stealing Mexican land during and after the U.S.–Mexican War.
30. *Roughing It*, 107.
31. Thomas J. Dimsdale. *The Vigilantes of Montana* (Norman: University of Oklahoma Press, 1953), 195.
32. Ronald M. James, *The Roar and the Silence: A History of Virginia City and the Comstock Lode* (Reno: University of Nevada Press, 1998).
33. Quoted from Dimsdale's book by Twain's narrator in *Roughing It*, 117.
34. James, 171.
35. *Roughing It*, 118.
36. *Ibid.*, 118–119.
37. *Roughing It*, 119.
38. Glenn Hendler, *Public Sentiments: Structures of Feeling in Nineteenth-Century American Literature* (Chapel Hill: University of North Carolina Press, 2001), 29.

39. *Ibid.*, 33. Hendler makes the point that Washingtonian Temperance Societies "were the first such groups to believe that habitual drunkards could be redeemed."
40. *Roughing It*, 112.
41. Dimsdale, 205.
42. *Roughing It*, 110.
43. *Ibid.*
44. *Ibid.*, 118–119.
45. James, 81.
46. *Ibid.*, 74. In 1863, this dollar figure was $12,486,238 in bullion. The previous year, when Twain began his western writing career, the figure was over six million dollars.
47. Note 3, SLC to the Postmaster of Virginia City, Mont. Terr...., 15 Sept 1870, Buffalo, N.Y. (*UCCL 00506*).
48. SLC to Orion Clemens, 10 March 1871, Buffalo, N.Y. (*UCCL 02453*).
49. SLC to Jane Lampton Clemens, 26 Oct 1861, Carson City, Nev. (*UCCL 00031*).
50. SLC to the Postmaster of Virginia City, Mont. Terr...., 15 Sept 1870, Buffalo, N.Y. (*UCCL 00506*).
51. "Lynching." *The Youth's Companion (1827–1929)*; May 12, 1864; 37, 19; American Periodicals Series, 74.
52. *Ibid.*
53. *Ibid.*
54. "Prefatory," *Roughing It.*
55. "Dispatches by the State Line," 3 September 1863, *Daily Morning Call*, from Branch, *Clemens of the "Call,"* 287.
56. *Roughing It*, 119.
57. *Ibid.*, 110.
58. *Ibid.*, 110–111.
59. "The United States of Lyncherdom," *The Complete Essays of Mark Twain*, ed. Charles Neider (Boston: Da Capo Press, 1991), 677. See also Terry L. Oggel's essay "Speaking Out About Race: 'The United States of Lyncherdom' Clemens Really Wrote," in *Prospects: An Annual of American Cultural Studies 25* (Cambridge University Press, 2000): 115–58.
60. "The United States of Lyncherdom," 676.
61. *Ibid.*, 677. Also of note is Colonel Sherburn from *Huckleberry Finn*. Sherburn is a murderer but is also brave and manly enough to back down a mob come to lynch him.
62. "Lynchings: By Year and Race," http://law2.umkc.edu/faculty/projects/ftrials/shipp/lynchingyear.html

63. "The United States of Lyncherdom," 677.
64. *Roughing It*, 347.
65. *Ibid.*, 348.
66. *Ibid.*, 349.
67. *Ibid.*
68. *Ibid.*, 359.
69. *Ibid.*, 360.
70. *Ibid.*
71. *Ibid.*, 365.
72. *Ibid.*
73. *Ibid.*, 361.
74. *Roughing It*, 103.
75. *Ibid.*, 105.
76. Dimsdale, 196.
77. *RI*, 119.
78. Charles Sumner, "Against Capital Punishment. Letter to a Committee of the Massachusetts Legislature," February 12, 1855.
79. Charles Sumner, "The Crime Against Kansas: The Apologies for the Crime; The True Remedy," 1856.
80. SLC to T. B. Pugh, 27 July 1873, Edinburgh, Scotland (*UCCL 00957*), n. 2.
81. Twain and Sumner also shared a disdain for President Grant. Sumner fought the president in Congress, and Twain satirized Grant's corrupt administration in *The Gilded Age* (1873).
82. "Annual Message of Captain Jim, Chief of Washoes, and Governor (de facto) of Nevada," 14 November 1862, Barney Woolf, Printer to the Third House, Carson City, MTP.
83. Editors at the Mark Twain Papers in Berkeley and the archivists at the Houghton Library at Harvard attribute the broadside to Samuel Clemens.
84. Branch and Hirst, 18.
85. "Annual Message of Captain Jim, Chief of the Washoes, and Governor (de facto) of Nevada," 14 November 1862, MTP.
86. SLC (Samuel Langhorne Clemens). "Mark Twain's Letters from Washington. Number III." Letter dated 20 December 1867. Virginia City *Territorial Enterprise*, 11 January, 2.
87. *Ibid.*
88. *Ibid.*
89. *Ibid.*
90. *The Hangman*, Vol. I., No. 18 (Boston, Massachusetts, Wednesday, July 30): 1845.
91. "SLC to Whitelaw Reid," 29 Apr 1871, Elmira, N.Y., MTP.
92. Charles Sumner, "Power of the Senate

to Imprison Recusant Witnesses," May 18, 1871, *Charles Sumner; His Complete Works* (Lee and Shepard, Boston), 1900.

93. For example, *The Innocents Abroad* (1869) sold more than 70,000 copies in the first year of its publication. "Sold by Subscription Only," http://rmc.library.cornell.edu/twain/exhibition/subscription/index.html. According to Rasmussen, *Huckleberry Finn* (1884) has sold more than 20 million copies in excess of fifty languages (229).

94. "Novel Entertainment," 31 May 1868, *Chicago Republican*, quoted in Reid and James, *Uncovering Nevada's Past: A Primary Source History of the Silver State* (Reno: University of Nevada Press, 2004), 60–61.

95. R. Kent Rasmussen cites Elwood R. McIntyre, "A Farmer Halts the Hangman: The Story of Marvin Bovee," *Wisconsin Magazine of History* 42, No. 1 [autumn 1958]: 3–12; Also, *Dict. of Wisconsin History* online; accessed 9 January 2013.

96. Edward Livingston, senator and eventually U.S. Secretary of State under Andrew Jackson from 1831 to 1833, solicited James Fenimore Cooper's help in a similar fashion a half century before Bovee used this method to attract Twain's attention.

97. Bovee to SLC, 7 April 1875, MTP.

98. "Note" on envelope of Bovee's letter to Twain, 7 April 1875, MTP.

99. Bovee to SLC, 10 February 1876, MTP.

100. "Note" on envelope of Bovee's letter to Twain, 10 February 1876, MTP.

101. Clemens never responded to Bovee's appeals. Nor did Clemens write about Bovee to his friends or family or mention the reformer in his *Autobiography*. The absence of evidence beyond Clemens's acerbic personal note could support the claim that Clemens did not like Bovee more than Clemens agreed with capital punishment.

102. SLC to OLC, 25 Sept 1872, London, England (*UCCL 00814*).

103. *Ibid.*

104. *Ibid.*

Chapter 5

1. "The Assassin in Nevada." *The National Police Gazette (1845–1906)* 22, no. 1122 (Mar 02, 1867): 4.

2. Historians have written much about Bulette's popularity, especially Marion S. Goldman, *Gold Diggers & Silver Miners: Prostitution and Social Life on the Comstock Lode* (Ann Arbor: University of Michigan Press, 1981). For a primary legal source, see *The Life and Confession of John Millian* (Virginia City: Lammon, Gregory, & Palmer, 1868). The publishers and attorney for Millian, Bulette's murderer, give a brief account of Bulette's life in the West. They note that the Virginia Engine Company No. 1 had made Bulette an honorary member. The publishers call Bulette "kind-hearted and benevolent," which is how she was known in the town (4).

3. John B. Reid and Ronald M. James, ed. *Uncovering Nevada's Past: A Primary Source History of the Silver State* (Reno: University of Nevada Press, 2004), 61.

4. Judith Butler's *Gender Trouble: Feminism and the Subversion of Identity* (New York: Routledge, 1990) has influenced my use of "gender performance." Butler assesses gender performance by noting that women appear within a system of language in which "...the female body is marked within masculinist discourse" (17). I have applied this idea to how Twain judges women, and men, and use his view of masculinity, and his own masculinity, to write about gender.

5. Ann M. Ryan, "The Voice of Her Laughter: Mark Twain's Tragic Feminism," *American Literary Realism*. Vol. 41, No. 3 (Spring 2009): 198. Clara became a controlling and a guiding force for Clemens after Livy died. Clara also disapproved of Clemens's affection for his "angelfish." Clemens had named his new home in Redding, Connecticut, "Innocence at Home" in honor of his angelfish who regularly gathered there. But when Clara returned to Connecticut from Europe, she renamed the home "Stormfield," which is the name Clemens used from then on, even when writing in his autobiography about a rash of burglaries at Stormfield.

6. For critical essays and books about Twain's relationships with women, to women, and gender analysis, see Ann M. Ryan, "The Voice of Her Laughter: Mark Twain's Tragic Feminism." *American Literary Realism*. Vol. 41, No. 3 (Spring 2009): 192–213; Linda A. Morris, *Gender Play in Mark Twain: Cross-Dressing and Transgression* (Columbia: University of Missouri Press, 2007); two books by Laura E. Skandera-Trombley, *Mark Twain*

in the Company of Women (Philadelphia: University of Pennsylvania Press, 1994) and *Mark Twain's Other Woman: The Hidden Story of His Final Years* (New York: Vintage Books, 2010); Susan K. Harris, "Four Ways to Inscribe a Mackerel: Mark Twain and Laura Hawkins," *Studies in the Novel.* Vol. 21, No. 2 (Summer, 1989): 138–153; and Linda A. Morris, *Gender Play in Mark Twain: Cross-Dressing and Transgression* (Columbia: University of Missouri Press, 2007).

7. Brook Thomas, *Cross-Examinations of Law and Literature* (Cambridge: Cambridge University Press, 1987), 15. For an additional discussion of use of evidence, see Alexander Welsh's *Strong Representations: Narrative and Circumstantial Evidence in England* (Baltimore: Johns Hopkins University Press, 1992).

8. Powers, 135.

9. Henry Nash Smith. *Mark Twain of the Enterprise: Newspaper Articles & Other Documents 1862–1864* (Berkeley: University of California Press, 1957), 78.

10. Powers, 136.

11. Goldman, 42.

12. James, 185.

13. Goldman, 38–42.

14. *Ibid.*, 46.

15. *Ibid.*, 38–39.

16. Henry Nash Smith, 78–79.

17. *Ibid.*, 79.

18. *Ibid.*

19. "Theatrical Record," *Daily Morning Call*, 3 January 1864.

20. Henry Nash Smith, 79.

21. *Ibid.*, 79–80.

22. Thomas Maguire built two opera houses—one in San Francisco and the second in Virginia City.

23. SLC to Orion Clemens, 28 Apr 1862, n. 8.

24. As in the cutting or operation of a *living animal*, yet another dehumanizing and desexualizing marker for Menken.

25. Lawrence I. Berkove, *Insider Stories of the Comstock Lode and Nevada's Mining Frontier 1859–1909: Primary Sources in American Social History* (Lewiston, New York: The Edwin Mellen Press, 2007), 984.

26. "Maguire's Opera House," *Virginia Daily Union*, 10 March 1864, MTP.

27. "Splendid Acting," *Stockton Daily Independent*, 14 March 1864, MTP.

28. "Untitled Note on Menken," *Unionville Humboldt Register*, 19 March 1864, MTP.

29. Though the term "drawers" seems like a masculine use of "underwear" in modern vernacular, according to the *Oxford English Dictionary* online, the term usually meant simply an undergarment, or "under-hose," or in "some early instances the word appears to mean stockings." Twain used the word to mean a thin suit that made Menken appear to be nude on stage.

30. Berkove, *Insider Stories*, 984.

31. Powers, 136. Twain may or may not have taken the opportunity to kick Menken instead of the dog, thereby abusing the "proper" creature and creating a reason to exit.

32. Berkove, *Insider Stories*, 985.

33. *Ibid.*

34. *Ibid.*, 984–85.

35. SLC to Pamela A. Moffett, 18 March 1864. Menken arrived in Virginia City on February 27 and performed throughout March.

36. *Ibid.*

37. Berkove, *Insider Stories*, 984.

38. SLC to Pamela A. Moffett, 18 March 1864.

39. "The Assassin in Nevada." *The National Police Gazette (1845–1906)* 22, no. 1122 (Mar 02, 1867): 4.

40. Twain, "Novel Entertainment," *Chicago Republican*, May 31, 1868.

41. The opposite would be "green," a term Twain applied to the inexperienced, often travelers and emigrants, from the East.

42. "The Assassin in Nevada," 4.

43. *Chicago Republican*, 31 May 1868, quoted in Reid and James, *Uncovering Nevada's Past: A Primary Source History of the Silver State*, 60.

44. "The Assassin in Nevada," 4.

45. Susan James, "Queen of Tarts," *The Historical Nevada Magazine* (Carson City: Nevada Magazine, 1998), 49.

46. "Julia Bulette." Courtesy of Nevada Historical Society.

47. "Appraisement of the Estate of Julia Bulette." Reid and James, *Uncovering Nevada's Past: A Primary Source History of the Silver State*, 58.

48. *Ibid.*, 57.

49. *Ibid.*, 59.

50. Susan James, "Julia Bulette's Probate Records." In Reid and James, *Uncovering Ne-*

vada's Past: A Primary Source History of the Silver State, 55.

51. Anne M. Butler, *Daughters of Joy, Sisters of Misery: Prostitutes in the American West, 1865–1890* (Urbana and Chicago: University of Illinois Press, 1987), 54–55.

52. Susan James, "Queen of Tarts," 53.

53. *Ibid.*, 50.

54. "The Assassin in Nevada," 4.

55. "A Mysterious Murder Chased Up." *The National Police Gazette (1845–1906)* 22, no. 1139 (Jun 29, 1867): 4.

56. *Ibid.*

57. Lawrence I. Berkove, *Insider Stories*, 521.

58. *Ibid.*, 522.

59. "The Assassin in Nevada," 4.

60. *Chicago Republican*, 31 May 1868, quoted in Reid and James, *Uncovering Nevada's Past: A Primary Source History of the Silver State*, 61.

61. "A Mysterious Murder Chased Up," 4.

62. Reid and James, 60.

63. *Ibid.*, 61.

64. *Roughing It*, 117–18.

65. Reid and James, 61.

66. Though Michel Foucault's discussion in *Discipline and Punish* develops from a European understanding of the State and not from a view of the U.S. model of federal and state governments, his analysis of a body on display as a "spectacular" symbol for power and crime deterrence influenced my reading of Twain's article about Millian's hanging. For Foucault, "the fact that the guilty man should moan and cry out under the blows is not a shameful side-effect, it is the very ceremonial of justice being expressed in all its force" (34).

67. James, "Queen of Tarts," 51.

68. Charles E. DeLong, *The Life and Confession of John Millian* (Virginia City: Lammon, Gregory, & Palmer, 1868), 15.

69. Reid and James, 61.

70. *Ibid.*, 60.

71. James, "Queen of Tarts," 51. In the late-seventeenth and early–eighteenth centuries, Cotton Mather and John Rogers, among other Puritan ministers, published broadsides that offered accounts of crimes (sins), confessions, execution sermons, and the executions of the sinners. Millian's confession to his attorney, his statement of confession and gratitude at the gallows, his prayer with a priest, and his public hanging follow a nearly identical pattern to the ritual of Puritan executions.

72. Goldman, 86.

73. *Ibid.*

74. "A Foul Fair," *Zion's Herald*. 11 May 1871, American Periodicals Series Online (Boston, Vol. 48, Issue 19): 223.

75. *Ibid.*

76. Jane G. Swisshelm, "The Fair Laura," 28 November 1872: 24 1252, *The Independent*, American Periodical Series Online.

77. *Ibid.*

78. SLC to Olivia L. Langdon, 30, 31 Oct, 1 Nov 1869, Pittsburgh, Pa. (*UCCL 00365*)

79. Courtesy of Bancroft Library, UC–Berkeley, BANC PIC 1963.002:0874—B, Lithograph, Kock & Harnett, ca. 1871.

80. Lithograph, Kock & Harnett, ca. 1871.

81. R. Kent Rasmussen, *Mark Twain A to Z*, 176.

82. Reviews of the Gilded Age play (*MTDP 00148*), n. 3.

83. New York *World* "Amusements" column on 17 September 1874. Reviews of the Gilded Age play (*MTDP 00148*). 1874.

84. In addition to the Edward Howard Rulloff trial in New York and Laura Fair's murder case and trial in California, Twain and Warner based many of the situations in *The Gilded Age* on actual legal and political scandals. For example, Judge O'Shaunnessy is based on the New York Judge John McCunn, whom Tammany groomed and installed. The scandal in Washington, D.C., and Kansas concerning free-state supporter Kansas Senator Samuel C. Pomeroy's bribery during his third-term re-election also inspired the novelists. For more on these legal and political scandals, see Bryant Morey French's "Mark Twain, Laura D. Fair and the New York Criminal Courts," *American Quarterly*. Vol. 16, No. 4, A Mark Twain Issue (Winter, 1964): 545–561.

85. Wai Chee Dimock, *Residues of Justice: Literature, Law, Philosophy* (Berkeley: University of California Press, 1997), 4.

86. *Ibid.*

87. In "Force of Law: The 'Mystical Foundation of Authority'" Jacques Derrida argues that the "undecidable, a theme often associated with deconstruction, is not merely the oscillation between two significations or two contradictory and very determinate rules, each equally imperative ... The undecidable is not merely the oscillation or the tension

between two decisions ... A decision that didn't go through the ordeal of the undecidable would not be a free decision, it would only be the programmable application or unfolding of a calculable process. It might be legal; it would not be just." *Deconstruction and the Possibility of Justice*, ed. Drucilla Cornell, Michel Rosenfeld, and David Gray Carlson (New York: Routledge, 1992), 24.

88. Bryant Morey French, "Mark Twain, Laura D. Fair and the New York Criminal Courts," *American Quarterly*, Vol. 16, No. 4, A Mark Twain Issue (Winter, 1964): 545–561.

89. Harris, 146.

90. *Ibid.*, 138.

91. Judith Butler, *Gender Trouble: Feminism and the Subversion of Identity* (New York: Routledge, 1990), 17.

92. Linda A. Morris, *Gender Play in Mark Twain: Cross-Dressing and Transgression* (Columbia: University of Missouri Press, 2007), 23.

93. Ron Powers, *Introduction*, xxi, Twain, Mark and Charles Dudley Warner. *The Gilded Age*. Ron Powers, ed. (New York: The Modern Library, 2006).

94. Twain and Warren, *The Gilded Age*, 443.

95. Ryan, 196.

96. Twain and Warren, 442.

97. *Ibid.*, 442.

98. *Ibid.*

99. Dimock, 8.

100. *Ibid.*, 444.

101. *Mark Twain Project Online: Authoritative Texts, Documents, and Historical Research*. http://www.marktwainproject.org/homepage.html

102. Susan K. Harris, 150. She argues that Laura represents "an ambitious female character," which "gets out of hand." Twain's response is to "kill her off," which ultimately denies "female autonomy."

103. *Ibid.*

104. Dimock, 10.

105. I am using Dimock's phrase, "the problem of justice" to describe Twain's method, though she does not use any of Twain's writing as evidence for her claims about literary justice. Instead, Dimock selects Kate Chopin's Edna, from *The Awakening*, as a female character to analyze how Chopin gives a "face and a voice" to this "problem." Still, Twain does something similar with his "Laura," especially because he played with the legal verdict on the stage after he had decided to "kill" his Laura outside of a legal verdict or punishment in the novel.

106. Michael Foster and Barbara Foster, *A Dangerous Woman: The Life, Loves, and Scandals of Adah Isaacs Menken, 1835–1868 America's Original Superstar* (Guilford, CT: Lyons Press, 2011), 298.

107. Twain and Warren, 444.

108. *Ibid.*

109. *Ibid.*

110. *Ibid.*

111. *Ibid.*

Afterword

1. Mark Twain and Charles Dudley Warner, *The Gilded Age*, ed. Ron Powers. (New York: The Modern Library, 2006) 446.

2. Judith Butler, *Excitable Speech: A Politics of the Performative* (New York: Routledge, 1997), 49.

3. Wai Chee Dimock, *Residues of Justice: Literature, Law, Philosophy* (Berkeley: University of California Press, 1997), 10.

4. Kate Chopin, *The Awakening*, ed. Nancy A. Walker (Boston and New York: Bedford/St. Martin's, 2000), 139.

5. Dimock, 221.

6. SLC to the Postmaster of Virginia City, Mont. Terr...., 15 Sept 1870, MTP.

7. *Roughing It*, 304.

8. *Ibid.*, 305.

9. SLC to Whitelaw Reid, 29 Apr 1871, Elmira, N.Y. (*UCCL 00607*).

10. Mark Twain, *The Adventures of Huckleberry Finn* (Colorado Springs: Piccadilly Books, 2010), 122.

11. Caron, 3.

12. *Ibid.*, 323.

13. *Ibid.*

14. Mark Twain, *Pudd'nhead Wilson and Those Extraordinary Twain: A Norton Critical Edition*, ed. Sidney E. Berger (New York: W.W. Norton & Company, Inc., 1980), 115.

15. Roy Blount, Jr. "Introduction," *A Connecticut Yankee in King Arthur's Court* (New York: The Modern Library, 2001), xxi.

16. Mark Twain, *A Connecticut Yankee in King Arthur's Court* (New York: The Modern Library, 2001), 446–47.

17. *Ibid.*, 446.

Bibliography

"Advertisement," *Placer Weekly Courier,* vol. 6, no. 30, January 17, 1863, MTP.
Anderson, Benedict. *Imagined Communities: Reflections on the Origin and Spread of Nationalism.* New York: Verso, 2006.
"Annual Message of Captain Jim, Chief of the Washoes, and Governor (de facto) of Nevada," 14 November 1862, Barney Woolf, Printer to the Third House, Carson City, MTP.
"Arrest of Rebel Officers' Wives," from "Our St. Louis Letter." San Francisco *Daily Morning Call,* 26 July 1864, MTP. On loan.
"The Assassin in Nevada." *The National Police Gazette (1845–1906)* 22, No. 1122 (Mar 02, 1867): 4. http://search.proquest.com/docview/127591975?accountid=14589.
Austin, J.L. *How to Do Things with Words.* Cambridge: Harvard University Press, 1962.
Austin, Mary Hunter. *The Land of Little Rain.* Boston & New York: Houghton Mifflin Company, 1903.
Bakhtin, M.M. "Discourse in the Novel," *Dialogic Imagination,* ed. Michael Holquist. Austin: University of Texas Press, 1981.
Banner, Stuart. *The Death Penalty: An American History.* Cambridge: Harvard University Press, 2002.
Barton, John Cyril. "The Anti-Gallows Movement in Antebellum America." *REAL* (Vol. 23. *Civil Liberties, Ltd,* ed. Brook Thomas. Verlag: 2006): 145–178.
Bell, Michael Davitt. *The Problem of American Realism: Studies in the Cultural History of a Literary Idea.* Chicago: University of Chicago Press, 1993.
Bennett, Emerson. *The Bride of the Wilderness.* Philadelphia: T.B. Peterson, 1854.
_____. *Mike Fink: A Legend of the Ohio.* Cincinnati: J.A. & U.P. James, 1853.
_____. Publisher's advertisement, *The Bride of the Wilderness.* Philadelphia: T.B. Peterson, 1854.
Benson, Ivan. *Mark Twain's Western Years.* New York: Russell & Russell, 1966.
Berkove, Lawrence I. *Insider Stories of the Comstock Lode and Nevada's Mining Frontier 1859–1909: Primary Sources in American Social History.* Lewiston, NY: The Edwin Mellen Press, 2007.
_____. "Nevada Influences on Mark Twain." *A Companion to Mark Twain,* ed. Messent and Budd. Malden, MA: Blackwell, 2005.
_____. *The Sagebrush Anthology.* Columbia: University of Missouri Press, 2006.
Bovee to SLC, 7 April 1875, MTP.
Bovee to SLC, 10 February 1876, MTP.
Branch, Edgar, and Robert H. Hirst. *Early Tales and Sketches and Sketches, Volume 2 1864–1865.* Berkeley: University of California Press, 1981.

_____. *Early Tales and Sketches, Volume 1 1851–1864*. Berkeley: University of California Press, 1979.
Branch, Edgar M. *Clemens of the "Call": Mark Twain in San Francisco*. Berkeley: University of California Press, 1969.
_____. *The Literary Apprenticeship of Mark Twain*. Champaign: University of Illinois Press, 1950.
_____. *Mark Twain's Letters: 1870–1871*. Berkeley: University of California Press, 1995.
Browne, J. Ross. "California Stage-Driver," illustration, *Harper's New Monthly Magazine*. February 1862.
_____. "Holding on to It," illustration, *Harper's New Monthly Magazine*. February 1861.
_____. "Outgoing and Incoming," illustration, *Harper's New Monthly Magazine*. February 1861.
_____. "A Peep at Washoe," [Third Paper], February 1861, *Harper's New Monthly Magazine*, Vol. 22, No. 129, pp. 289–290.
_____. "A Queston of Title," illustration, *Harper's New Monthly Magazine*, January, 1861.
_____. "Snow Slide," illustration, *Harper's New Monthly Magazine*. February 1861.
_____. "We are Waiting for You," illustration, *Harper's New Monthly Magazine*, January, 1861.
Butler, Anne M. *Daughters of Joy, Sisters of Misery: Prostitutes in the American West. 1865–1890*. Urbana and Chicago: University of Illinois Press, 1987.
Butler, Judith. *Excitable Speech: A Politics of the Performative*. New York: Routledge, 1997.
_____. *Gender Trouble: Feminism and the Subversion of Identity*. London: Routledge, 2006.
Caron, James E. *Mark Twain: Unsanctified Newspaper Reporter*. Columbia: University of Missouri Press, 2008.
Chopin, Kate. *The Awakening*, ed. Nancy A. Walker. Boston and New York: Bedford/St. Martin's, 2000.
Clemens, Samuel Langhorne *see* SLC
Cohen, Daniel A. *Pillars of Salt, Monuments of Grace: New England Crime Literature and the Origins of American Popular Culture, 1674–1860*. Amherst: University of Massachusetts Press, 1993.
Collins, Wilkie. "Mrs. Bullwinkle," The New-York *Saturday Press*, 2 June 1866, MTP.
Cooper, James Fenimore, *The Ways of the Hour: A Tale*. New York: W.A. Townsend and Company, 1861.
Coryell, Irving. "Josh, of 'The Territorial Enterprise.'" *The North American Review*, Vol. 243, No. 2 (Summer, 1937): 287–295.
Coulombe, Joseph L. *Mark Twain and the American West*. Columbia: University of Missouri Press, 2003.
Cox, J. Randolph. *The Dime Novel Companion: A Source Book*. Westport, CT: Greenwood, 2000.
Davis, David Brion. *From Homicide to Slavery: Studies in American Culture*. New York: Oxford University Press, 1988
_____. *Homicide in American Fiction, 1798–1860: A Study in Social Values*. Ithaca: Cornell University Press, 1968.
_____. "The Movement to Abolish Capital Punishment in America, 1787–1861." *The American Historical Review* (Vol. 63, No. 1, 1957): 23–46.
Davis, Sam P. *The History of Nevada*. Reno and Los Angeles: The Elms Publishing Co., Inc., 1913.
DeLong, Charles E. *The Life and Confession of John Millian*. Virginia City, NV: Lammon, Gregory, & Palmer, 1868.
Denning, Michael. *Mechanic Accents: Dime Novels and Working-Class Culture in America*. New York: Verso, 1987.
De Quille, Dan. *The Big Bonanza*. Las Vegas: Nevada Publications, 1947.
_____. "Time for Her to Come Home," *Amador Weekly Ledger*, 14 November 1863, MTP.
Derrida, Jacques. "Force of Law: The 'Mystical Foundation of Authority.'" *Deconstruction and the Possibility of Justice*, ed. Drucilla Cornell, Michel Rosenfeld, and David Gray Carlson. New York: Routledge, 1992.
_____. *Limited Inc*. Evanston: Northwestern University Press, 1988.
_____. *Writing and Difference*. Chicago: University of Chicago Press, 1978.
"Devil," def., 4.b., *Oxford English Dictionary Online*.

Bibliography

Dimock, Wai Chee. *Residues of Justice: Literature, Law, Philosophy.* Berkeley: University of California Press, 1997.
Dimsdale, Thomas J. *The Vigilantes of Montana.* Norman: University of Oklahoma Press, 1953.
Douglass, Frederick. "Self-Made Men." *Address Before the Students of the Indian Industrial School at Carlisle, Pa.* The Frederick Douglass Papers at the Library of Congress. http://memory.loc.gov/cgibin/ampage?collId=mfd&fileName=29/29002/29002page.db&recNum=0& itemLink=%2Fammem%2Fdoughtml%2FdougFolder5.html&linkText=7 March 11, 2011.
"Esmeralda Correspondence." 20 August 1862, Sacramento *Bee*, MTP. (Signed Veni, Vidi).
Evans, Albert S. "Our San Francisco Correspondence," *News*, 22 July 1864, p. 2. Quoted by Branch, *Clemens of the "Call,"* 260.
Fatout, Paul. *Mark Twain Speaking.* Iowa City: University of Iowa Press, 1976.
Foster, Michael, and Barbara Foster, *A Dangerous Woman: The Life, Loves, and Scandals of Adah Isaacs Menken, 1835–1868 America's Original Superstar.* Guilford, CT: Lyons Press, 2011.
Foucault, Michel. *Discipline and Punish.* New York: Vintage, 1995.
"A Foul Fair," *Zion's Herald.* 11 May 1871, Boston, Vol. 48, Issue 19: 223. American Periodicals Series Online.
French, Bryant Morey. "Mark Twain, Laura D. Fair and the New York Criminal Courts," *American Quarterly.* Vol. 16, No. 4, A Mark Twain Issue (Winter, 1964): 545–561.
Fulton, Joe B. *The Reconstruction of Mark Twain: How a Confederate Bushwhacker Became the Lincoln of Our Literature.* Baton Rouge: Louisiana State University Press, 2010.
Gard, Wayne. *Frontier Justice.* Norman: University of Oklahoma Press, 1949.
"Girls," *Daily Morning Call*, 3 January 1864, MTP.
Goldman, Marion S. *Gold Diggers & Silver Miners: Prostitution and Social Life on the Comstock Lode.* Ann Arbor: University of Michigan Press, 1981.
Gonzales-Day, Ken. *Lynching in the West, 1850–1935.* Durham: Duke University Press, 2006.
Greeley, Horace. "The Movement in Favor of Peace," *Daily Morning Call*, 26 July 1864, MTP.
Haines, Herbert. *Against Capital Punishment: The Anti-Death Penalty Movement in America, 1972–1994.* Oxford and New York: Oxford University Press, 1996.
Halttunen, Karen. *Murder Most Foul: The Killer and the American Gothic Imagination.* Cambridge: Harvard University Press, 1998.
Harris, Susan K. "Four Ways to Inscribe a Mackerel: Mark Twain and Laura Hawkins," *Studies in the Novel.* Vol. 21, No. 2 (Summer, 1989): 138–153.
Hendler, Glenn. *Public Sentiments: Structures of Feeling in Nineteenth-Century American Literature.* Chapel Hill: University of North Carolina Press, 2001.
Holmes, Oliver Wendell, Jr. "The Path of the Law," 10 *Harvard Law Review* 457: 1897.
Hopkins, Ernest Jerome. "Introduction," *The Complete Short Stories of Ambrose Bierce.* Lincoln: University of Nebraska Press, 1979.
James, Ronald M. *The Roar and the Silence: A History of Virginia City and the Comstock Lode.* Reno: University of Nevada Press, 1998.
James, Susan. "Julia Bulette's Probate Records." In Reid and James, *Uncovering Nevada's Past: A Primary Source History of the Silver State.* Reno: University of Nevada Press, 55–59.
_____. "Queen of Tarts," *The Historical Nevada Magazine*, Carson City: Nevada Magazine, 1998, 47–53.
Jehlen, Myra. "Gender," *Critical Terms for Literary Study*, Second Edition, ed. Frank Lentricchia and Thomas McLaughlin. Chicago: The University of Chicago Press, 1995.
"Julia Bulette," Courtesy of the Nevada Historical Society.
"Life, trial, and execution of Edward H. Ruloff: perpetrator of eight murders, numerous burglaries, and other crimes; who was recently hanged at Binghamton, N.Y...." Courtesy of Fenimore Art Museum, "Murder Pamphlet Collection," 1871.
Lillard, Richard G. "Contemporary Reaction to 'The Empire City Massacre,'" *American Literature*, Vol. 16, No. 3 (Nov., 1944): 203.
Lippard, George. "Preface to this Edition," ed. David S. Reynolds. *The Quaker City, Or, the Monks of Monk Hall: A Romance of Philadelphia Life, Mystery, and Crime.* Amherst: University of Massachusetts Press, 1995.

"Lynching." *The Youth's Companion (1827–1929)*; May 12, 1864; 37, 19; American Periodicals Series: 74.
"Lynchings: By Year and Race," http://law2.umkc.edu/faculty/projects/ftrials/shipp/lynchingyear.html
"Maguire's Opera House," *Virginia Daily Union*, 10 March 1864, MTP.
Mark Twain Project Online: Authoritative Texts, Documents, and Historical Research. 5 Oct. 2009. The Regents of the University of California. 5 July, 2009. http://www.marktwainproject.org/homepage.html
Mark Twain's Letters from Virginia City, ed. Guy Louis Rocha. Nevada State Library and Archives. 30 April, 2010. http://nsla.nevadaculture.org/index.php?option=com_content&view=article&id=1573%3Amark-twains-letters-from-virginia-city&catid=215%3Acorrections&Itemid=1
Marshall, George M. "Our Traveler's Letters," 7 July 1864, Virginia City *Union*, 1, MTP. Signed "Marshall."
Masur, Louis P. *Rites of Execution: Capital Punishment and the Transformation of American Culture, 1776–1865*. New York and Oxford: Oxford University Press, 1989.
McGrath, Roger D. *Gunfighters, Highwaymen, & Vigilantes: Violence on the Frontier*. Berkeley and Los Angeles: University of California Press, 1984.
McIntyre, Elwood R."A Farmer Halts the Hangman: The Story of Marvin Bovee," *Wisconsin Magazine of History* 42, No. 1 [autumn 1958]: 3–12; *Dict. of Wisconsin History* online; accessed 5 May 2011.
McPherson, James M. *Battle Cry of Freedom: The Civil War Era*. New York: Oxford University Press, 2003.
Miller, J. Hillis. *Speech Acts in Literature*. Stanford: Stanford University Press, 2001. Morris, Linda A. *Gender Play in Mark Twain: Cross-Dressing and Transgression*. Columbia: University of Missouri Press, 2007.
Morris, Roy, Jr. *Lighting Out for the Territory: How Samuel Clemens Headed West and Became Mark Twain*. New York: Simon & Schuster, 2012.
"The Movement in Favor of Peace," 26 July 1864, *Daily Morning Call*, MTP.
"Muck-raker." *Oxford English Dictionary Online*.
"Muck-raking." *Oxford English Dictionary Online*.
"A Mysterious Murder Chased Up." *The National Police Gazette (1845–1906)* 22, No. 1139 (Jun 29, 1867): 4. http://search.proquest.com/docview/127589747?accountid=14589.
Nicoletta, Julie. "Redefining Domesticity: Women in Lodging Houses on the Comstock," *Comstock Women: The Making of a Mining Community*, ed. Ronald M. James and C. Elizabeth Raymond, Reno: University of Nevada Press, 1998.
Online Nevada Encyclopedia. http://www.onlinenevada.org/julia_bulette
Orion and SLC to Mary E. (Mollie) Clemens, 29, 30, and 31 Jan 1862, Carson City, Nev. (*UCCL 00035*).
Paine, Albert Bigelow. *Mark Twain: A Biography: The Personal and Literary Life of Samuel Langhorne Clemens*. New York and London: Harper & Brothers, 1912.
Parins, James W. *John Rollin Ridge: His Life and Works*. Lincoln: University of Nebraska Press, 2004.
Parker, Theodore. *Lessons from the World of Matter and the World of Man*, Vol. 14 of *The Collected Works of Theodore Parker*, ed. Rufus Leighton, London: Trubner and Company, 1872.
"Picture of a Southern Empire," reprinted from *The London Daily News* in the *Placer Weekly Courier*, Vol. 6, No. 30, January 17, 1863, MTP.
"Population of the Largest Urban Places: 1860," U.S. Bureau of the Census.
Powers, Ron. *Mark Twain: A Life*. New York: Free Press, 2005.
Pray, Isaac Clarke. *Memoirs of James Gordon Bennett and His Times: By a Journalist*. New York: Stringer & Townsend, 1855.
Rasmussen, R. Kent, cites Elwood R. McIntyre, "A Farmer Halts the Hangman."
Reid, John B., and Ronald M. James, ed. *Uncovering Nevada's Past: A Primary Source History of the Silver State*. Reno: University of Nevada Press, 2004.

Reviews of the Gilded Age play (*MTDP 00148*), n. 3.
Reynolds, David S. *Beneath the American Renaissance: The Subversive Imagination in the Age of Emerson and Melville*. Cambridge: Harvard University Press, 1988.
_____. Introduction, *The Quaker City, or, the Monks of Monk Hall: A Romance of Philadelphia Life, Mystery, and Crime*. Amherst: University of Massachusetts Press, 1995, xxv.
Reynolds, David S., and Kimberly R. Gladman, ed. "Introduction" to *Venus in Boston and Other Tales of Nineteenth-Century City Life*. Amherst: University of Massachusetts Press, 2002.
Ridge, John Rollin. *The Life and Adventures of Joaquin Murieta, the Celebrated California Bandit*. Norman: University of Oklahoma Press, 1955.
Roark, Jarrod. "Beneath Mark Twain: Detecting Sensational Residues in Twain's Early Writing." *Mark Twain Annual*. The Pennsylvania State University Press, Vol. 12, No 1, 2014, pp. 14–29.
Rocha, Guy. "Myth #20—Red Light Legend and Lore: Julia Bulette." Former Nevada State Archivist, State Library and Archives. http://nsla.nevadaculture.org/index.php?option=com_content&task=view&id=682&Itemid=418
Rottenberg, Dan. *Death of a Gunfighter: The Quest for Jack Slade, the West's Most Elusive Legend*. Yardley, PA: Westholme Publishing, 2008.
Rowe, John Carlos. "Mark Twain's Rediscovery of America in *A Connecticut Yankee in King Arthur's Court*." *Literary Culture and U.S. Imperialism: From the Revolution to World War II*. New York: Oxford University Press, 2000, 121–139.
Ryan, Ann M. "The Voice of Her Laughter: Mark Twain's Tragic Feminism." *American Literary Realism*. Vol. 41, No. 3 (Spring 2009): 192–213.
"Sam Clemens," 1863, Age 27, Carson City, Nevada, courtesy of the Mark Twain Papers, Bancroft Library.
Scharnhorst, Gary. "Introduction" to *The Luck of Roaring Camp and Other Writings*. New York: Penquin Books, 2001.
_____. "Twain and the Literary Construction of the West." *A Companion to Mark Twain*, ed. Messent and Budd. Malden, MA: Blackwell, 2005.
Schudson, Michael. *Discovering the News: A Social History of American Newspapers*. New York: Basic Books, 1978.
Schuele, Donna C. "'None Could Deny the Eloquence of This Lady' Women, Law, and Government in California, 1850–1890," ed. John F. Burns and Richard J. Orsi. *Taming the Elephant: Politics, Government, and Law in Pioneer California*. Berkeley: University of California Press, 2003.
SLC "Note" on envelope of Bovee's letter to Twain, 10 February 1876, MTP.
_____. "Note" on envelope of Bovee's letter to Twain, 7 April 1875, MTP.
SLC (Samuel Langhorne Clemens). "Mark Twain's Letters from Washington. Number III." Letter dated 20 December 1867. Virginia City *Territorial Enterprise*, 11 January, 2.
SLC to Charles Warren Stoddard, 23 Apr 1867, New York, N.Y. MTP.
SLC to Dan De Quille, 15 July 1864, MTP.
SLC to Elisha Bliss, Jr., 15 May 1871, Elmira, N.Y. (*UCCL 00612*) and n. 5, MTP.
SLC to Horace Greeley, 17 August 1871, Hartford, CT, MTP.
SLC to Horace Greeley, 17 August 1871, Hartford, CT, n. 2.
SLC to Jane Lampton Clemens, 2 April 1862, MTP.
SLC to Jane Lampton Clemens, 20 March 1862, MTP.
SLC to Jane Lampton Clemens, 26 Oct 1861, Carson City, Nev. (*UCCL 00031*).
SLC to Jane Lampton Clemens, 30 January 1862, MTP.
SLC to Jane Lampton Clemens, 4 Nov 1868, New York, N.Y. (*UCCL 02762*).
SLC to Jane Lampton Clemens and Family, 20 Nov 1867, New York, N.Y., MTP.
SLC to Jane Lampton Clemens and Pamela A. Moffett, 16 Feb 1863, Virginia City, Nev. MTP.
SLC to Jane Lampton Clemens and Pamela A. Moffett, 17 May 1864, Virginia City, Nev. (*UCCL 00077*).
SLC to Jane Lampton Clemens and Pamela A. Moffett, 25 October 1861, MTP.SLC to Jane Lampton Clemens and Pamela A. Moffett, 8 and 9 Feb 1862, Carson City, Nev. (*UCCL 00036*).

SLC to Jane Lampton Clemens and Pamela A. Moffett, 25 Sept 1864, San Francisco, Calif., MTP.
SLC to Jane Lampton Clemens and Pamela A. Moffett 11 and 12 April 1863, Virginia City, Nev. Terr., MTP.
SLC to Jane Lampton Clemens and Pamela A. Moffett 11 and 12 April 1863, Virginia City, Nev. Terr. (MS: NPV and CU-MARK, *UCCL* 00063), n. 1.
SLC to Mary E. Clemens, 29 January 1862, MTP.
SLC to OLC, 25 Sept 1872, London, England, Note 6, MTP.
SLC to Orion and Henry Clemens, 26–28 Oct 1853, Philadelphia, Pa., MTP.
SLC to Orion and Mary E. (Mollie) Clemens, 16 and 17 January 1862, MTP.
SLC to Orion and Mary E. (Mollie) Clemens, 19 and 20 Oct 1865, San Francisco, Calif., MTP.
SLC to Orion and Mary E. (Mollie) Clemens, 19 and 20 Oct 1865, San Francisco, Calif. (*UCCL 00092*).
_____. *(UCCL 00092)*, n. 6.
SLC to Orion and Mary E. (Mollie) Clemens, 28 Sept 1864, San Francisco, Calif., MTP.
SLC to Orion, 11 May 1862, MTP.
SLC to Orion, 24 April 1862, MTP.
SLC to Orion Clemens, 10 March 1871, Buffalo, N.Y. (*UCCL 02453*).
SLC to Orion Clemens, 24 and 25 Apr 1862, Aurora, Nevada (*UCCL 00045*).
_____. *(UCCL 00045)*, n. 8.
SLC to Pamela A. Moffett, 15 August 1862, MTP.
SLC to Pamela A. Moffett, 18 March 1864, MTP.
SLC to Pamela A. Moffett, 8 February 1862, MTP.
SLC to T. B. Pugh, 27 July 1873, Edinburgh, Scotland (*UCCL 00957*) and n. 2, MTP.
SLC to the Postmaster of Virginia City, Mont. Terr...., 15 Sept 1870, Buffalo, N.Y. (*UCCL 00506*), MTP.
SLC to Whitelaw Reid, 29 Apr 1871, Elmira, N.Y., MTP. See also *Mark Twain's Letters, 1870– 1871*, ed. Victor Fischer, Michael B. Frank, and Lin Salamo. Berkeley: University of California Press, 1995.
Slotkin, Richard. *The Fatal Environment: The Myth of the Frontier in the Age of Industrialization, 1800–1890.* Norman: University of Oklahoma Press, 1985.
Smith, Henry Nash. *Mark Twain of the Enterprise: Newspaper Articles & Other Documents 1862–1864.* Berkeley: University of California Press, 1957.
Spear, Charles. *The Prisoners' Friend: A Monthly Magazine Devoted to Criminal Reform, Philosophy, Literature, Science and Art.* Vol. 1, No. 1, Boston: C. Spear, 1849.
"Splendid Acting," *Stockton Daily Independent,* 14 March 1864, MTP.
Stern, Milton R. *Contexts for Hawthorne: The Marble Faun and the Politics of Openness and Closure in American Literature.* Champaign: University of Illinois Press, 1991.
"The Story of Marvin Bovee." *Mark Twain A–Z: The Essential Reference to His Life and Writings.* New York: Oxford University Press, 1995.
_____. *Wisconsin Magazine of History* 42, No. 1 [autumn 1958]: 3–12; *Dict. of Wisconsin History* online; accessed 5 May 2011.
Streeby, Shelley. "Sensational Fiction," *A Companion to American Fiction,* ed. Shirley Samuels. Oxford: Blackwell, 2002, 179–190.
Sumner, Charles. "Against Capital Punishment. Letter to a Committee of the Massachusetts Legislature," February 12, 1855. *Charles Sumner; His Complete Works.* Boston: Lee and Shepard, 1900.
_____. "The Crime Against Kansas: The Apologies for the Crime; The True Remedy," 1856, *The Works of Charles Sumner: Vol. 4.* Boston: Lee and Shepard, 1875.
_____. "Power of the Senate to Imprison Recusant Witnesses," May 18, 1871, *Charles Sumner; His Complete Works: Vol. 19.* Boston: Lee and Shepard, 1900.
Sweets, Henry. "John M. Clemens Justice of the Peace dedicated 50 years ago." Hannibal *Courier-Post,* 1 May 2009. http://www.hannibal.net/article/20090501/NEWS/305019857.
Swisshelm, Jane G. "The Fair Laura," *The Independent.* 28 November 1872: 24, 1252, American Periodical Series Online.

"THAT 'SELL,'" 29 or 30 October 1863, Gold Hill *Daily News*, MTP.
"Theatrical Record," *Daily Morning Call*, 3 January 1864.
Thomas, Brook. *Cross-Examinations of Law and Literature*. Cambridge: Cambridge University Press, 1987.
_____. "Forward." *Research in English and American Literature*, Vol. 18, *Civil Liberties, Ltd*, ed. Brook Thomas. Verlag: (2002).
Turner, Erin. *Badasses of the Old West: True Stories of Outlaws on the Edge*. Guilford, CT: TwoDot, 2010.
Turner, Frederick Jackson, "The Significance of the Frontier in American History," 1893, excerpted from *The American Studies Hypertexts Project* at the University of Virginia, 7.
Twain, Mark. *The Adventures of Huckleberry Finn*. Colorado Springs: Piccadilly Books, 2010.
_____. "After the Hackmen," *Daily Morning Call*, 7 August 1864, MTP.
_____. "Another Innocent Man Killed," 16 September 1862. Cited by Barbara Schmidt, text recovered by Michael Marleau. Reprinted in *Mark Twain Journal* (Fall 2004), 11–12.
_____. "Another Obscene Picture Knave Captured—He Solicits the Custom of School Girls," *Daily Morning Call*. Reprinted in *Clemens of the "Call": Mark Twain in San Francisco*, ed. Edgar M. Branch. Berkeley: University of California Press, 1969.
_____. "Another Victim," *Daily Morning Call*, 26 July 1864, MTP.
_____. "Arrest of Charles L. Weller for Treasonable Utterances," *Daily Morning Call*, 26 July 1864, MTP.
_____. "Arrested for Theft," *Daily Morning Call*, 6 August 1864, MTP.
_____. "Assassination in Carson," 11 December 1863, MTP. Text from Ivan Benson, *Mark Twain's Western Years*. New York: Russell & Russell, 1966, 178.
_____. "Attention, Hackmen," *Daily Morning Call*, 6 August 1864, MTP.
_____. "Beasts in the Semblance of Men," 12 June 1864, *Daily Morning Call*, MTP.
_____. "A Big Thing in Washoe City," *Placer Weekly Courier*, 17 January 1863, MTP.
_____. "A Big Thing in Washoe City," *Placer Weekly Courier*, vol. 6, no. 30, January 17, 1863, MTP.
_____. "A Bloody Massacre Near Carson," 28 October 1863, *Territorial Enterprise*, reprinted in the San Francisco *Daily Evening Bulletin*, 31 October 1863, MTP.
_____. "A Brisk Business in the Shooting and Slashing Way at Washoe," 10 March 1864, San Francisco *Evening Bulletin*, MTP.
_____. "Brutal Affrays in Washoe," 19 April 1864, *Territorial Enterprise*.
_____. "Concerning Hackmen," 26 July 1864, *Daily Morning Call*. Reprinted in *Clemens of the "Call": Mark Twain in San Francisco*, ed. Edgar M. Branch. Berkeley: University of California Press, 1969.
_____. *A Connecticut Yankee in King Arthur's Court*. New York: The Modern Library, 2001.
_____. "Death—Robbery," 2 December 1863, *Daily Morning Call*, from Ivan Benson, *Mark Twain's Western Years*. New York: Russell & Russell, 1966, 178.
_____. "Demoralizing Young Girls," San Francisco *Daily Morning Call*, 23 July 1864, MTP. On loan.
_____. "Dispatches by the State Line," 3 September 1863, *Daily Morning Call*. Reprinted in *Clemens of the "Call": Mark Twain in San Francisco*, ed. Edgar M. Branch. Berkeley: University of California Press, 1969.
_____. "End of the Rape Case," 30 July 1864, *Daily Morning Call*. Reprinted in *Clemens of the "Call": Mark Twain in San Francisco*, ed. Edgar M. Branch. Berkeley: University of California Press, 1969.
_____. "False Report," *Daily Morning Call*, 9 July 1863, MTP.
_____. "For Sentence," San Francisco *Daily Morning Call*, 26 July 1864, MTP.
_____. "Hackmen Arrested," *Daily Morning Call*, 28 June 1864, MTP.
_____. "Homocide—Coroner's Inquest," 7 July 1864, *Daily Morning Call*, MTP.
_____. "Horrible Affair," *Territorial Enterprise*, between 16 and 18 April 1863. Reprinted in *Early Tales & Sketches, Vol. 1 1851–1864*. Berkeley: University of California Press, 1979, 246–47.
_____. "I TAKE IT ALL BACK." 29 October 1863, *Territorial Enterprise*. Text reprinted in

Lawrence I. Berkove, *The Sagebrush Anthology.* Columbia: University of Missouri Press, 2006, 20.
____. "The Indian Troubles on the Overland Route," *Weekly Appeal,* 5 October 1862. Reprinted from the *Territorial Enterprise,* 1 October 1862, MTP.
____. "Insolent Hackmen," *Daily Morning Call,* 18 August 1864, 3, c. 1, MTP.
____. "Judicial Strategy," *Daily Morning Call,* 6 August 1864, MTP.
____. "Late from Washoe," *Sacramento Daily Union,* 22 July 1862, MTP.
____. "Letter from Mark Twain," 28 April 1864, *Territorial Enterprise,* MTP.
____. "Letter from Mark Twain," reprinted in Branch and Hirst, *Early Tales and Sketches, Volume 1,* 293–294.
____. "Letter from San Francisco," Sacramento *Union,* 3 November 1865. Reprinted in Branch and Hirst, *Early Tales and Sketches, Volume 1: 1851–1864,* 33.
____. "Lewd Merchandise," San Francisco *Daily Morning Call,* 26 July 1864, MTP.
____. "Man Shot," *Daily Morning Call,* 9 July 1863, MTP.
____. "A Merited Penalty," San Francisco *Daily Morning Call,* 24 July 1864, MTP.
____. "The Movement in Favor of Peace," *Daily Morning Call,* 26 July 1864, MTP.
____. "Obscene Information," San Francisco *Daily Morning Call,* 29 July 1864, MTP.
____. "Obscene-Picture Dealers," San Francisco *Daily Morning Call,* 24 July 1864, MTP.
____. "Offices," 19 November 1863, *Daily Morning Call,* MTP.
____. *Pudd'nhead Wilson and Those Extraordinary Twain: A Norton Critical Edition,* ed. Sidney E. Berger, New York: W.W. Norton & Company, Inc., 1980.
____. "Rape," 23 July 1864, *Daily Morning Call.* Reprinted in *Clemens of the "Call": Mark Twain in San Francisco,* ed. Edgar M. Branch. Berkeley: University of California Press, 1969.
____. "Regular Correspondent of the Daily Call," Complete Set of "Mark Twain's" Letters to SF *Call* for 1863, MTP.
____. "The Roderick Case," *Daily Morning Call,* 9 October 1864, MTP.
____. "A Rough Customer," *Daily Morning Call,* 8 October 1864, MTP.
____. *Roughing It.* New York: Penguin, 1981.
____. "A Strange Dream," The New-York *Saturday Press,* 2 June 1866, MTP.
____. "Trial of a Hackman," *Daily Morning Call,* 22 September 1864, 3, MTP.
____. "Trip Over the Mountains," 7 July 1864, Virginia City *Union,* 1, MTP.
____. "The United States of Lyncherdom," *The Complete Essays of Mark Twain.* Charles Neider, ed. Boston: Da Capo Press, 1991
____. Untitled. Virginia *Union,* 7 July 1864, MTP.
____. "Vending Obscene Pictures," San Francisco *Daily Morning Call,* 26 July 1864, MTP. On loan.
Twain, Mark, and Charles Dudley Warner. *The Gilded Age,* ed. Ron Powers, New York: The Modern Library, 2006.
"Untitled," from "Facts and Fancies," *Daily Morning Call,* 26 July 1864, MTP.
"Untitled Note on Menken," *Unionville Humboldt Register,* 19 March 1864, MTP.
Whitman, Walter. "Revenge and Requital. A Tale of a Murderer Escaped." *The United States Magazine, and Democratic Review.* Vol. XVII, No. LXXXV (July and August, 1845): 111.
"A Wolf in the Fold, or a Fair Trial of Laura." Bancroft Library, UC–Berkeley, BANC PIC 1963. 002:0874-B, Lithograph, Kock & Harnett, ca. 1871.
Young, James Harvey. "Anna Dickinson, Mark Twain, and Bret Harte." *The Pennsylvania Magazine of History and Biography.* Vol. 76, No. 1 (Jan., 1952): 39–46.

Index

Adventures of Huckleberry Finn (1884) 12, 211
The Adventures of Tom Sawyer (1876) 78, 110
affrays 24, 27, 43, 191, 192, 211
Ainsworth, W. Harrison 6, 151; *Jack Sheppard* (1839) 151; *Rookwood* (1834) 151, 154
alcohol use (liquor, whisky) 24, 29, 192
Alger, Horatio, Jr. 14, 194
Alta California (periodical) 6, 146
American Publishing Company 115
Anderson, Benedict 104, 198, 205
Angelfish Club 147
Anthony, Susan B. 169
anti-gallows sentimen 11, 81, 109, 113, 142, 147, 167, 170, 199
The Awakening (1899) 181, 204, 206

badmen 11, 15, 17, 27, 28, 30, 33, 35, 39, 49, 122, 129, 133, 178
Bakhtin, Mikhail 191, 193, 205
Barstow, William H. 156
Barton, John Cyril 198, 199, 205
beasts (i.e., male criminals) 4, 10, 69, 77, 78, 80–82, 85–90, 92, 94, 96–98, 100, 104–108, 181, 197, 211
Beecher, Henry Ward 136
Beni, Jules 118
Benjamin, Walter 82
Bennett, Emerson 4–6, 8, 186, 205; *The Bride of the Wilderness* (1854) 6, 190, 205; *The League of Miami* (1860) 5; *Mike Fink: A Legend of the Ohio* (1853) 5, 6, 205; *Wild Scenes on the Frontier; or; Heroes of the West* (1859)
Bennett, James Gordon 7, 8, 190, 208
Bennett, Sir John 144
Berkove, Lawrence I. 29, 76, 77, 184, 189, 192, 195, 196, 199, 202, 203, 205, 212

Billings, Josh 136
Blakely, Captain Ned 11, 113, 117, 130–135, 145, 147, 199
Bliss, Elisha, Jr. 115, 199, 209
Blitz, Officer Bernard S. 82, 90–94, 99, 107
"A Bloody Massacre Near Carson" 8, 41, 44, 190, 193, 211; *see also* hoaxes
Branch, Edgar 14, 17, 101, 190–198, 200, 205–207, 211, 212
The Broadway Belle, and Mirror of the Times (periodical) 5
Brooklyn Daily Eagle 112
Browne, Charles Farrar 8; *see also* Ward, Artemus
Browne, J. Ross 59–61, 63–65, 78, 195, 206; "A Peep at Washoe" (1860–1861) 59, 61, 63–65, 195, 206
bohemia 49, 50, 152, 157, 159
Booth, J.B. 155
Booth, John Wilkes 155
Bovee, Marvin Henry 113, 141–144, 201, 205, 208–210; *Christ and the Gallows, or Reasons for the Abolition of Capital Punishment* (1869) 142
The Bride of the Wilderness (1854) 6, 190, 205
Bryant, Morey French 174, 203, 204, 207
Buffalo, NY 108, 172, 200, 210
Buffalo Bill, the King of the Border Men (1869) 5
Bulette, Julia 142, 146–149, 160–166, 168, 175, 177–179, 201, 202, 207–209
Buntline, Ned 4, 5, 8, 183, 184, 186, 187; *Buffalo Bill, the King of the Border Men* (1869); *The Mysteries and Miseries of New York* (1848)
Butler, Anne M. 203, 206
Butler, Judith 23, 175, 191, 201, 204, 206
Byron, George Gordon (Lord Byron) 150,

213

151, 154; *Mazeppa* (play based on Lord Byron's poem) 149, 150, 153, 155

California Police Gazette 7
California Rangers 119
The Californian 7, 8, 16, 47
Camp, Martha 163, 164, 168
Campbell, John 39, 40, 190
capital punishment 9, 108, 109, 112, 113, 116, 135, 141–145, 147, 175, 199, 201, 206–208, 210
Caron, James 2, 37, 184, 189, 192, 204, 206
Carson City, Nevada 2, 51–53, 58, 68, 74, 109, 189, 194, 195, 200, 202, 205, 207–209
Carson City Morning Appeal 68
Carton, Sydney 113, 114
"The Celebrated Jumping Frog of Calaveras County" (1867) 60
Central Overland Company 117–119, 124
Chicago Republican 146, 161, 164, 165, 201–203
Chincha Islands, Peru 131–133
Chopin, Kate 181, 204, 206; *The Awakening* (1899) 181, 204, 206
Christ and the Gallows, or Reasons for the Abolition of Capital Punishment (1869) 142
Citizen Soldier: A Weekly Newspaper Devoted to the Interests of Volunteers and Militias of the United States (periodical) 5
City Crimes; or Life in New York and Boston: A Volume for Everybody; Being a Mirror of Fashion, a Picture of Poverty, and Startling Revelation of the Secret Crimes of Great Cities (1849) 5
Civil War 5, 53, 55, 69, 70, 73, 74, 82, 98, 118, 144, 196, 208
Clapp, Henry, Jr. 8, 48–50, 194
Clemens, Clara 147, 201
Clemens, Jane 34, 55, 56, 109, 189, 190, 192–197, 200, 209, 210
Clemens, Jean 147
Clemens, Jennie 54
Clemens, John Marshall 115, 152
Clemens, Mollie 16, 54, 55, 57, 190–192, 194, 195, 208, 210
Clemens, Pamela 33, 55–57, 74, 152, 190–197, 202, 209, 210
Clemens, Orion 1, 16, 17, 33, 49, 53–56, 58, 64, 69, 73, 74, 85, 115, 117, 124, 126, 139, 190–192, 194–196, 200, 202, 208, 210
Clemens, Susy 147
coaches 1, 10, 51–56, 58–60, 62, 64, 66, 67, 69–71, 75–77, 79, 117, 138, 198, 206; *see also* stages and stagecoaches
Collins, Wilkie 14, 50, 206
Compromise of 1850 54
Comstock Lode, Comstock Lead 41, 42, 124, 189, 193, 194, 201, 202, 205, 207, 208
Confederacy 53, 75, 77, 79
A Connecticut Yankee in King Arthur's Court (1889) 12, 142, 185, 204, 209, 211
Conway, Moncure 144, 145
Cooper, James Fenimore 110, 112, 114, 198, 201, 206; *Last of the Mohicans* (1826) 6; *The Spy* (1821) 114; *The Ways of the Hour* (1850) 112, 198, 206
Copperheads 72, 74, 75, 78
Coulombe, Joseph L. 15, 184, 189–191, 206
courts (i.e., legal justice system) 12, 20, 31, 87, 103, 112, 122, 126, 130–135, 140, 141, 172–174, 178, 186, 187, 203, 204, 207
Cox, Randolph J. 190, 206
Czolgosz, Leon 130

Dagget, Rollin 7, 9, 161, 164
David, Brion Davis 199, 206
Davis, Sam P. 9, 50, 68, 70, 120, 186, 195; *History of Nevada* (1913) 68, 195, 206
death penalty 11, 35, 110, 113–115, 140–143, 192, 199, 205, 207
DeLong, Charles E. 168, 203, 206
Democratic Review 112, 212
demoralization 4, 10, 80, 81, 83, 85, 87, 89, 91, 93–97, 99, 101–105, 107, 181, 197, 198, 211
Denning, Michael 85, 196–198, 206
De Quille, Dan 9, 44, 47, 50, 67, 68, 70, 146, 156–159, 186, 187, 206, 209; *The History of the Big Bonanza* (1876) 68; *see also* Wright, William
Derrida, Jacques 203, 206
Desmore, Gilbert B. 172
desperadoes 1, 11, 15, 16, 27, 32–36, 39, 40, 56, 60, 113, 116–118, 120–122, 124–129, 131, 147, 166
devil 10, 35, 37, 50–55, 57–59, 61, 62, 64, 65, 67–69, 71–73, 75, 77–79, 84, 100, 112, 125, 159, 194, 206
Dickens, Charles 14, 114, 194; *A Tale of Two Cities* (1859) 114
Dickinson, Anna 110, 136, 212
Dimock, Wai Chee 174, 177, 178, 181, 203, 204, 207
Dimsdale, Thomas J. 120–123, 127, 129, 199, 200, 207; *The Vigilantes of Montana* (1866) 119, 120, 122, 123, 127, 199, 207
Doten, Alf 9
Douglass, Frederick 110, 136, 138, 207
Doyle, Ralph 95, 102
Dramatic Chronicle (periodical) 13
Drury, Wells 29
Dumas, Alexandre 6

Eden *see* Garden of Eden
Elmira, NY 11, 108, 109, 198–200, 204, 209, 210

Index

Emerson, Ralph Waldo 14, 110, 136
Emerson Bennett's Weekly 5
Engine Company No. 1 161, 163
Esmeralda Rifles 73
Evans, Albert S. 72, 73, 196, 207
extra-legal justice 3, 4, 11, 28, 30, 31, 34, 40, 45, 113, 116, 117, 119, 122, 123, 125–130, 133, 134, 137, 147, 165, 173, 176, 180, 182, 185, 193

Fair, Laura 149, 168–175, 177, 178, 187, 203, 204, 207, 210, 212
Fatout, Paul 191, 207
Finn, Huck 3
Fitch, Thomas 9
Flag of Our Union (periodical) 7
Florida, Missouri 115
Ford, Teresa 86–88, 105
Foster, Barbara 204, 207
Foster, Michael 204, 207
Foucault, Michel 203, 207
Frank Leslie's Illustrated Newspaper 7
The French Spy 149
Fulton, Joe B. 183, 189, 190, 207

The Galaxy (periodical) 146
Garden of Eden 10, 11, 56, 60, 74, 82, 85, 102, 105, 107, 187
gender 2, 9–11, 21, 38, 53, 54, 62, 64, 69, 70, 76, 81, 83, 84, 98, 103, 106, 107, 146–150, 152, 154, 159, 160, 165, 166, 175, 176, 178, 180, 181, 183, 184, 189, 191, 201, 202, 204, 206–208
Gilbert, Henry 56
Gilbert, Margaret 56
The Gilded Age (1873) 3, 11, 12, 110, 147–149, 158, 168, 170, 172–174, 177, 178, 180, 181, 183, 184, 200, 203, 204, 209, 212
Gillan, Barney 87–89, 91, 94, 96, 97, 99, 107
Gold Hill, Nevada 8, 39, 41–43, 57, 60, 123, 124, 194
Gold Hill Daily News 45. 46, 72, 193, 211
The Golden Circle 75
Golden Era (periodical) 6, 7, 48
Goldman, Marion S. 168, 201–203, 207
Gonzales-Day, Ken 193, 207
Goodman, Joseph 9, 50, 52, 74, 146, 157–159, 161, 164, 182, 186
Goodwin, C.C. 9
Gough, John B. 136
Grant, Ulysses S. 24, 109, 137, 200
Greeley, Horace 51, 52, 79, 194, 196, 198, 207, 209
Gridley, Reuel Colt 72, 75
gun violence 19, 20, 31, 32, 35–37, 116, 118, 123, 132, 193, 194, 208, 209

hackmen and hacks 10, 11, 76, 77, 80–83, 85–99, 101–105, 107, 197, 211, 212

Haines, Herbert 207
Halttunen, Karen 199, 207
hanging (legal and extra-legal execution) 4, 9, 11, 32, 34, 45, 51, 95, 96, 110, 112, 114–120, 122–130, 132–135, 137, 140–142, 144, 151, 161, 163, 165–169, 178, 179, 182, 198, 203, 207
The Hangman (periodical) 140, 200
Hannibal, Missouri 72, 115, 177, 199, 210
Harper's New Monthly Magazine 59, 61–65, 195, 206
Harris, Susan K. 84, 174, 175, 183, 196, 202, 204, 207
Hart, Fred 9
Harte, Brett 7–9, 16, 40, 47, 50, 110, 136, 137, 187, 212; "The Luck of the Roaring Camp" (1868) 9, 190, 209
Hawkins, Laura (fictional character from *The Gilded Age*) 12, 147–149, 158, 168, 172–179
Hawkins, Laura (Samuel Clemens's boyhood friend) 177
Hendler, Glenn 53, 78, 199, 200, 207
Heroes of the West (1859) 5
Hirst, Robert 17, 190–196, 198, 200, 205, 212
History of Nevada (1913) 68, 195, 206
The History of the Big Bonanza (1876) 68
hoaxes 4, 8, 9, 15, 16, 24, 37–47, 50, 112, 114, 180, 181, 192–195; *see also* "A Bloody Massacre Near Carson"; "A Horrible Affair"
Hoffman, John Thompson 116
Holmes, Oliver Wendell, Jr. 207
Holy Land 62
Hopkins, Ernest Jerome 207
"A Horrible Affair" 8, 38, 40, 43, 45, 190, 192, 211; *see also* hoaxes
The House Breaker (1848) 5
Howells, William Dean 3, 14, 49, 189, 194
Humboldt, Nevada 25, 156
humor 1–8, 10, 14, 18, 19, 22, 23, 26–28, 31, 37, 38, 44, 46–50, 52, 53, 67, 70, 71, 83, 94, 102, 103, 105, 106, 130, 142, 145, 156, 157, 159, 160, 184, 189, 191, 194

Idaho Territory 56, 119, 120, 123, 125, 126, 140
The Innocents Abroad (1869) 7, 84, 115, 201

The Jack Harold Series 5
Jack Sheppard (1839) 151
James, Henry 3, 189
James, Ronald M. 19, 191–194, 196, 199, 201–203, 207, 208
James, Susan 201–203, 207
Jehlen, Myra 183, 207
Jerusalem 62
"Jim Smiley and His Jumping Frog" (1865) 8, 14, 48, 49

216 Index

Judson, Edward Zane Carroll, Sr. 4; see also Buntline, Ned

Kerr, Orpheus 157, 159
King Umberto I of Italy 130
The Knights of the Columbian Star 75

Lafayette, Marquis de 140
Lake Bigler 57, 60
Lambertson, George 95–97, 102, 107
Langdon, Olivia (Livy) 147, 170, 201, 203
Last of the Mohicans (1826) 6
The League of Miami (1860) 5
lex talionis 120, 132, 141, 199
The Life and Adventures of Joaquin Murieta, the Celebrated California Bandit (1854) 5, 209
Lillard, Richard G. 43, 193, 194, 207
Lincoln, Abraham 75, 78, 79, 184, 189, 198, 207
Lippard, George 3, 4, 6, 8, 10, 83–85, 104–106, 112, 183, 184, 186, 187, 196–198, 207; *The Quaker City; or, The Monks of Monk Hall: A Romance of Philadelphia Life, Mystery, and Crime* (1845) 5, 83, 84, 106, 112, 196–198, 207, 209
Longfellow, Henry Wordsworth 136
Los Angeles Vigilante Committee 127
Lowell, James Russell 14
Love, Harry 119
The Loyal Leaguers 75
"The Luck of the Roaring Camp" (1868) 9, 190, 209
lynching, lynch mobs 1, 8, 40, 112, 126–130, 134, 135, 147, 149, 182, 183, 187, 190, 193, 200, 207, 208, 212
Lyon, Isabel 147

The Man of Two Lives (1871) 110
Manifest Destiny 102
Marion Rangers 75
Marleau, Michael 191, 211
Masur, Louis P. 199, 208
Matthiessen, F.O. 3
Mazeppa (fictional character) 15, 151, 153, 154–156
Mazeppa (play based on Lord Byron's poem) 149, 150, 153, 155
McEwen, Arthur 9
McGee, Joe 18, 36, 37
McGrath, Roger D. 193, 208
McGuire's Opera House 150
McKinley, William, Jr. 130
McMahon, Dennis 39
McNabb, Jack 32–35, 37, 116, 117, 124, 125, 127–130
McPherson, James M. 196, 208
McQuinn, Margaret 87–91, 94, 99, 102, 105, 147, 182
Mead, George Herbert 82

Measure for Measure (1604) 114
Menken, Adah Isaacs 50, 148–160, 164, 165, 168, 175, 177–179, 202, 204, 207, 212
Merrick, Frederick 110
Mike Fink: A Legend of the Ohio (1853) 5, 6, 205
Miller, J. Hillis 208
Millian, John 142, 146, 148, 149, 160, 161, 163–168, 177–179, 201, 203, 206
mining 1, 8, 14, 16, 19–22, 24, 27, 29, 42, 43, 50, 54–58, 60, 64, 66, 68, 70, 74, 87, 103, 105, 114, 115, 118, 123–125, 131, 152, 155, 160, 164–166, 189, 192, 194, 202, 205, 208
Moffett, Pamela A. 159, 190, 192–196, 202, 209, 210
Moffett, William A. 55, 58
Monk, Hank 51, 52
Monroe County Court 115
Montana Vigilantes 120, 122, 123, 127, 199, 207
Morgan, Hank 3, 142, 185–187
Morris, Linda A. 175, 183, 201, 202, 204, 208
Morris, Roy, Jr. 190, 192, 196, 208
Murieta, Joaquin 119
The Mysteries and Miseries of New York (1848) 5

Nasby, Petroleum 136
National Police Gazette 7, 161, 163, 164, 201–203, 205, 208
National Weekly Story Paper 5
Ned Buntline's Own (periodical) 5
New York Herald 7, 141, 146
New York Ledger 5, 184, 206
New York Round Table 13, 48, 49, 194
New-York Saturday Press 8, 14, 48–50, 190, 194, 206, 212
New York Supreme Court 11, 108, 110, 170
The New York Times 141, 146
New-York Tribune 7, 110, 112, 114, 116, 140–142, 172, 182, 198
Newgate Prison, London 144
Nicoletta, Julia 194, 208
Noakes, Bill 132–135, 141, 145
nom de plume 8, 9, 22, 36

obscenity 10, 80, 84, 85, 92, 94–104, 156, 197, 198, 211, 212
Occidental Hotel, San Francisco 79
The Overland Monthly (periodical) 16
Owsley, William 115

Paine, Albert Bigelow 208
Parins, James W. 190, 208
Parker, Theodore 208
"A Peep at Washoe" (1860–1861) 59, 61, 63–65, 195, 206
periodical marketplace 2–4, 6, 7, 183

Index

Peterson, T.B. 6, 190, 205
"Petrified Man" 8; *see also* hoaxes
Phillips, Wendell 110, 136
philology 110
Pike's Peak, Colorado 58, 59
Piper's Opera House 146
pistols 13, 14, 18, 19, 24–26, 29, 31–33, 35, 36, 39, 48, 54, 71, 138, 190
Placer Weekly Courier 60, 66, 195, 205, 208, 211
police 18, 20, 28–33, 36, 39, 40, 45, 80, 85, 91, 93, 94, 96, 97, 99, 103, 128, 146, 163, 179, 187, 196
Powers, George R. 104
Powers, Ron 151, 175, 191, 193, 202, 204, 208, 212
Pray, Isaac Clarke 7, 190, 208
Prisoner's Friend (periodical) 113
prostitution 1, 4, 11, 81, 82, 87, 95, 98, 100, 102–104, 106, 136, 142, 146–149, 152, 160–164, 166, 168, 169, 171, 175, 181, 203, 206, 207
Pudd'nhead Wilson (1894) 185, 204, 212
Pugh, T.B. 136, 198, 200, 210

Quarry Farm, New York 108

railroads 54, 124, 197
rape 4, 12, 19, 51, 52, 80, 82–92, 94–96, 99, 102, 103, 105, 147, 181, 182, 197, 211, 212
Rawls, John 174
Raymond, Elizabeth C. 194, 208
Raymond, John T. 172
Realism (literary movement) 3, 174, 189, 201, 205, 209
Reed, Thomas 39
Reid, John B. 201–203, 207, 208
Reid, Whitelaw 112–115, 125, 141, 172, 198–200, 204, 210
"The Reliable" 37, 60, 66, 137
Reynolds, David S. 3, 83, 84, 189, 190, 196, 198, 207, 209
Ridge, John Rollin 4–8, 5, 186, 190, 199, 208, 209
riverboat 16, 36, 55
robbery 19, 20, 29, 35, 36, 51–53, 55, 56, 68, 69, 71–73, 75–78, 81, 86, 94, 117, 120, 125, 129, 192, 211
Roberts, Mary 100, 182
Rocha, Guy 208, 209
Rocky Mountain News 126
Roderick, Benjamin 99, 100, 198, 212
Rookwood (1834) 151, 154
Rosseau, Jean 96–98
Romance (literary movement) 3, 151, 189
Roosevelt, Theodore 102; *The Winning of the West* (1889) 21, 102
Rottenberg, Dan 194, 209
Roughing It (1872) 3, 11, 17, 20–22, 27, 33, 35, 36, 51, 54, 61, 62, 71, 72, 79, 102, 109, 110, 113, 115–117, 119, 124, 126–130, 135, 144, 158, 166, 167, 170, 180, 182, 184, 190–192, 194, 195, 198–200, 203, 204, 212
Rowe, John Carlos 209
Rulloff, Edward Howard (also spelled Ruloff) 11, 110, 112–117, 125–127, 129, 130, 135, 137, 139–142, 145, 147, 167, 174, 182, 183, 187, 198, 203, 207
Ryan, Ann M. 147, 174–176, 183, 201, 204, 209

Sacramento Bee 6, 191, 207
Sacramento, California 20, 21, 58, 62
Sacramento Union 48, 61, 193, 194, 212
Sagebrush writers 76, 184, 189, 192, 193, 195, 196, 199, 205, 212
St. Louis, Missouri 55, 75, 99, 104, 196, 205
saloons 15, 18–21, 24–27, 30–33, 36, 37, 41, 127, 170, 192
San Francisco Bulletin 42, 44
San Francisco Daily Morning Call 5, 6, 20, 36, 44, 67, 69, 75, 80, 86, 98, 99, 101, 127, 149, 154, 191, 192, 196–198, 200, 202, 205, 207, 208, 211, 212
San Francisco Dramatic Chronicle 7, 13
San Francisco's Committee of Vigilance 127
San Jose, California 76, 77
Sandwich Islands (Hawaii) 14, 61, 62, 74
The Saturday Evening Post 5
Sawyer, Tom 3
Scharnhorst, Gary 189, 190, 193, 196, 199, 209
Schmidt, Barbara 191, 211
Schudson, Michael 82, 196–198, 209
Schuele, Donna C. 209
Secessionists 53, 69–78, 81, 101
seducers and seduction 83, 85, 99, 105, 106, 170, 176, 177
"Self-Murder" 33, 49; *see also* suicide
sensationalism 115
Setchell, Dan 48
Sexton, Margaret 57
Shakespeare, William 114, 194; *Measure for Measure* (1604) 114
Shepheard, Judge 82, 90, 93, 96–99, 103, 107
Sherburn, Colonel 40, 115, 119, 149, 158, 182, 183, 187, 200
shootouts 19, 25, 30, 33, 36, 43
Slade, Joseph A. 11, 56, 113, 116–131, 133–135, 140, 147, 149, 158, 166, 167, 182, 183, 187, 194, 209
Slotkin, Richard 102, 118, 198, 199, 210
Smarr, Sam 115
Smith, Henry Nash 74, 75, 192, 194, 196, 198, 202, 210

Smythe, Fitz 73; *see also* Evans, Albert S.
Social Darwinism 102
Spear, Charles 8, 113, 140, 210
Spirit of the Times (periodical) 5, 84
Spring Valley Water Company 42–44, 190
The Spy (1821) 114
stages and stagecoaches 1, 10, 51–56, 58, 60, 66–73, 75–77, 79, 81, 85, 125, 128, 138, 198, 206
Stanton, Elizabeth Cady 169
Stockton Daily Independent 16, 202, 210
Streeby, Shelley 190, 210
Sue, Eugene 6
suicide 14; *see also* "Self-Murder"
Sumner, Charles 109, 110, 113, 135–138, 140, 141, 198, 200, 201, 210
Sweets, Henry 199, 210
Swisshelm, Jane Grey Cannon 170, 203, 210

A Tale of Two Cities (1859) 114
Thackeray, William Makepeace 6
Thatcher, Becky 149, 177
Thomas, Brook 149, 189, 199, 202, 205, 211
Thompson, George 3–5, 7, 8, 83, 183, 186; *Being a Mirror of Fashion, a Picture of Poverty, and Startling Revelation of the Secret Crimes of Great Cities* (1849) 5; *City Crimes* 5; *The House Breaker* (1848) 5; The Jack Harold Series 5
Trans-Atlantic marketplace 4
Trollope, Anthony 49, 194
Trombley, Laura Skandera 147, 183, 201
Turbin, Dick 151, 154
Turner, Erin 199, 211
Turner, Frederick Jackson 21, 102, 191, 211

Union (during the Civil War) 54, 69, 72–75, 78, 79, 98, 99, 197
Unionville Humboldt Register 16, 212
"The United States of Lyncherdom" (1901) 129, 135

vigilance committee 9, 11, 31, 32, 34, 45, 72, 73, 117, 119, 120, 122–130, 134; *see also* vigilantes

vigilantes 45, 116, 119, 120, 122, 123, 133, 196, 199, 207, 208; *see also* vigilance committee
The Vigilantes of Montana (1866) 119, 120, 122, 123, 127, 199, 207
Villain, Jean Marie A. 160; *see also* Millian, John
Virginia City, Nevada 1, 6, 8, 18, 21, 24, 28, 34, 40, 41, 45, 50, 70, 71, 73, 74, 99, 123–127, 131, 133, 142, 146, 148, 152, 155–157, 159, 162–165, 169, 192–196, 199–204, 206–210, 212
Virginia City Evening Chronicle 68
Virginia City Territorial Enterprise 1, 4, 5, 9, 14, 16, 21, 24, 40, 52, 67, 79, 127, 138, 142, 146, 149, 150, 156, 157, 160, 190–212
Virginia City Union 14, 195, 208, 212
Virginia Daily Union 156, 202, 208
Virginia Evening Bulletin 29, 45
vox populi 15, 23, 28, 49, 50

Ward, Artemus 8, 9, 49, 50
Warner, Charles Dudley 172, 203, 204, 212; *The Gilded Age* (1873) 3, 11, 12, 110, 147–149, 158, 168, 170, 172–174, 177, 178, 180, 181, 183, 184, 200, 203, 204, 209, 212
Washington Morning Chronicle 141
Washington Temperance Society 122, 200
The Ways of the Hour (1850) 112, 198, 206
Webb, Charles Henry 7, 8, 47–49
Wells, Fargo and Company 68, 71, 77
Wheeler, Andrew Carpenter 172, 173
The White House 107
Whitman, Walt (Walter) 3, 14, 49, 112, 194, 198, 212
Wild Scenes on the Frontier; or, Heroes of the West (1859) 5
Williams, Jack 35–37, 124, 125
The Winning of the West (1889) 21, 102
Wright, William 9, 44, 67, 69, 193, 195; *see also* De Quille, Dan

Yellow Bird 4; *see also* Ridge, John Rollin
Young, James Harvey 212
The Youth's Companion (periodical) 126, 200, 208

www.ingramcontent.com/pod-product-compliance
Lightning Source LLC
Chambersburg PA
CBHW021353300426
44114CB00012B/1208